always a beginner

Finding art + awareness

Perrin Brew Stewart

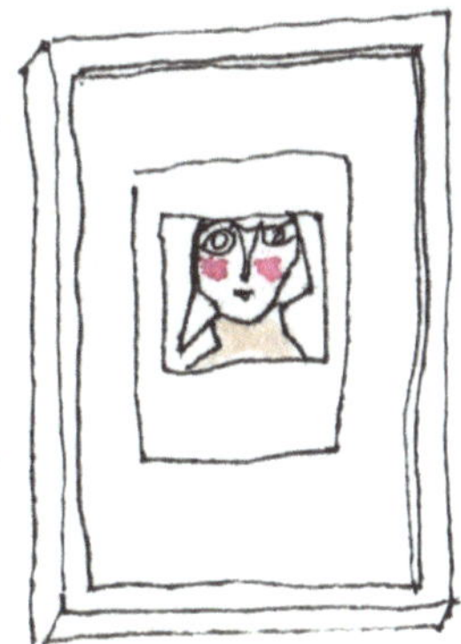

ISBN: 979-8-9917358-0-3
Printed in the United States of America
Cover + Interior Art + Design: Perrin Stewart
First printing, 2024
www.perrinpublishing.com

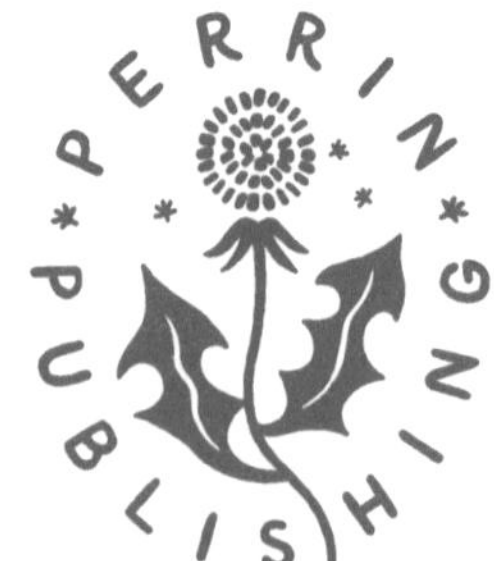

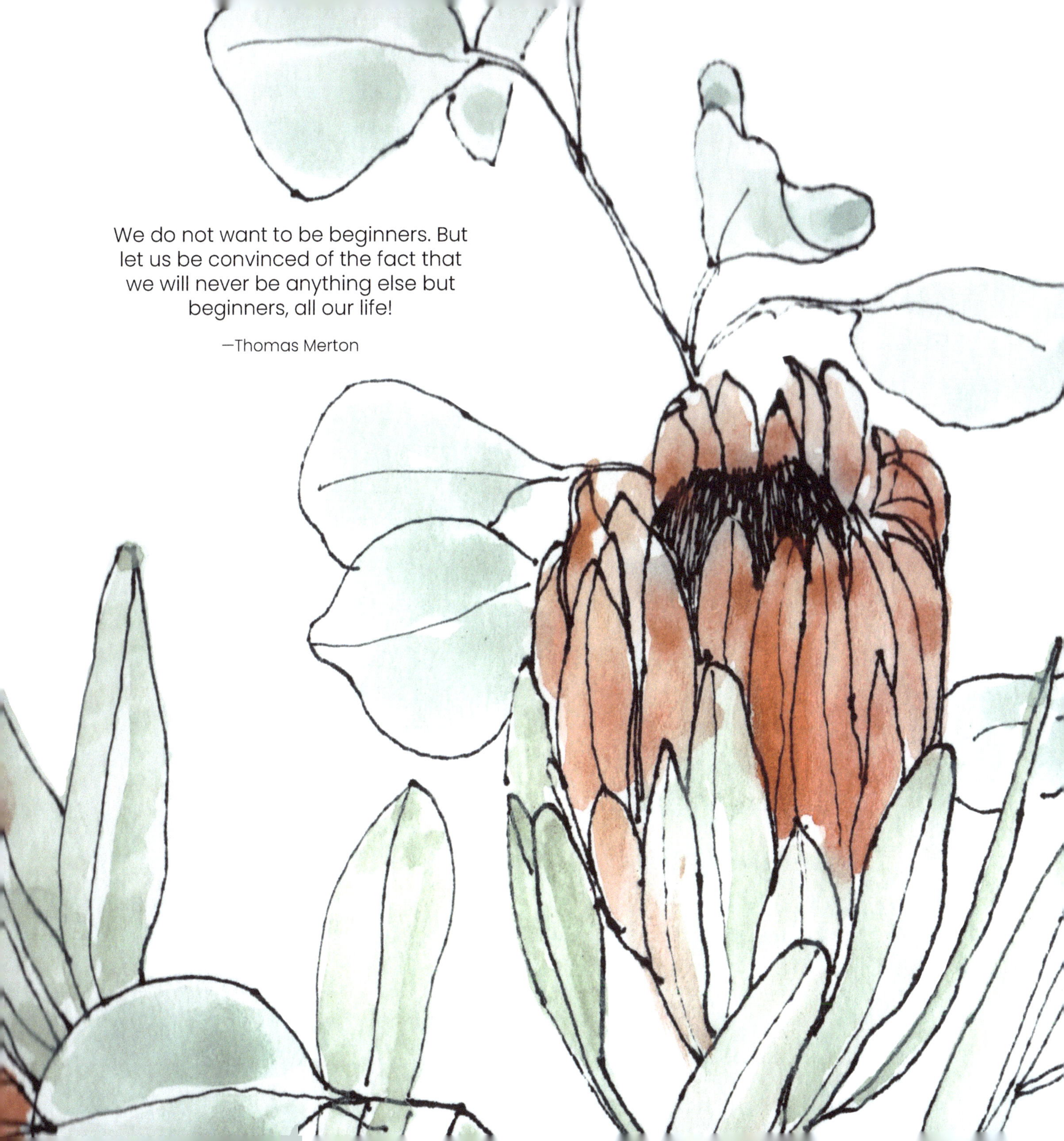
We do not want to be beginners. But
let us be convinced of the fact that
we will never be anything else but
beginners, all our life!

—Thomas Merton

The beginning of this book

I initially wrote this book for myself. Five years ago, when I first started painting and drawing, I kept running into roadblocks. I often felt frustrated and discouraged. I had neither skills nor knowledge, and I didn't have any idea what to make or how to make it. I was, and still am, intimidated by people who have studied and practiced making things most of their lives. It would have been so easy to stop trying and simply enjoy art made by others.

It wasn't learning new techniques or becoming more proficient that kept me going; instead, it was concepts I borrowed from mindfulness. My original intention was for this book to serve as a reminder: a reminder of what works and what gets in my way. For me, just learning a lesson isn't enough. I have to remember again and again. This book captures what I need to remember.

Being a beginner is always difficult, and art, in particular, has a lot of baggage. Weaving awareness into the process of art-making is helpful in a very practical way. When I sit down to make something, there is a background conversation that colors my experience. Suddenly, there are voices in my head already evaluating and judging what I am doing. I don't think this is unusual; when we sit down to make something, most of us suddenly become aware of thoughts that can interfere with the making itself. Recognizing that background conversation allows me to reexamine buried ideas and opens up new possibilities. When you are able to notice the things that are getting in your way, you naturally unlock your own inspiration and creativity.

I wish I could tell you I have it all figured out. I don't. But then again, what I have learned is that having it all figured out is not the point. The point is in the doing. And that there really is a mix of awareness and practical strategies that make the doing easier.

When I shared what I had written with family and friends, I realized that my desire to make art and the difficulties I experienced were common. So many of us want to make something, yet so much gets in the way.

This book is meant for people like me who want to make things after a creative dry spell and need some help getting going. Because many of the obstacles a beginner encounters never entirely go away, it is also intended for people who are more practiced in art-making. It is also for those curious about art and awareness and the connections between the two.

It's meant to be both practical and philosophical, a companion through the discomfort, joys, and possibilities of art-making. Making art provokes discomfort that continually needs to be overcome, and this book aims to help you through that process.

More than anything, this book is an invitation to myself to simply keep going. And, dear reader, it is also an invitation to you.

It's an invitation to approach creative work in a way that makes art-making more accessible and more fun. It's also an invitation to see and celebrate the many ways that awareness and art intertwine, each encouraging and illuminating the other.

Table of contents

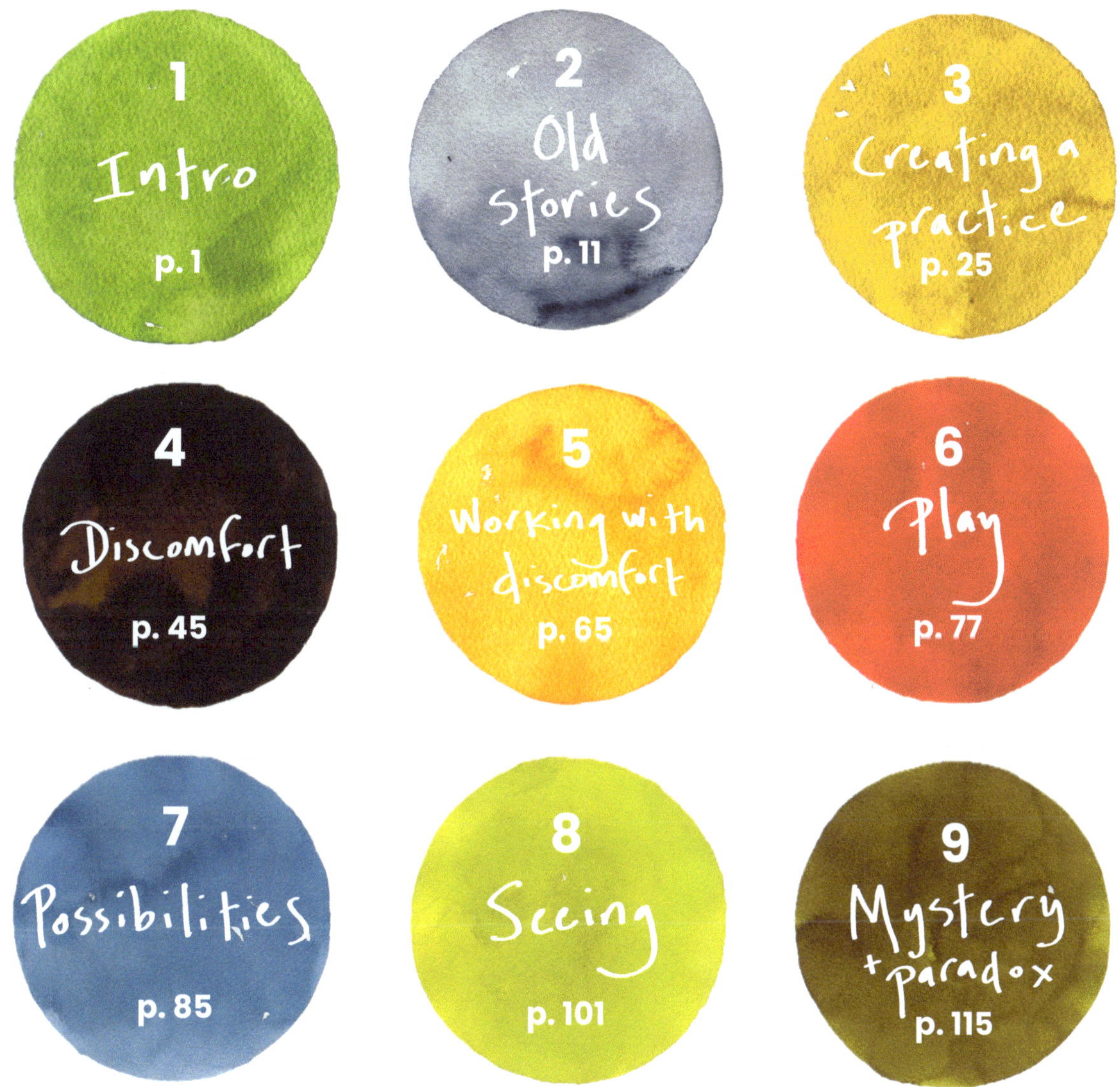

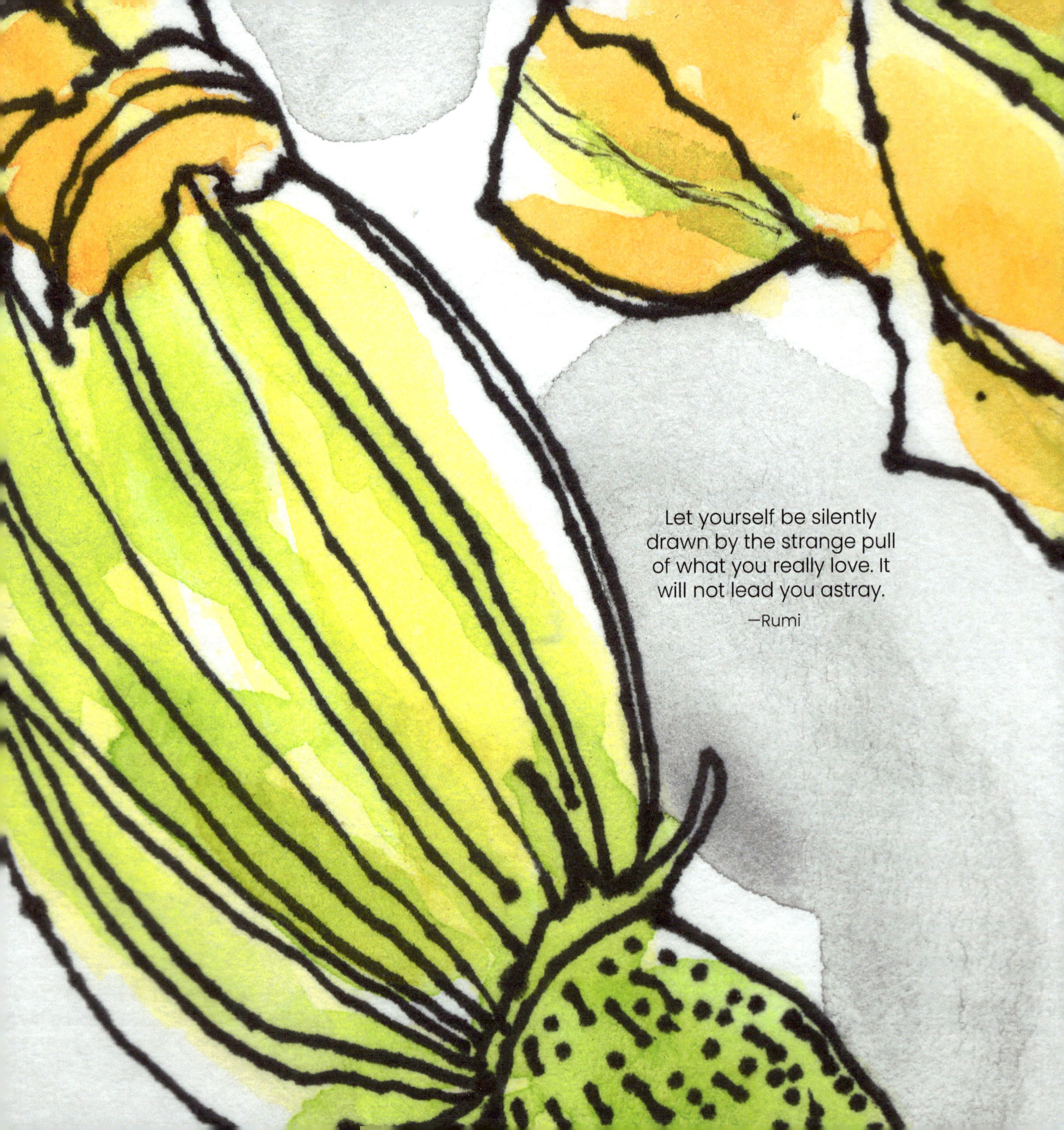
Let yourself be silently
drawn by the strange pull
of what you really love. It
will not lead you astray.
—Rumi

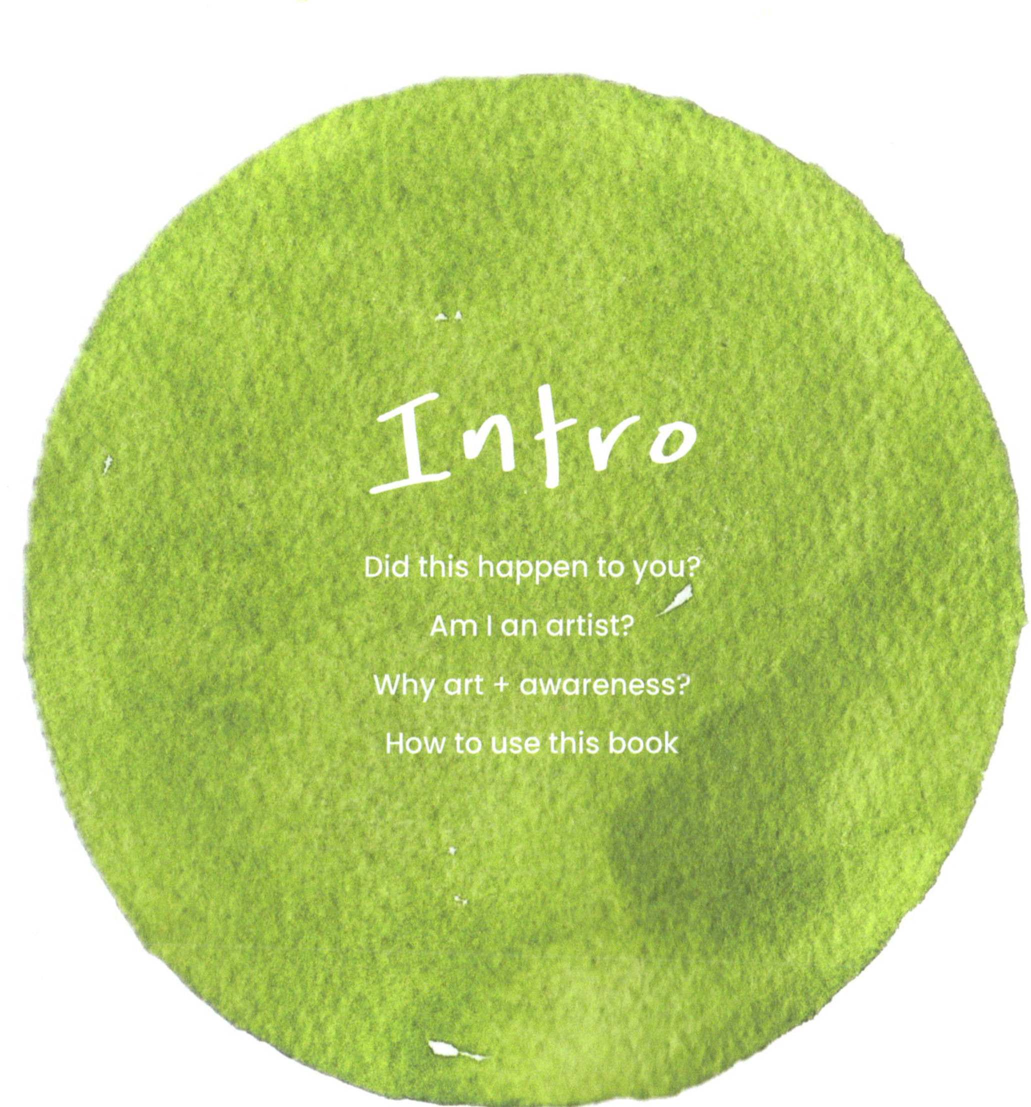

Intro

Did this happen to you?

Am I an artist?

Why art + awareness?

How to use this book

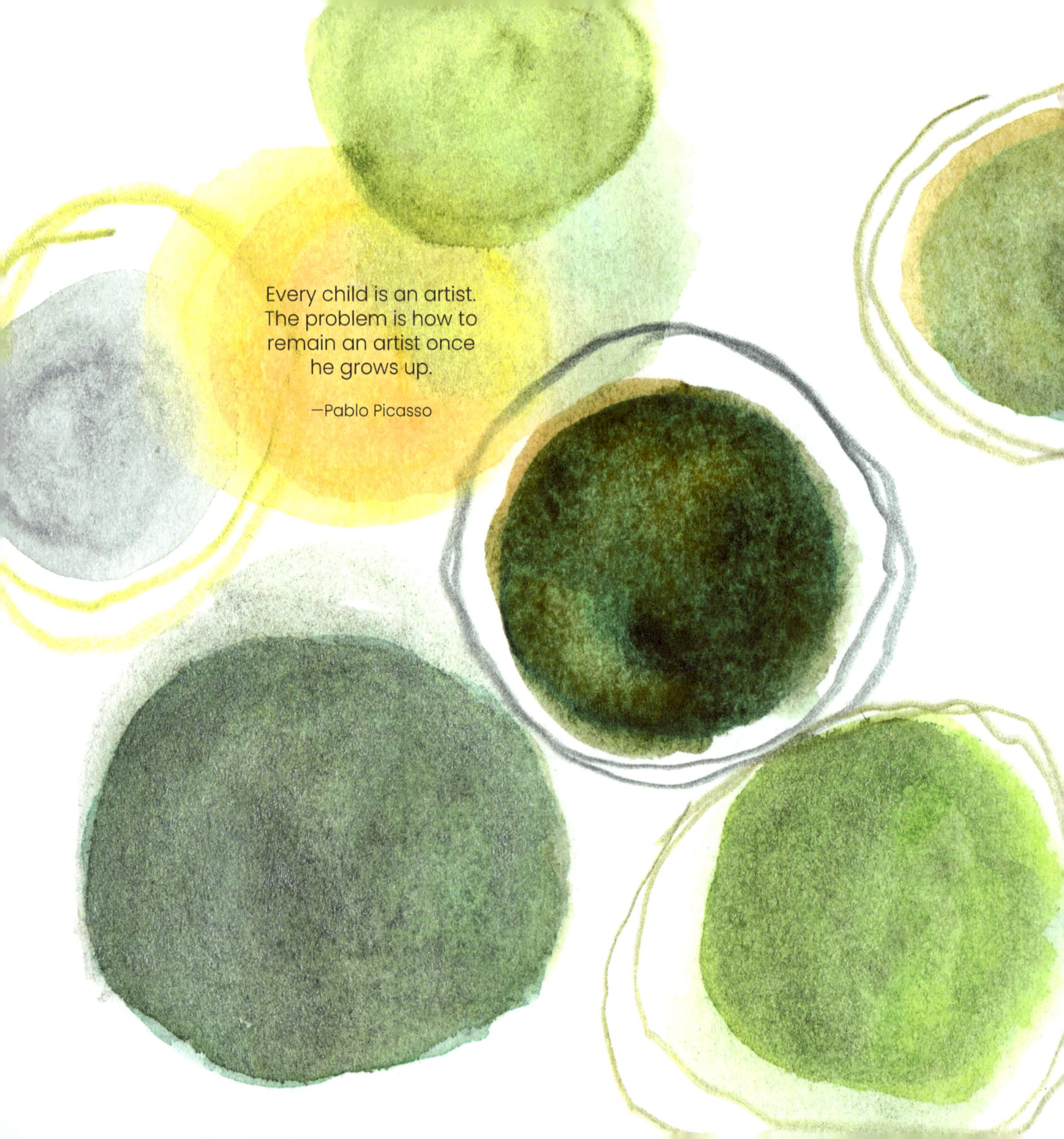
Every child is an artist.
The problem is how to
remain an artist once
he grows up.

—Pablo Picasso

Did this happen to you?

As a young child, I would happily draw anything. There weren't "good" or "bad" drawings; there was just drawing, and I didn't think much about it. I just drew. But at some point, I stopped drawing everything and only drew stylized mushrooms, frogs, and flowers.

I didn't know it, but I had entered a "drawing crisis." This crisis commonly happens around the age of nine or ten, when kids realize their drawings don't look realistic and become discouraged. Many of us stop drawing at this point.

At the same time, the world becomes filled with new challenges and opportunities. Here is a photo from a time when I wore the same red plaid dress pretty much every day and could beat anyone, boy or girl, in a running race on the school playground. Later, schoolwork became more challenging, but back then, school was easy, playing on the playground was easy, and art was hard. I didn't know how to get better at art, and frankly, I was just better at other stuff.

Also, my early report cards developed a common theme. "Perrin needs to slow down. She does good work, but she works too fast." Drawing and observation require patience. Maybe I needed to get older, perhaps even fifty years older, to finally slow down enough to observe the world around me.

So here I am, so many years later, with the desire to make art but no experience or skills. And I've found that once you get older, it's harder to be a beginner. There is a disconnect between how you view yourself as a generally competent person and your ability to draw something common, like a cat or a car. If you draw poorly, it must mean you can't do art, right? And how incredibly embarrassing it is to draw like a child!

A pivotal moment in my reentry into the world of drawing came when I discovered the book *Syllabus* by Lynda Barry. A cartoonist, writer, teacher, and illustrator, Barry helped me see the magic in drawings done by adults who haven't drawn for a while. She said, "There is a realness in them that is hard to come by."

I also laughed out loud when Barry recounts the horror and embarrassment she's witnessed that adults express about their drawings. That was 100 percent me.

try this

Grab a piece of paper and spend five minutes drawing a car, an animal, or a superhero. Do you want to keep your drawing or throw it away?

resource

The book *Syllabus* by Lynda Barry opened up a world of possibility for me. Consisting entirely of handwritten syllabi, notes, and illustrations from her college courses, *Syllabus* has numerous assignments and suggestions that I find tremendously freeing and helpful.

Am I an artist?

I married someone you can easily call an artist: a man who studied Fine Arts in college and can draw charming comic strips, build delightful wooden toys, and paint stunning portraits. But my art adventures mostly ended fifty years ago when, like so many of us, I stopped drawing.

The years were busy. When the kids moved out, work slowed, and I finally had some time, I had this little voice inside me that urged me to create. The voice was urgent but also unsure.

My husband suggested a printing class at a local community art school. I was nervous but signed up. The instructor was lovely, but I was a disaster. I was very anxious—let's just say that after the first day of class, it was only when I got home that I realized I had been wearing one shoe and one slipper all day. I was way over my head. It was an oil monoprint class, and there was a precise way of using the press, and you had to keep everything clean. It was very hard to relax. I made some big messes.

But it got me looking at the art school course catalog, and one day, I saw a nature journaling class. It was called "Nature Journaling—For the Joy of It" and was taught by a woman named Jude Siegel. It was described as "a relaxing, delightful way to record what charms you, with simple drawing and watercolor, and some writing. Learn to see in a new way, to create pages that reflect experiences, observations, musings. Not for mastery, but as a personal, creative way to 'pay attention, be astonished, tell about it.' –Mary Oliver."

I mustered my courage and signed up. Jude's class opened up art again for me. She would say simple things like, "It is your journal. You can do anything you want." It's crazy how liberating that was. And she would add, "If you don't like something, you can paste over it or just turn the page." With this newfound encouragement, I started working in journals.

But I found there was still so much that got in my way. Starting something new is often frustrating and challenging. That first burst of inspiration can be easily swallowed by discouragement.

I made my way forward by combining practical habits with mindfulness concepts. I sorted out some easy-to-do practices and started viewing art in a new way. My art-making has become very different from what I envisioned it would be.

Am I an artist? That question that seemed so important now seems odd. What I can say is that I make art almost every day.

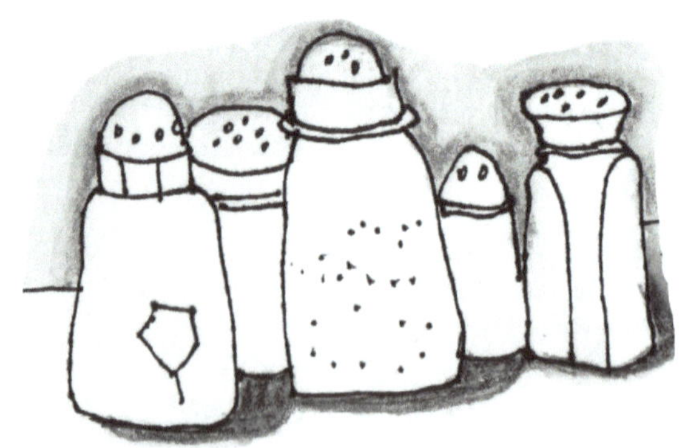

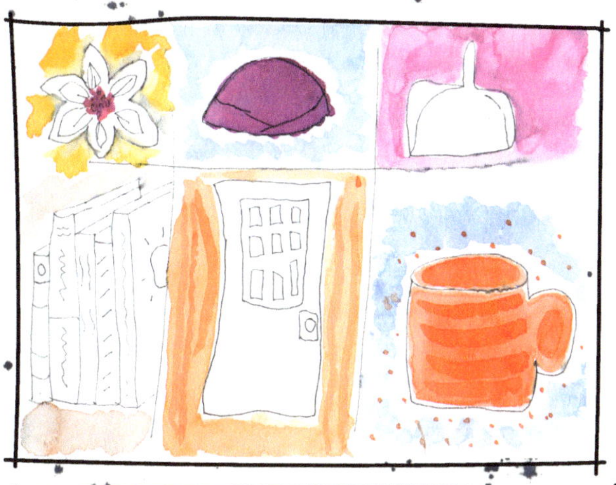

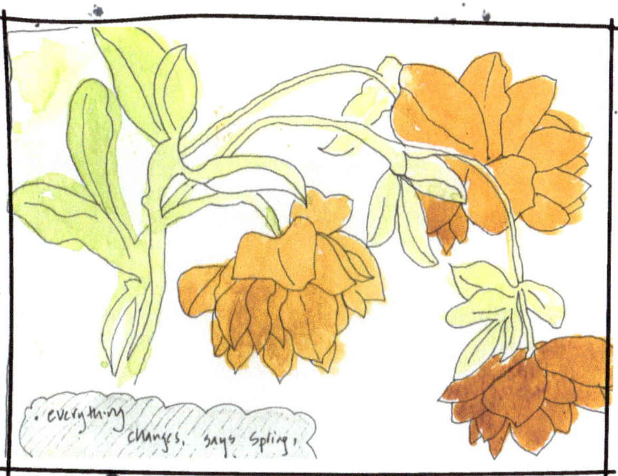

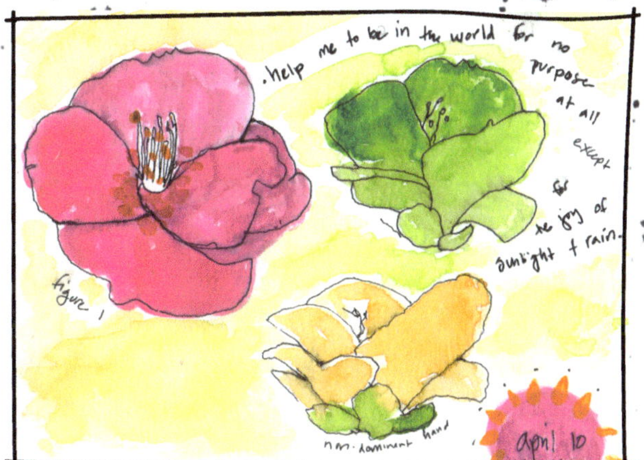

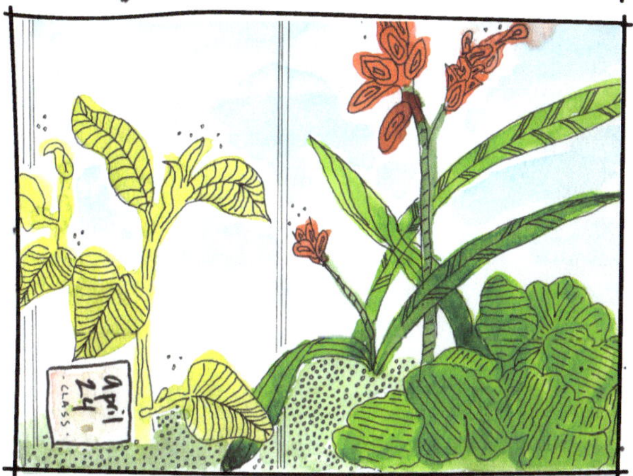

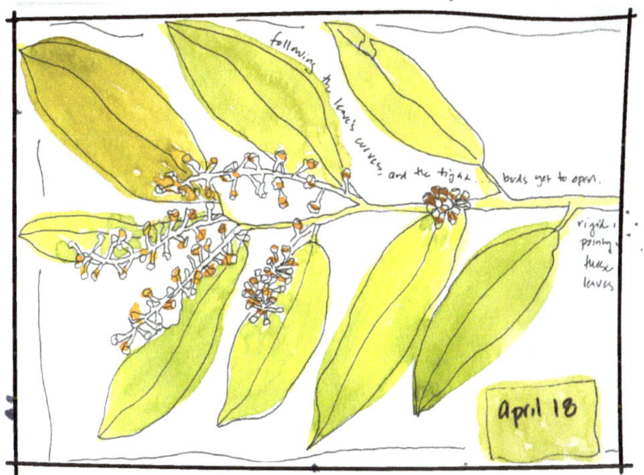

Some pages from that first class with Jude

try this

Take a few minutes today to look at some art or a photograph, listen to music actively, or read a poem. Keep your mind open and relaxed, and just enjoy it. You don't have to do anything with it.

At the end of the day, you can remember that you made a little space for something that you enjoy, something that matters to you.

Why art + awareness?

The connections between art and awareness are both myriad and wonderful; this book explores many of those connections. But most essentially, both art and awareness strengthen the ability to see.

I should be good at seeing because I do it all the time, but in reality, I overlook much of what is right in front of me. I don't think this is unusual; most of us habitually construct our lives in our heads. Consumed by thinking, memories, or planning for the future, we are often blind to what is right here, right now.

Similarly, our brains use shorthand to help us navigate the world. They are continually simplifying and predicting what we see. We look just long enough—and no longer—to get to where we are going. We just don't have to look carefully.

Art-making invites attention, which encourages looking, which, in turn, encourages noticing and seeing. Awareness is also about paying attention and noticing what you are paying attention to. Art and awareness prompt different kinds of looking that can help us see the world more clearly.

Paying attention and carefully looking can result in a deeper appreciation of life. In *The Zen of Seeing*, the Zen artist Frederick Frank describes the sort of seeing he experiences when he draws something: "It is in order to really see, to see ever deeper, ever more intensely, hence to be fully aware and alive, that I draw ... I have learned that what I have not drawn, I have never really seen, and that when I start drawing an ordinary thing, I realize how extraordinary it is, sheer miracle."

You could say that Frank's description of seeing as becoming more aware and alive is at the center of what this book is all about. But you could also say there is no center, and it is all about the journey and the fun. Either way, attention, awareness, and art all circle around, encouraging each other while strengthening our ability to see.

Much has been written about attention and awareness, but here is the simple way I think about it.

I find that to recognize awareness, I have to pay attention. My attention is something that I feel I have some control over. The world is a wild mix of experiences; some pass unnoticed, while others yell for attention. Since what I pay attention to is what I notice and what colors my world, it makes sense for me to hone my ability to pay attention.

It is often said that what you pay attention to grows stronger, that attention is a form of love, and that the key to greater awareness is simply noticing what you are paying attention to. I think all these are true.

Attention is an excellent tool. I think of it like a camera's zoom function. I can pull back and notice many things or instead focus tightly on a single thing.

Awareness, on the other hand, is not something I create or control. It is always there, often unseen, in the background— attention reveals it.

When I look more closely, learn something new, or understand something from a new perspective, I gain what I think of as a little awareness. Then, there is the big awareness that permeates everything.

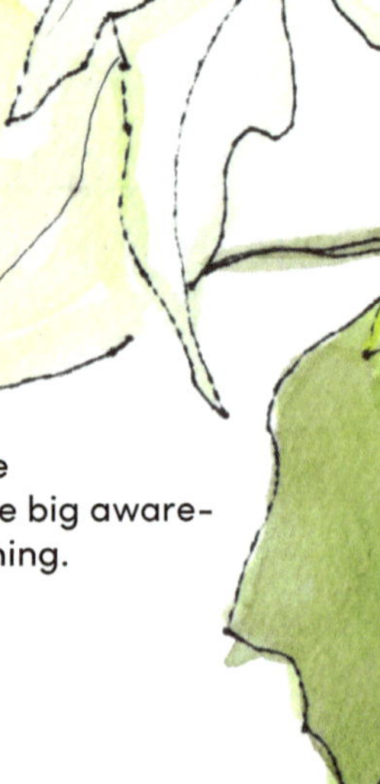

Mindfulness teachers use many different terms for this sort of awareness: natural awareness, spatial awareness, primordial awareness, and awake awareness, just to name a few. All of them speak to an awareness that is felt, quite hard to define, and a bit mysterious while simultaneously being common, close at hand, and present at all times.

Definitions of awareness aside, I have learned that making art helps me pay attention, which makes me more aware. Awareness helps me keep making art, and it goes on and on—a lovely little circle.

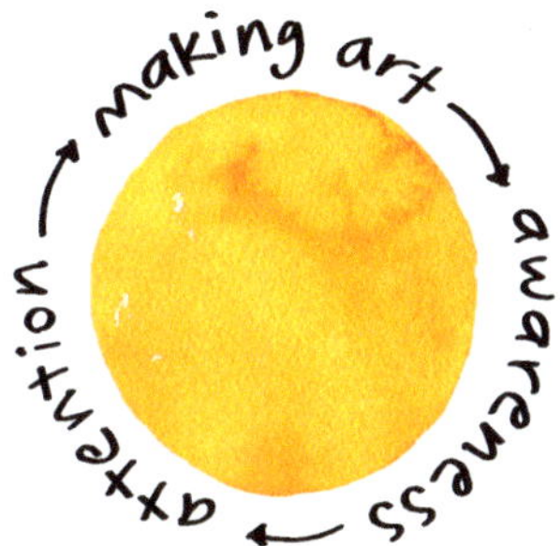

resource

If you want to learn more about nondual awareness, the *Waking Up app* is a treasure chest. In this app, Sam Harris gives an introductory meditation course on nondual awareness to get listeners started. From there, you can explore the app's many meditation practices, conversations, and lectures from teachers, spiritual leaders, scientists, and philosophers. I find it to be consistently educational, helpful, and engaging. There is so much there!

try this

Sitting quietly for five minutes can help you notice what you are paying attention to.

You could try meditating. It is not for everyone, but it can change how you see yourself and the world.

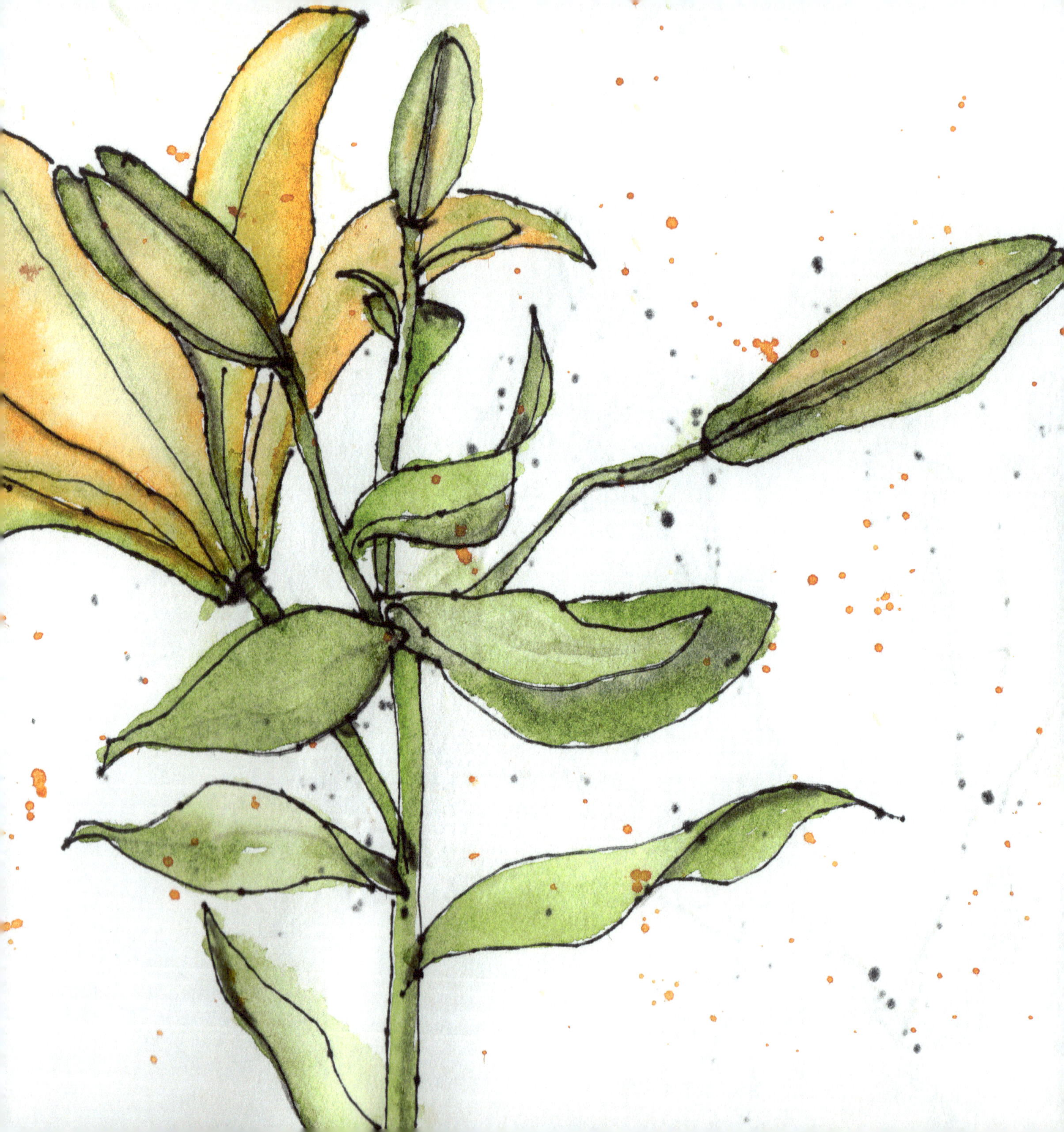

How to use this book

This book aims to jump-start your creativity right away. Need some help starting a daily practice? The "Creating a practice" chapter on page 25 has lots of suggestions. Keep getting stopped in your tracks by your reaction to what you have made? Turn to page 46 to find some skillful ways to approach evaluation.

The book begins with a look at the old stories that can get in our way and then moves on to helpful tips about structuring a creative practice. A section on discomfort comes next since discomfort often quickly accompanies making. From there, I share the fun and possibilities I have discovered in art-making. After that, the book gets a bit more "philosophical." Art-making is provocative; it uncovers paradoxes, possibilities, and new ways of seeing the world. The connections between awareness and art-making are both fascinating and helpful to explore. The end of the book takes a look at some of these connections.

Scattered throughout are activities to try, resources, and tips. These sections are suggestions, not assignments. Trust yourself to find the ones that work for you. You might end up looping back around or pushing forward. You don't need to start at the beginning and read to the end—you could just open the book up and see what catches your eye.

Woven throughout are concepts from awareness. You can't truly separate philosophy from practice. I often consider philosophy as the foundation or the iceberg beneath the water. The suggestions and lists are only the tip of the iceberg. Often, it is the philosophical ideas that give those suggestions staying power. When frustration inevitably shows up or when you wonder what the heck you are doing, philosophical concepts will be there to bolster your practice.

And when your inspiration and enthusiasm slip away, this book is here to remind you that you don't actually need either of those things.

These ideas are not linear, and this book isn't either. Many of these concepts feed into each other in a sort of continuous loop. There is also a certain amount of returning again and again to certain ideas—they bear repeating; that is the practice. I hope some of these concepts and practices become embedded in your life, but I also hope you never expect to complete them. The doing is the magic.

And what works for me might not work for you. Take what works and discard what doesn't. Your creative journey is just as wonderful and individual as you are.

resource

Throughout the book, you will find resources listed. I found these books, apps, websites, and classes particularly helpful. (A more complete list of resources is also included at the end of the book.)

try this

You will also find things to try. These are activities that help me keep my creative self awake and alive. However, they really are things to try rather than assignments. Find the ones that work for you!

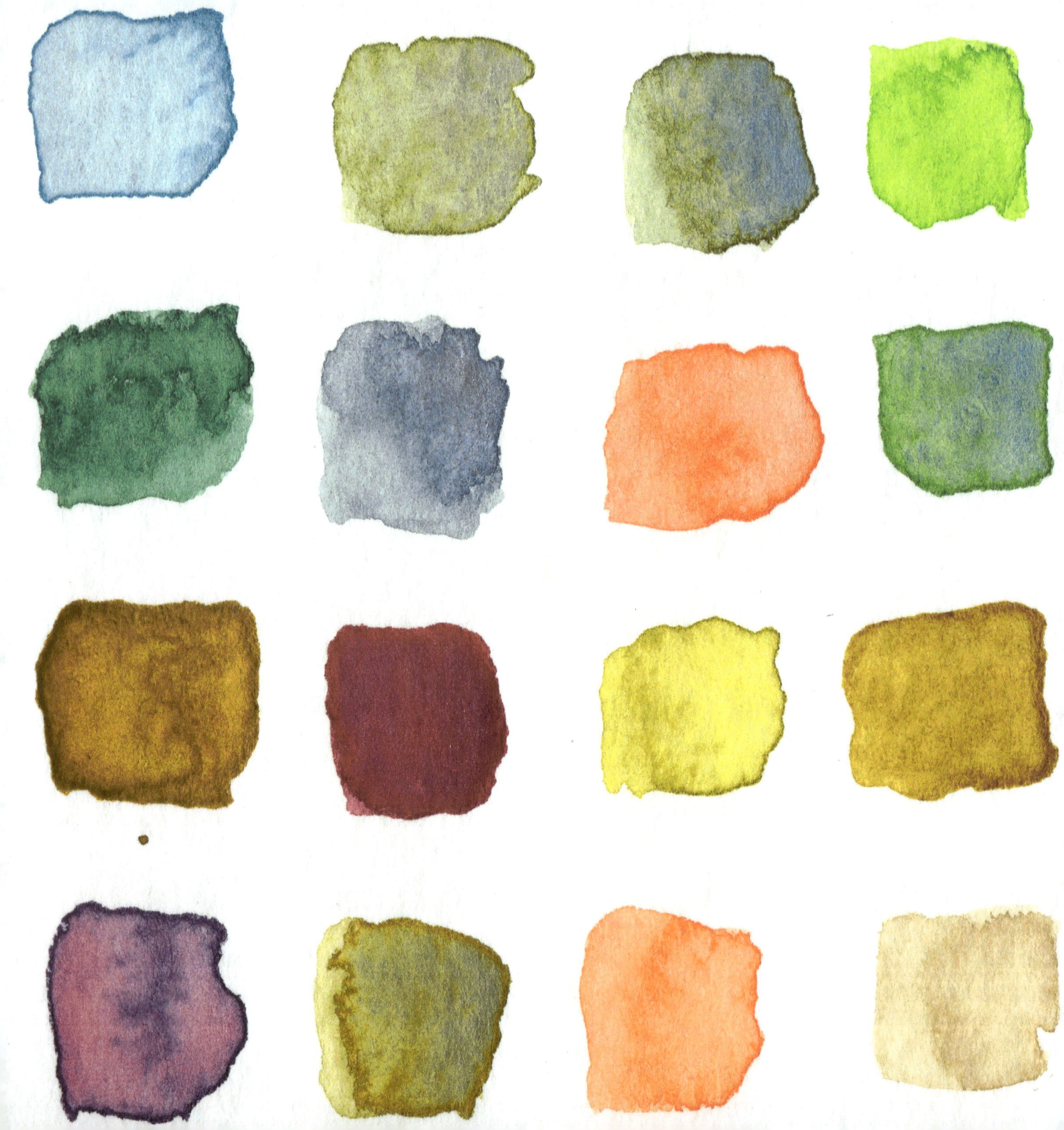

Old stories

Talent

Comparison

Competency + efficiency

Utility

Being good

Evaluation

Talent

Years ago, I was playing Pictionary with my family, and the clue was "horse." I drew something so ridiculous that it reduced the entire family into a helpless laughing fit. (Strangely enough, my daughter Ella—drawing on some sixth sense—guessed horse, which is part of what made it incredibly funny.) The word "horse" still makes us all laugh.

Pictionary advertises the game as a chance to get together with friends "to find out who's an artist and who really isn't!" Does that mean I am not an artist? If I had talent, wouldn't I have known how to draw a horse?

If I try to draw any number of things, they look pretty silly. If I had talent, the thinking goes, I wouldn't be struggling so much. If I had talent, I would be satisfied with more of my art-making. If I had talent, I could draw on street corners, confident when someone looked over my shoulder. Okay, that is clearly not my experience, so why am I continuing to try to make art? I guess because I have realized "talent" is a word and an idea that sounds good and supportive but is really a bomb.

The other day in class, a fellow student, Margaret, made a gorgeous painting of hydrangeas and hellebores. Her painting was carefully, meticulously, and lovingly rendered. Someone said, "Wow, Margaret, you have real talent." And yet, I was also taken with another student, Francine's, painting. Francine's painting featured stiff, garish flowers with shocking colors; her work was so different, so uncommon!

And so I wondered, does Francine not have talent? Is this so-called "talent" the ability to paint something in a more conventional way? And did the comment about Margaret having talent mean no one else in the class did? And will Margaret now be afraid to share a painting that is not as finished or as realistic because she would be seen as no longer having talent? Is being seen as talented as big of a trap as being seen as untalented?

It reminds me of a study by Claudia Mueller and Carol Dweck on affirming language and its impact on performance. A group of 400 fifth-graders were given a test. Half were told they did well because they were smart; the other half were told they did well because they worked hard. The kids were tested again later, and the half that had been told they did well because they were talented did more poorly than the half who had been told they did well because they worked hard.

Upon further inspection, the whole idea of talent seems odd. There are lots of things we need to be taught to do: typing, reading, driving a car, writing. It wouldn't make sense to teach kids skills only in areas where they demonstrate "talent." And would we know what talent even looked like in any of these areas? Is talent derived from familiarity or experience?

I don't expect to pick up a flute and know how to play it. Why should I expect myself to know how to draw a horse? Sure, I have an aptitude for some things in art but absolutely zero for others. I began to realize talent was a story I could simply let go of.

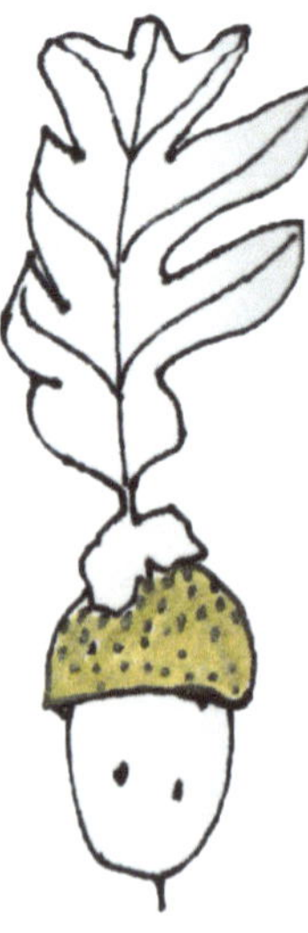

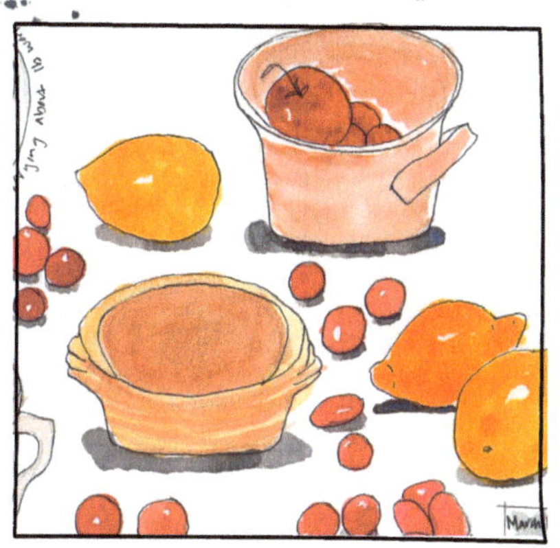

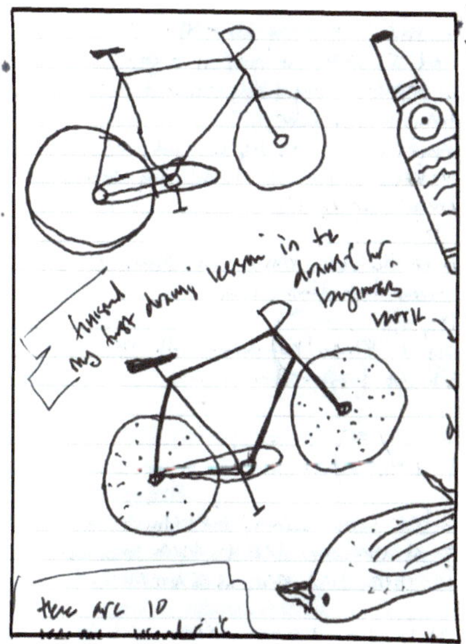

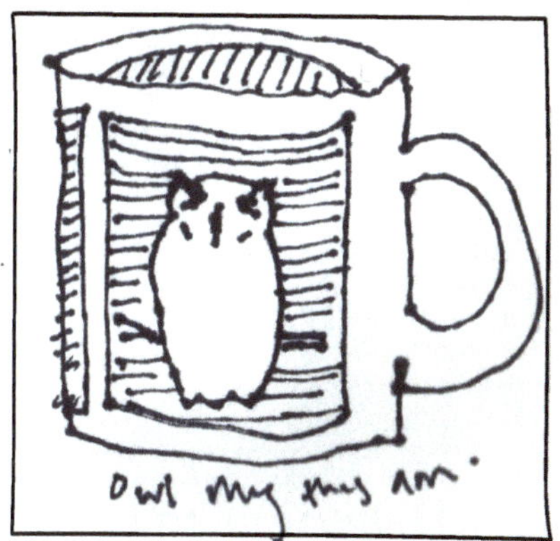

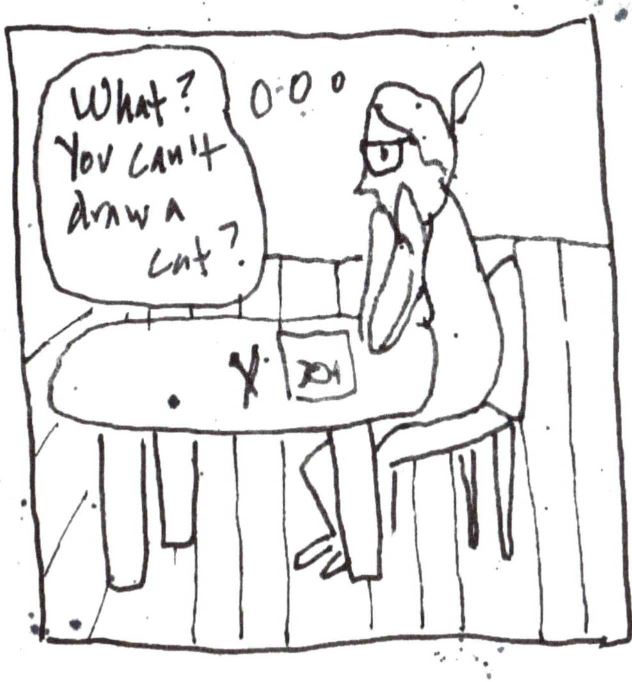

try this

Get some sort of little notebook and start writing some things, really anything. It doesn't matter what you write. (Sometimes, an inexpensive book can be less intimidating than a fancy one.)

There is something satisfying about using paper and pen when so much of our lives are on screens.

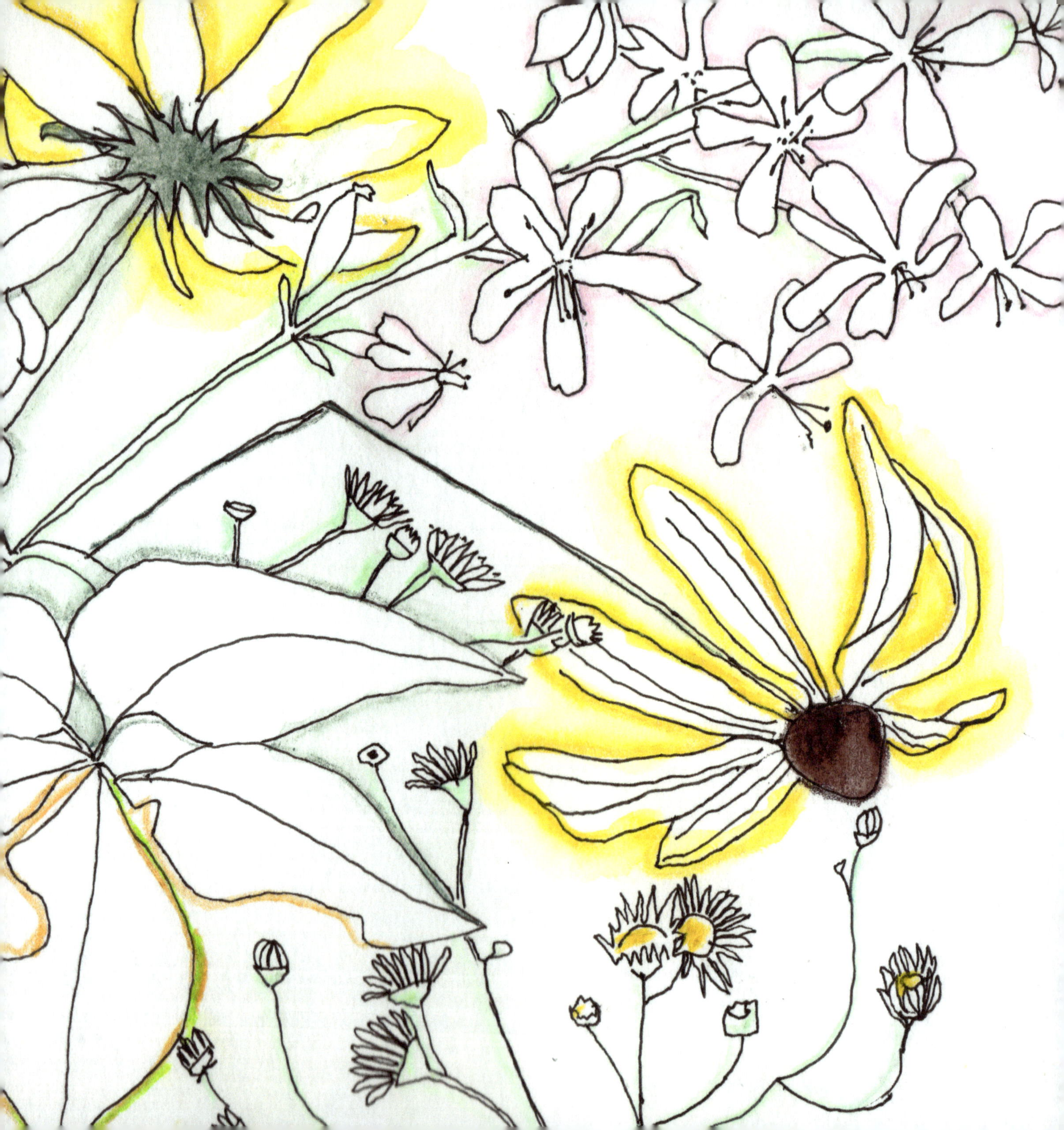

Comparison

Comparing our work to others happens so easily, so naturally, and it can be so discouraging. While I know we all come to art-making from different places, it is hard not to get sucked into comparing my work to others. And comparison can feel bad. As Theodore Roosevelt famously said, "Comparison is the thief of joy."

The other day in watercolor class, a couple of students, Denise and Mathilda, shared their paintings—gorgeous landscapes with both breadth and detail—and I thought, *I have no idea how they did that ... I have absolutely no idea how they were able to paint that.* It feels crummy to compare your work to others' and find it lacking.

But in looking at those landscapes, I didn't think that Denise and Mathilda had more talent than I do (because you know how I feel about talent); instead, I felt as if there was a vast distance between what they knew and what I knew.

It is hard to tell how great that distance truly is.

I see only the surface when I view someone else's art. What I don't see is the time spent making the piece. I also don't see all the experience they have behind them. I am looking at the tip of the iceberg. It is hard to remember that the work likely took many hours to complete because I take it all in in a moment. It is easy to think it was created just as quickly. I also remind myself that most people share what they consider their best work; the rest I am unlikely to see.

It could be that next week, I will learn something that will help close the distance.

This brings me to the good side of comparison. Comparison is not helpful to me when I use it to judge my competence, but it is useful as a way to gain information.

In class, I asked Denise how she had painted her trees, and she said, "Oh, with a filbert brush." I had never heard of them, but she said filberts were her favorite kind of brush. Then, she demonstrated how she used them to make the foliage. She was glad to share her technique, and I learned something valuable. It created a happy little moment. So, I guess Roosevelt wasn't completely right.

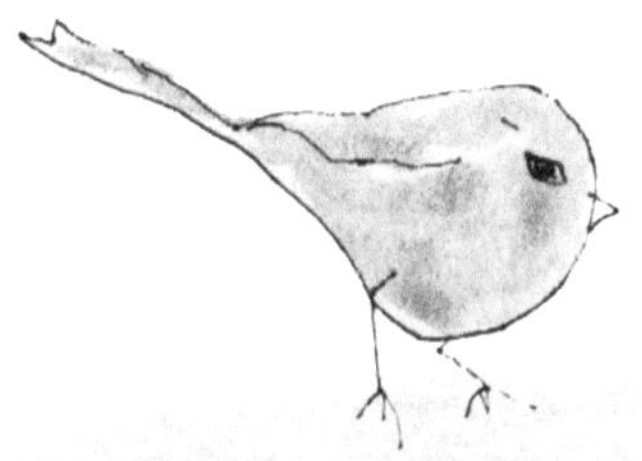

try this

Try some different pens and pencils. A scritchy pen or pencil drives me crazy, whereas I am absolutely in love with the smooth lines some pens and pencils make. By trying and comparing different pens and pencils, you will discover what *you* like.

You can start by trying out whatever you find in your drawers.

Competency + efficiency

This might sound obvious, but we live in a world that values competence. When people are told they are good at something, they tend to keep doing it. Encouragement can be scarce when we are not good at something.

We are drawn to competence. I love watching people draw or paint with confidence and skill. It can be mesmerizing. My friends Emma and Noah often watch videos of people detailing cars or repairing antiques. There is something very soothing about watching other people do things well. It makes the work look easy, efficient, and almost effortless.

The trouble is that beginners are seldom competent or efficient. Is there anything less efficient than a beginner? Who wants to be the person bumbling along, taking more effort or time than others do? And who wants to make something that looks like a kid could have made it?

When I started making art, it was a virtual wilderness of disappointment. It would have been easy to give up.

I don't think that's unusual. In her book *Big Magic*, Elizabeth Gilbert notes, "If you want to be an artist of any sort, it seemed to me, then handling your frustration is a fundamental aspect of the work—perhaps the single most fundamental aspect of the work."

Ira Glass's quote about the frustration felt by beginners is helpful and widely shared— Jude Siegel handed it out in our first class: "Nobody tells this to people who are beginners, I wish someone told me... For the first couple years you make stuff, it's just not that good. It's trying to be good, it has potential, but it's not ... A lot of people never get past this phase, they quit ... It's gonna take awhile. It's normal to take awhile. You've just gotta fight your way through."

I came home and pasted Ira's quote in my journal. If disappointment was simply part of the gig, well then, maybe I was okay. I needed to accept that there were things I simply didn't know how to do and that things weren't going to turn out the way I thought they should.

I had to accept the fact that I was neither competent nor efficient; there was simply no other way to start. And I can learn to put a question mark after the value of competence and efficiency because maybe they are not as important as they initially appear. The idea that we should only do things we are efficient or competent at is ruthless and impoverished. After all, if my prerequisite to doing something is being good at it, then there are a good many things I will never do. When competence and efficiency become barriers, they may not be such great things after all.

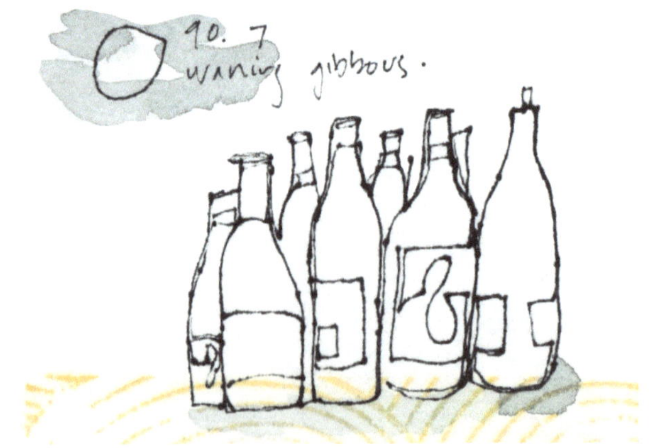

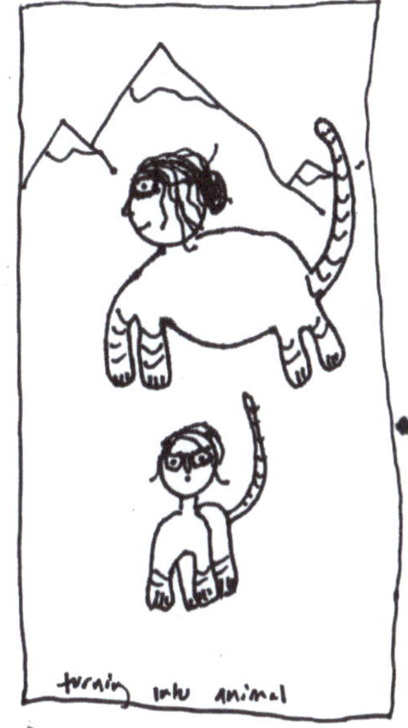

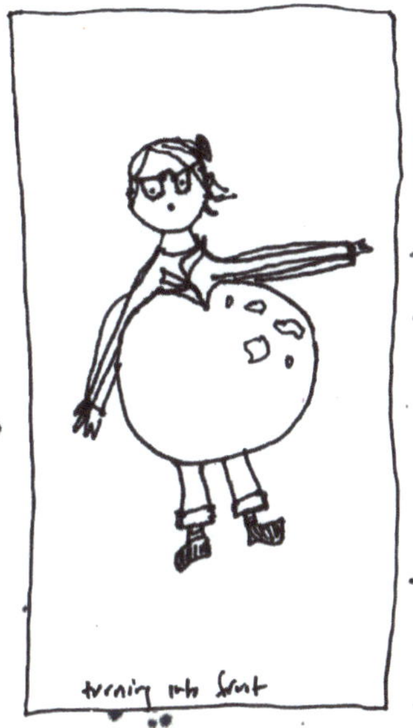

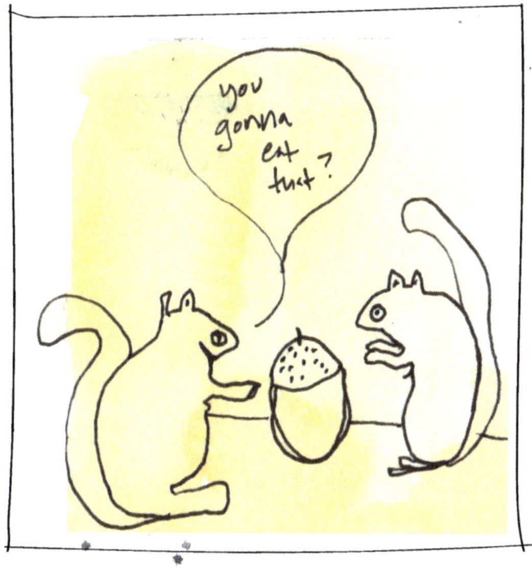

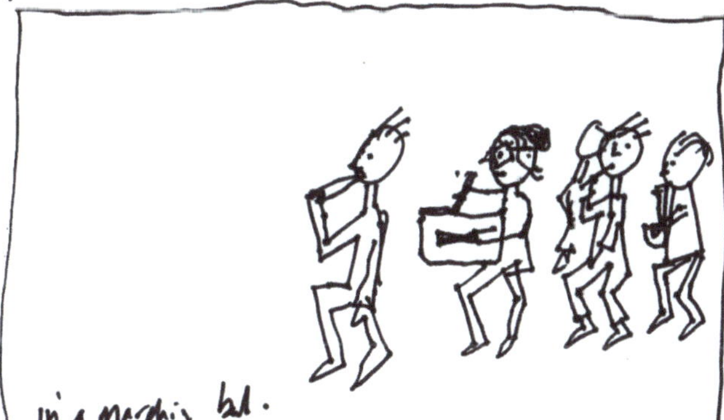

Some sketches based on prompts from Lynda Barry's book, Making Comics.

try this

See if you can notice what stories run through your head when you make something. You don't have to stop the thought or change the thought; simply notice that it is there. You can note, Hmmm, that's a thought, but you don't need to entertain it any more than that.

Most of us have some sort of background chatter. Simply becoming aware of this background talk is helpful.

Utility

When I sit down to draw, a voice in my head often asks: *Is this* really *what you should be doing right now?* Like everyone, I have an endless supply of to-do lists and can think of boundless, productive ways to spend my time. *Isn't it selfish to spend all that time on yourself?* The voice asks. *Isn't this mostly medio-cre art-making a waste of your limited time here on Earth?* Anxieties about how I use my time are often tied to utility.

We live in a culture that values usefulness. It's easy to treat ourselves, others, and time as resources. There is a powerful, invisible belief that the most important thing for humans to do is to produce, to be good at things, to make money, and to get things done.

Questions about how we spend our time come from many different sources. When I was a kid, my dad put a note on the fridge: "Is this the way you want to live your life?" He meant it as a kindly reminder to be intentional, but somehow, I interpreted it to mean that the way I was going about everything might be wrong. Was I spending time and energy on the wrong things?

Mary Oliver famously asks, "Tell me what is it you plan to do with your one wild and precious life?"

What a lot of pressure!

And what to say when people ask me, "What will you do with your art?"

With so much to do and so little time, how can doing something with little apparent value or use be okay?

But then again ... how can I not spend time on this?

Mary Oliver writes: "The most regretful people on earth are those who felt the call to creative work, who felt their own creative power restive and uprising, and gave it neither power nor time."

You often hear that when people reach the end of their lives, one of their most powerful regrets is that they didn't live the life they wanted but instead led the life that others expected of them.

When I reach the end of my life, I would like to say, "Yes, I spent my time on earth in a way that was valu-able to me."

Of course, I want to be useful. I want to help and do my bit to make the world a better place. Being useful to others is an essential and wonderful part of being human, but measuring everything I do by the external metric of utility seems both reductive and misguided.

The danger of always being useful is that you may miss a chance to simply grow and become. This is often illustrated by an image of an old gnarled tree. The tree's bent branches and twisted wood are of no use as lumber, so it is not cut down. It is left alone to grow old and thus survives. The tree does not have to be useful; it can just be.

And then I start wondering: Can I even tell what is truly useful? How can I know where things will end up? Who is making up the standards for useful ac-tivities? If I spend my day focused on getting things done, will I not see that my neighbor is suffering? If I do what I am called to, will that end up being the most useful thing of all?

One of Leo Lionni's children's fables describes a mouse named Frederick who stands quietly in the busy days of fall when the other mice are storing food for the winter. The other mice ask him reproachfully why he isn't helping, and he tells them he is storing up colors. When the bleak days of winter come, Frederick remembers, for all the other mice, the colors and warmth of summer.

Like so many things, usefulness becomes less certain and more mysterious once examined. But because the yardstick of utility is ever-present in our culture, the question of how you can allow yourself to do something (that perhaps only you see as valuable) surfaces again and again in this book.

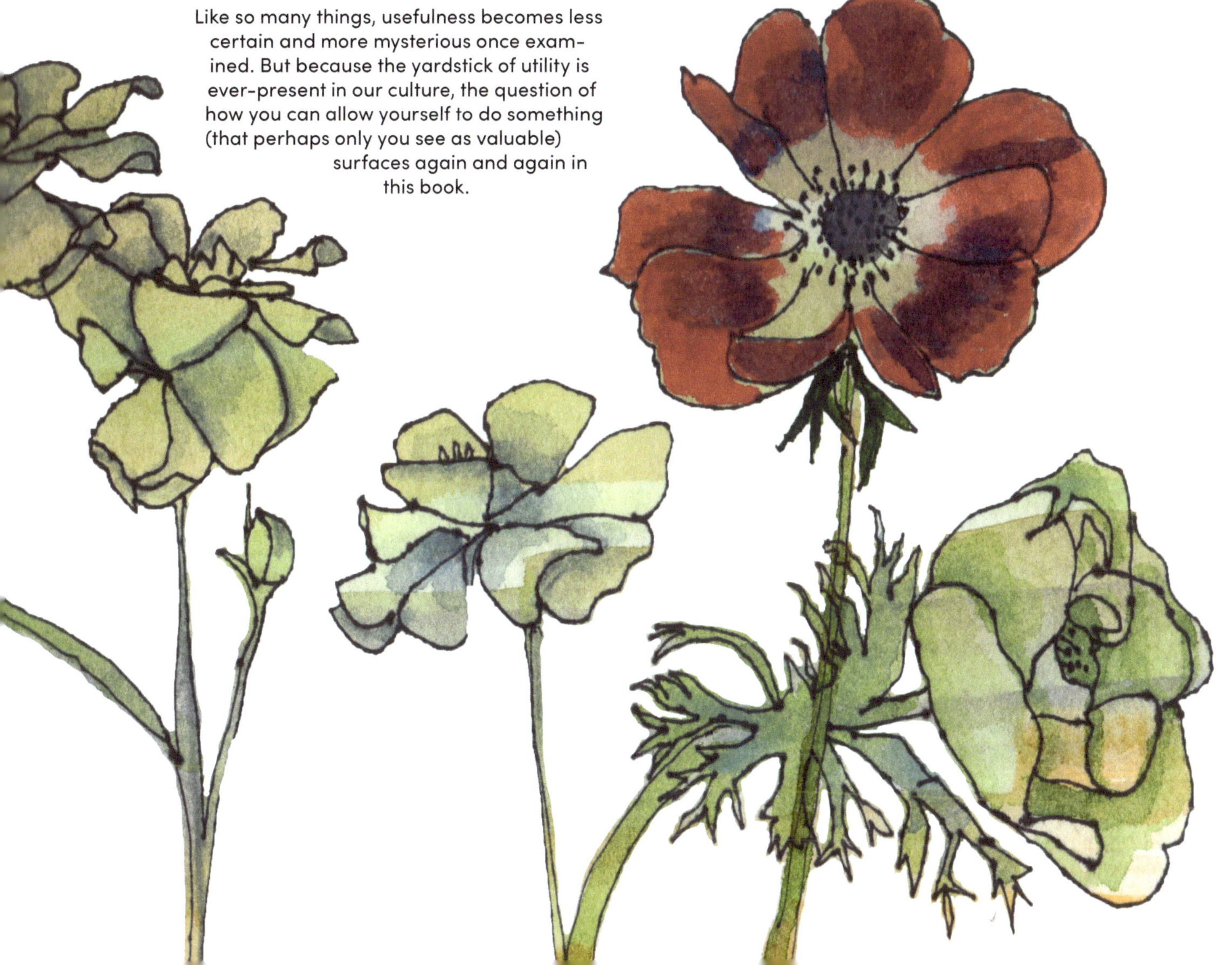

Being good

When I first started making art and learning about mindfulness, I envisioned that someday I would reach a point where both my art and I would be good!

Because I could see all the places, I fell short. I liked so little of what I made; I could only focus on all the things that weren't working. And the more aware I became, the greater the distance seemed to grow between who I was and who I wanted to be. I tried to be patient but was impatient; I wanted to let go of things but still held on tightly; I tried to listen but ended up talking instead. Some days, it seemed the list went on and on.

And yet ... I so wanted to be a good, mindful, artistic person! My awareness that I fell short on all accounts made me feel bad. That somehow didn't seem right—and it certainly wasn't fun or self-compassionate.

When I read the chapter entitled "And It's Okay" in Diana Winston's wonderful *The Little Book of Being,* I was surprised how much it resonated—especially this quote: "Some students relentlessly beat themselves up when they lose touch with natural awareness or when their meditation practice is shot and they return to habitual mind states. Do me a favor: please don't do that ... Just take a breath, relax, and do your best to let go. You can do it. It's okay. It's okay. It's okay."

That was what I was doing. I was beating myself up. Diana invited me to stop. That shifted things for me. Whereas before, I had pictured myself as needing to become a sort of blissed-out, perfect, monk-like person, I started wondering if, instead, I could just become more accepting of who I actually am.

As Buddhist teacher Pema Chödrön writes, "When people start to meditate or to work with any kind of spiritual discipline, they often think that somehow they're going to improve, which is a sort of subtle aggression against who they really are." She explains, "The point is not to try to change ourselves. Meditation practice isn't about trying to throw ourselves away and become something better. It's about befriending who we are already."

I realized I didn't want my art-making to become a means of beating myself up. If I approached my art-making focused on the final product, casting a punitive eye at everything I made, I would get frustrated and stop. Diana's reassurance of "It's okay. It's okay" could also extend to my art.

I could decide to be okay with who and where I was; judging myself as falling short was just not helping. Learning to let all that go is what would help. There is a lot wrapped up here: compassion, acceptance, non-seeking. These characteristics can be downright elusive! Woven throughout this book are practices and considerations that help me find them.

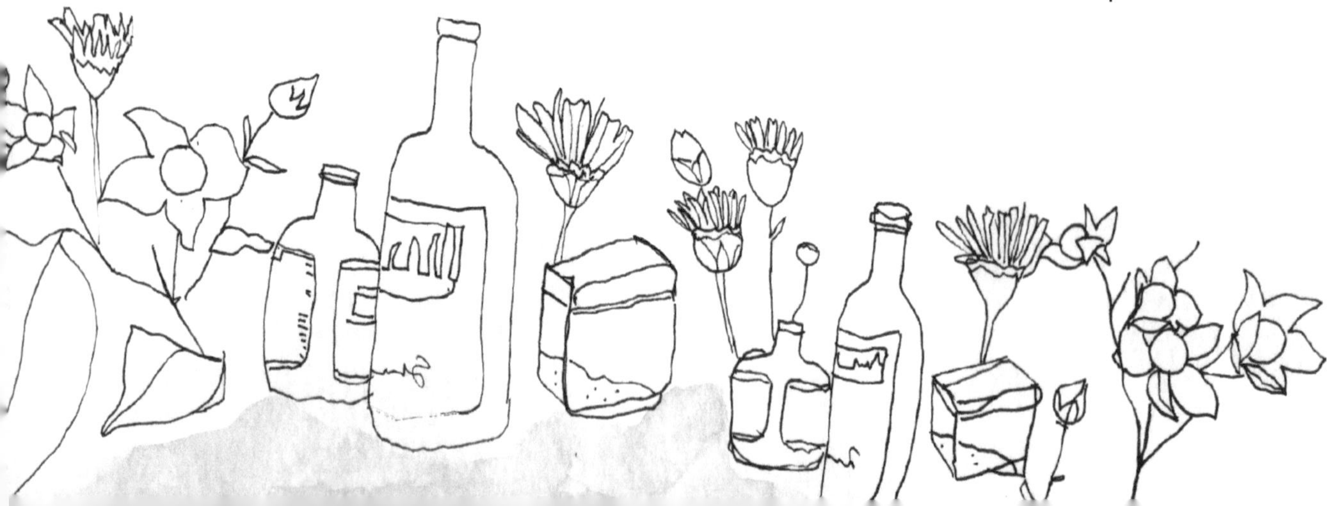

"It's okay. It's okay. It's okay."

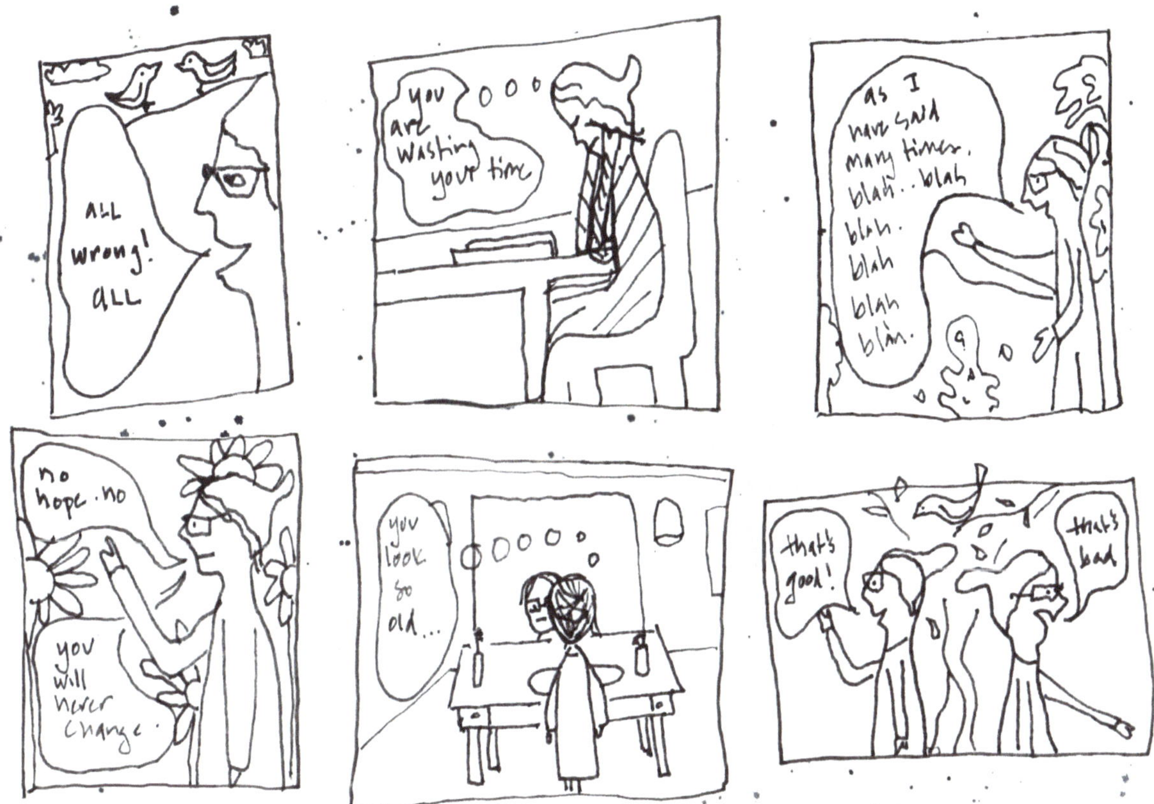

resource

Diana Winston's *The Little Book of Being* was a revelation to me. A compassionate, accessible introduction to natural awareness, *The Little Book of Being* provides teachings and meditation practices that point to this innate awareness.

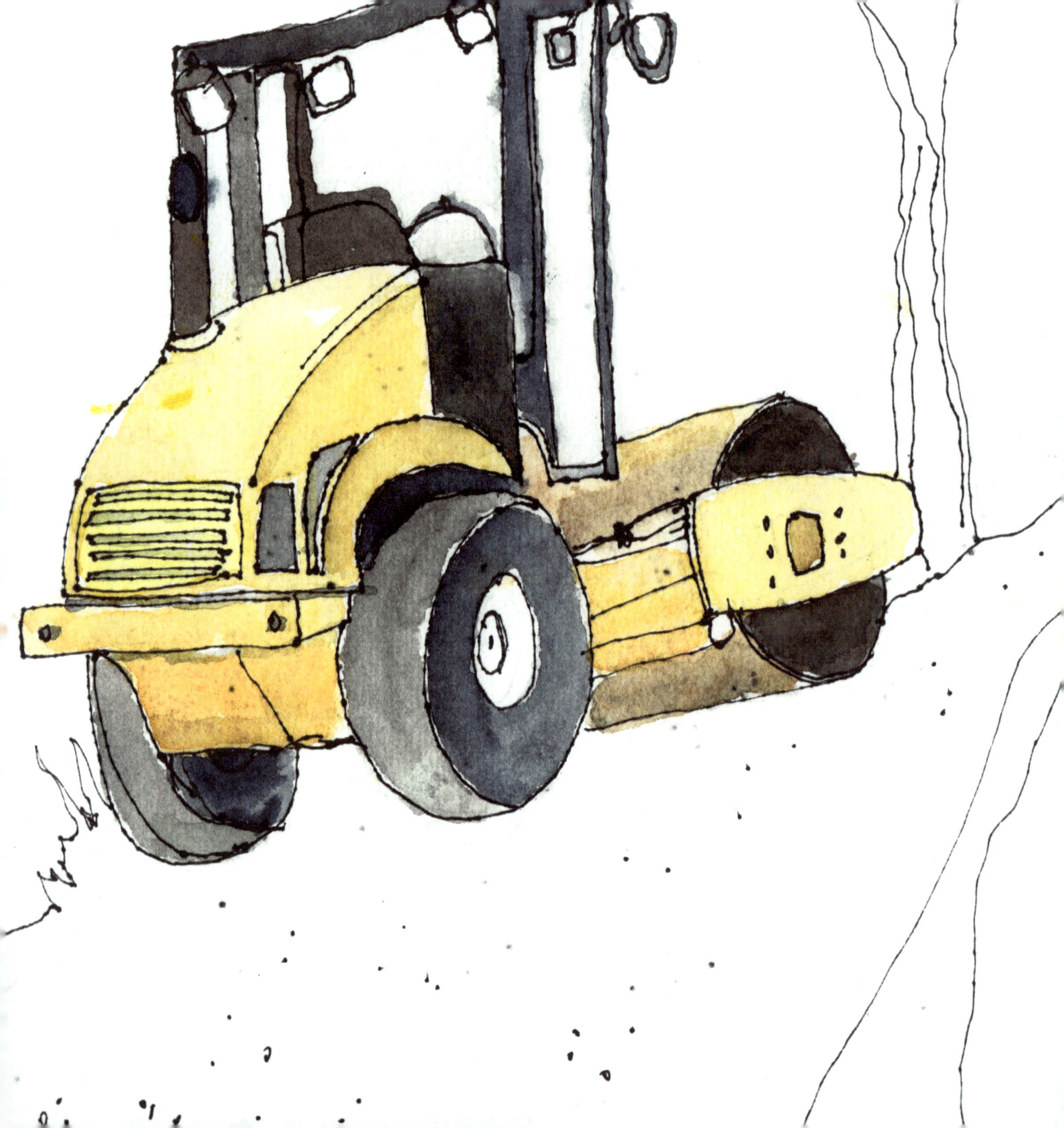

Evaluation

Anything we make can solicit an immediate response. Every time I put my pen to paper, something emerges, newly visible and nakedly subject to evaluation. Almost immediately, two questions arise:

Is it good?

Do I like it?

These questions come so naturally that they seem to be the most important questions. But learning to view them warily can be helpful.

The old story here is that these are the only questions that matter and that there is some instant correct answer based on a binary analysis of art as good or bad, likable or unlikeable.

But what we make is far more complex and interesting than these two questions would have us believe. There are probably thousands of questions you could ask about any sort of art, but learning to ask different questions, rather than limiting ourselves to an automatic reaction, is key.

If you are getting stuck by your reactions to what you make, jump right to page 46. Here, I look closely at how to work with evaluation because learning to evaluate your work skillfully is fundamental to having fun and progressing.

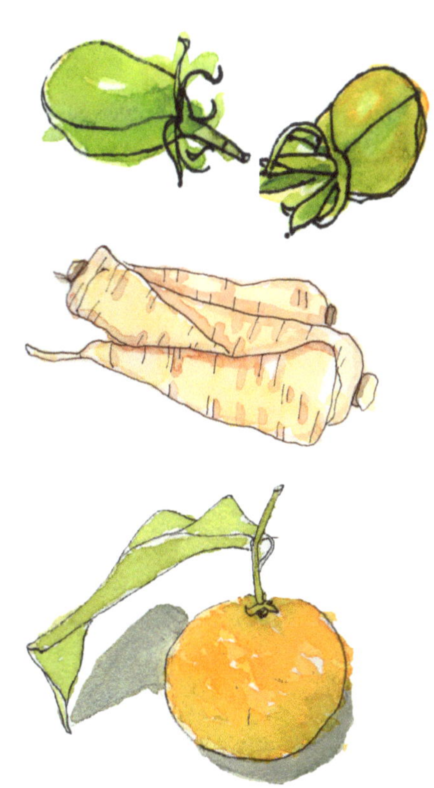

try this

Fruit and vegetables are easily accessible and fun subjects to draw. If you have some on hand, pick a couple out and draw them.

When you are finished, do you have an immediate reaction to your drawing?

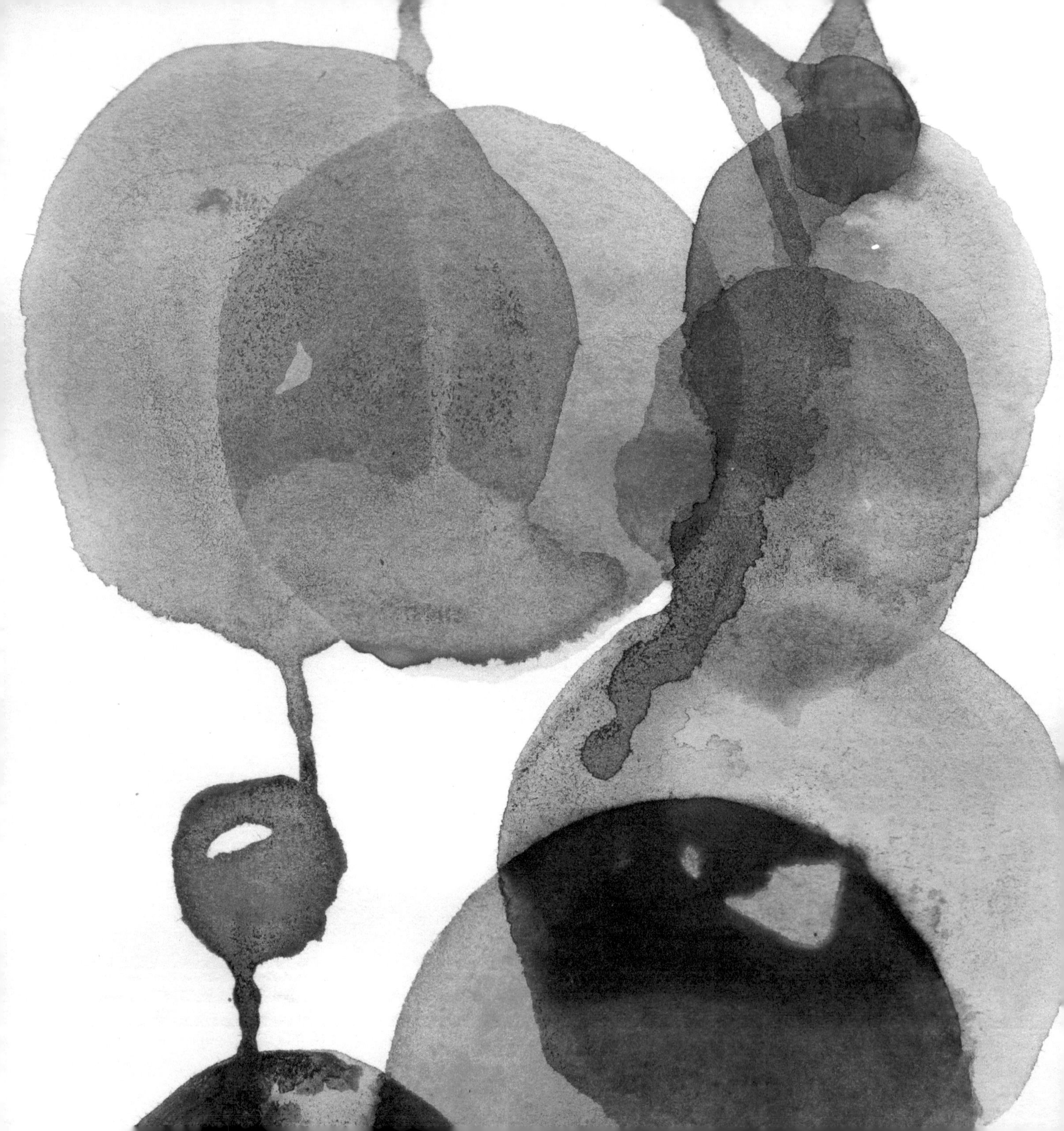

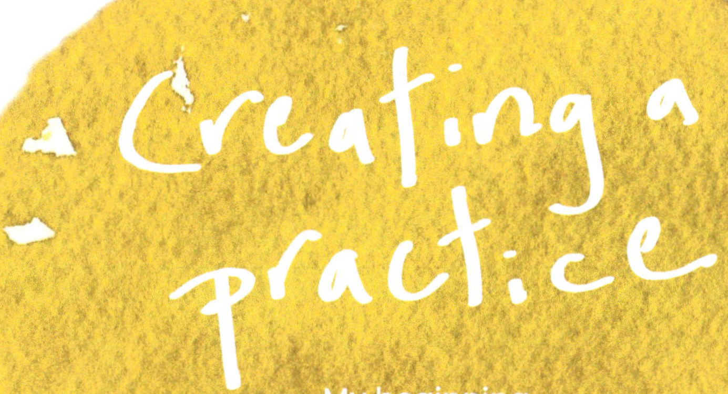

My beginning

Make a structure

Three permissions

Five tips to get started

Why a practice works

When practice becomes a habit

Focusing on process

Ways to begin

my beginning

I learned about the power of having a little creative structure when I started slowly building a drawing habit, not knowing that was what I was doing.

It started with a desire to simply write things on paper, so I started writing in notebooks. I began by allowing myself to write anything: grocery lists, vacation plans, to-do lists, anything! It didn't need to be beautiful or profound; I simply wanted to put pen to paper.

Then, I started journaling daily. Most days, I began by writing down the temperature, the weather forecast, when the sun came up and went down, and the phase of the moon. Some days, that's still all I write.

Around that time, I was inspired, and still am, by Amy Krouse Rosenthal. She wrote "Why You Should Marry My Husband" in the New York Times, which was published after she died of cancer. It was astonishing and made me want to know more about her. Amy was an author of children's books, among other things. She also made a homemade video called "17 things i made," which features dirty dishes, photos of her kids, books she wrote, and a peanut butter sandwich. Her work is warm, whimsical, and a love song to the world. She made me want to make things. When I told my daughter Haley about Amy, I cried. Haley said she thought I should write and illustrate children's books.

On October 13, 2017, I wrote, "just had an idea about creating a 'book of life' which would be a big unlined scrapbookish book. Each day I would add stuff: recipes I made, runs we did, notes about movies or soccer matches or dinners out or people seen." And I sketched a slice of frittata and a bowl of pumpkin coconut soup! I also wrote that I am "grateful for the magic of creativity that has landed on me this am."

My notebooks started to change. I began mapping moments in my day as little islands with words. Then I started adding a few little sketches ... and then more sketches.

Before I knew it, I had stumbled into a practice.

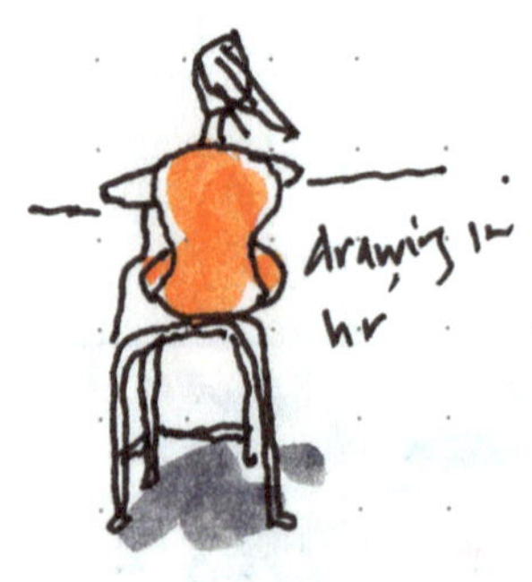

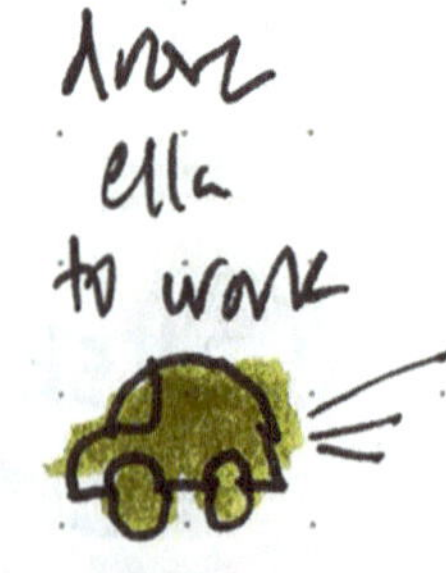

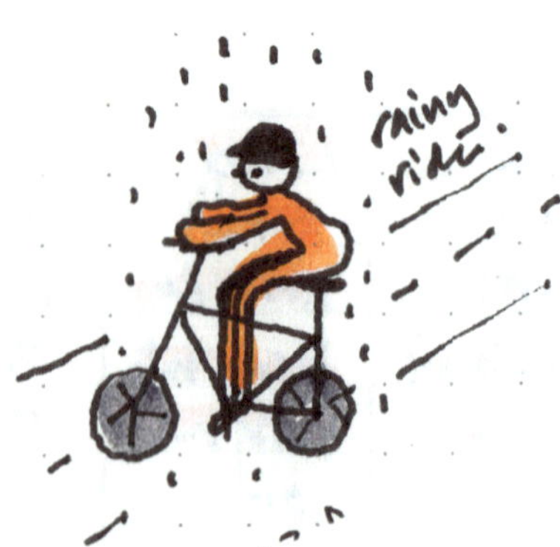

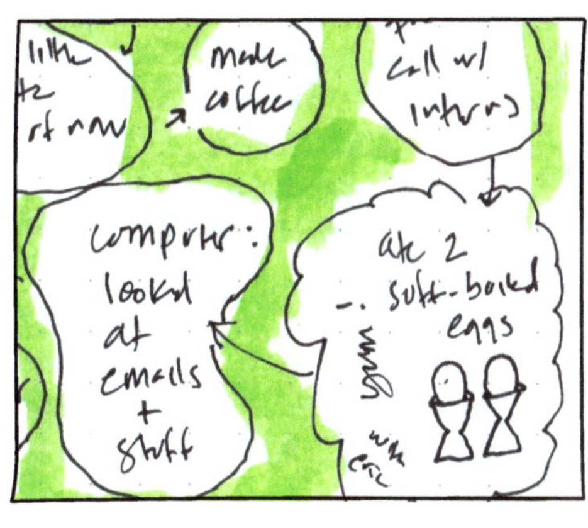
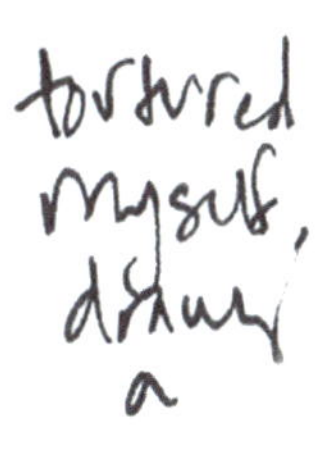
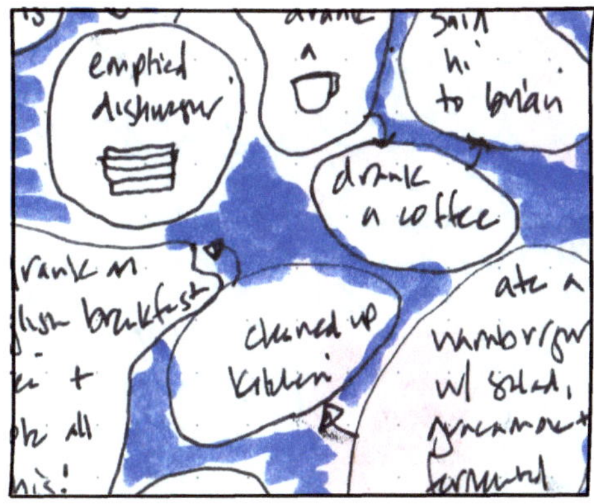
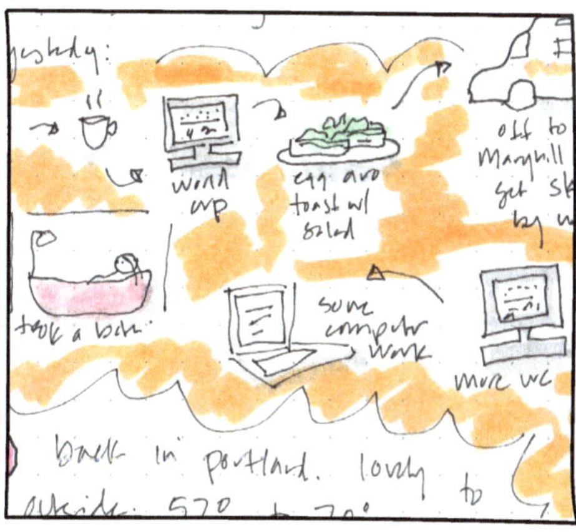
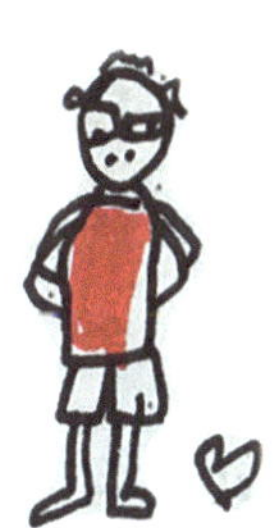
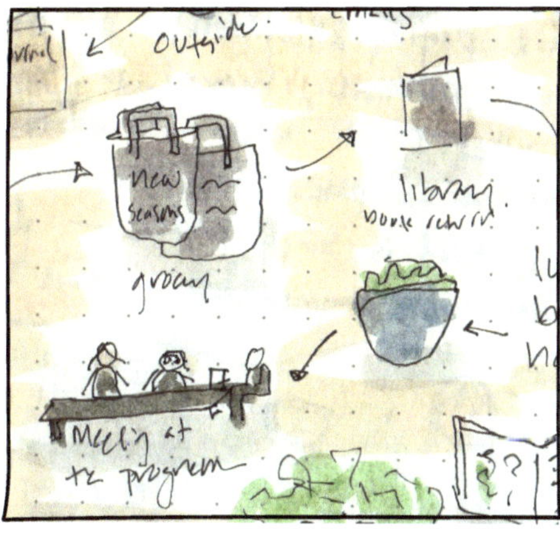
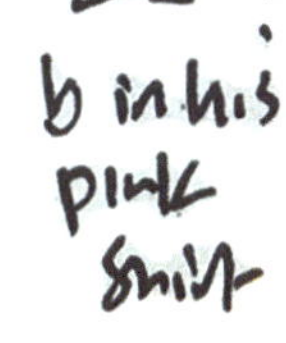
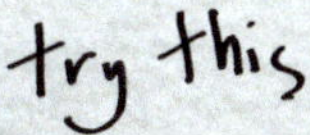
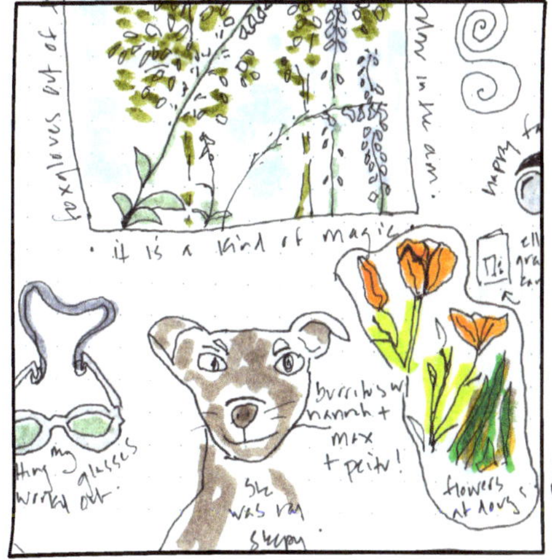
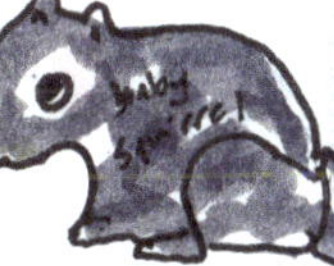

try this

Get a few supplies. Just a notebook and a pen or pencil will do. Set them out where you can see them in the morning. Carve out just a wee bit of time in the morning. Maybe with a quiet cup of coffee or tea? You could just write the date and doodle.

It is not about what you write or draw; it is about the doing. You are aiming for a sense of satisfaction from just feeling the pen or pencil connect with the paper. It is okay to be happy just to see a line created.

Make a structure

In many ways, I think this is the beating heart of this book. Practice is at the center of it all. There is something about the regularity of a practice that invites change in a way that more sporadic activity doesn't. And it doesn't have to be in a gotta-do-hours-a-day-or-you-are-never-going-to-be-any-good kinda way. That is not helpful. If I make my expectations big, I will only disappoint myself.

Setting up a little creative structure provides the scaffolding of a practice. The scaffolding is the time and space you set aside to practice. The only expectation is that you will sit down with a pen and paper in hand. You can relinquish all your worries, hopes, or dreams about what you will create and just sit down. I like to think of this time and space as a structure that can carry all that weight. I can sidestep myself (talk myself into sitting down) and all my worrying (Is this any good?) by leaning into structure. *Just sit down, pick up the pen, and let the next thing happen,* I tell myself.

My small, regular habit is still writing down the weather and details about the sun and moon every morning. I like to draw a simple little sun (or clouds if it is a cloudy day) and the phase of the moon. I am looking for something that will give me a toehold in the moment that is happening right now, but just as importantly, it helps me avoid the paralysis of a blank page. Some days, life gets busy, and that's all I can do. And that's okay! But most days, I can fit in more.

It can be hard to rely on willpower, inspiration, or creativity to keep a habit going—it is so much easier to rely on the structure of a habit.

Setting aside ten minutes a day seems like it wouldn't make much of a difference, but consistent practice has a power beyond its apparent simplicity. It is so easy to get caught up in the tumult of everyday life, moving ceaselessly from this thing to that. Creating a little pool of quiet in the day gives my life a depth it wouldn't otherwise have. Even a small, simple habit gives me some time to be aware of what I am paying attention to—something that can easily escape me in the business of life. A small habit helps me remember what I value doing and then gives me a chance to do it.

A habit of drawing or writing helps train my eyes, mind, and hand. Just like playing the piano or tennis, regular practice builds momentum. But still, it can be hard to get started and then continue. To be successful, I have learned to lean into the doing and let go of everything else.

I have also learned to grant myself three permissions. These permissions help me navigate the inevitable moments of self-doubt and weariness. They help me keep creating despite the everyday demands of life.

try this

Sometimes, when trying to get into the rhythm of a new habit, I make a little chart for myself. You could make a little thirty-day chart and give yourself a star or a check mark for each day you sit down and do a little practice. It can be a page in a journal, or you can hang it on your wall or put it on your desk where you can see it and get a gentle little reminder. Yes, it's a little geeky, but it can work.

Three permissions

1. It doesn't have to be good.

It's helpful to start without a lot of expectations. Before I sit down to journal, I say to myself: *I am just going to sketch quickly, have a little fun here, try to draw whatever—say, a coffee cup. I am not working on a masterpiece; this is NEVER gonna go on anyone's wall, and I only have a few minutes. I am not going to try to slay the dragon; I am just going to put a little ink on the page. It can be totally wonky—that is just fine.*

2. I don't have to know what I am doing.

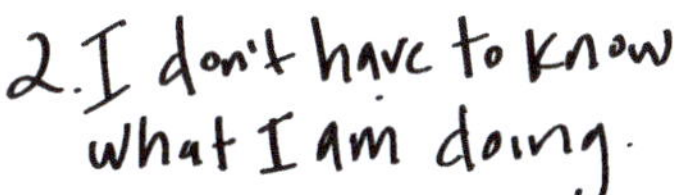

Welcoming uncertainty opens the door. It is easier for me to start something when I know that it is okay not to know exactly what I am doing or where I am going. After all, the flip side of uncertainty is possibility. As a fellow student in my mixed media class said: "If I knew what it was going to look like when I started, then I would be doing it wrong." It is about not getting stopped because I have no idea what I am doing.

3. I am an audience of one.

You really can follow your own instincts and interests and not care what anyone else thinks. It's allowed.

When my first teacher, Jude Siegel, said I could do anything I wanted in my journal, it was so free-ing—and still is. Because my journal is just for me, I can set my own expectations and follow my interests, which takes a lot of the pressure off. I remind myself that I am not doing this for anyone other than myself. It might seem a bit harsh to put it this way, but no one really cares what I do in my journal.

What these permissions do is lower the bar and make it easier to just do. They also point to a philosophical recognition that there is real freedom when I can give up the need to have anyone (including myself) justify or validate my work. Not worrying about what others might think certainly makes it easier to create!

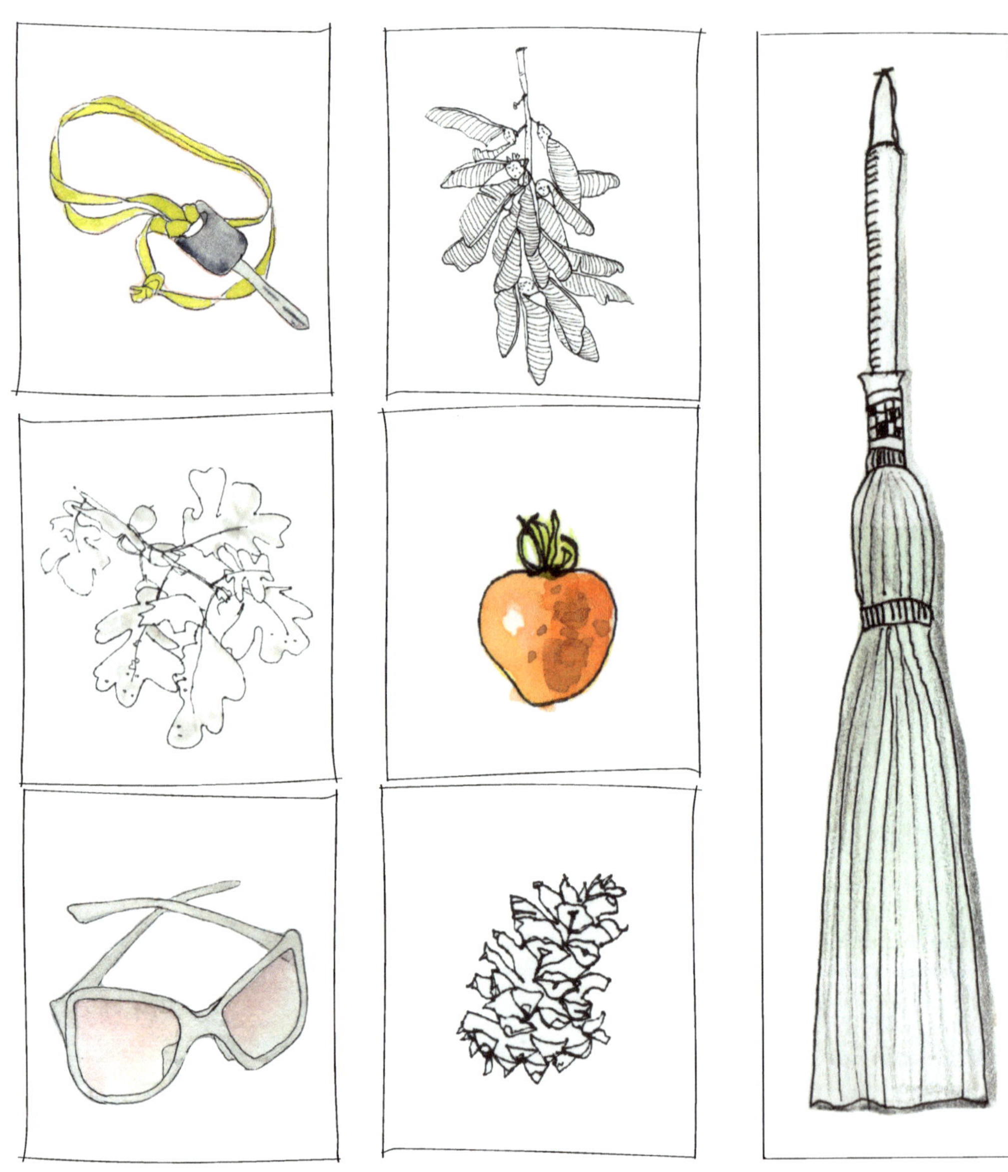

try this

Need a mantra? You could try "Just start."

Five tips to get started

1. Start small

Draw something small and ordinary, I tell myself. It is all practice. *Have fun, be kind*, I add. It is so much harder to start something big. If I want to go big, I first figure out how to start small. Otherwise, it is hard to start.

2. Pick anything

It doesn't matter what I draw. Even if I have drawn it many times before. It still works. Sometimes, I have to convince myself of this.

I like to think of it as the way I feel about exercise. Sure, it is nice to try some new routines, but that doesn't mean that going the same way I have gone hundreds of times before isn't going to make me happier and healthier. And when I really pay attention, every outing is different. You just gotta pick something and not think about it too much. As Lynda Barry says in *Syllabus*, "On my mind is the question raised by some of my students about what things are worth drawing and writing about—I don't believe thinking can give you the answer to this. Though it <u>feels</u> like it can long enough to stop us from trying."

3. Start simple

I like starting with a simple drawing of something I see in real life. I really try to look at what I am drawing and just follow and enjoy the shapes, lines, and shades. Beginning with a simple observational drawing helps me center myself and connect my mind and hand. I find it calming, and I can quickly get absorbed into the object. As Lynda Barry says, I try to follow "something small carefully and <u>sincerely</u>." I try to look more at what I am drawing and less at my paper. This way, I see more, and it reinforces that what I am after is process rather than results.

4. Keep going

Things go wonky, and I just keep going. Worrying about accuracy or continually restarting keeps me from discovering what happens if I keep going. I make mistakes and draw a new line or just move on. When I worry about accuracy, I seem to get a little lost, and I definitely have less fun.

5. Goof around

I have to remind myself not to take myself too seriously! Honestly, what am I so worried about? I remind myself just to try stuff. Making goofy stuff is wonderfully fun and freeing when I let myself do it. Also, making things regularly means nothing is too precious; it is hard to get wound up about a single drawing if you do a lot of them.

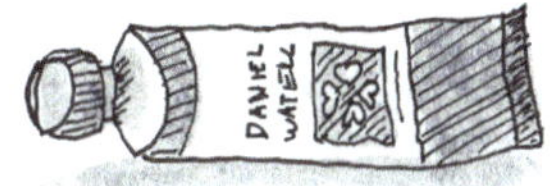

try this

Go outside and look for something to bring in to draw: a leaf, a seed pod, a broken-off branch. I do this a lot. It gets me outside, gets me looking, and then gives me something interesting to draw.

Drawing natural objects can be forgiving. Drawing a wayward line doesn't stand out as much as when your line wanders while drawing a manufactured object or a person.

You must have a room, or a certain hour or so a day,
where you don't know what was in the newspapers
that morning, you don't know who your friends are, you
don't know what you owe anybody, you don't know
what anybody owes to you.

This is a place where you can simply experience and
bring forth what you are and what you might be. This
is the place of creative incubation. At first you may find
that nothing happens there. But if you have a sacred
place and use it, something eventually will happen.

—Joseph Campbell

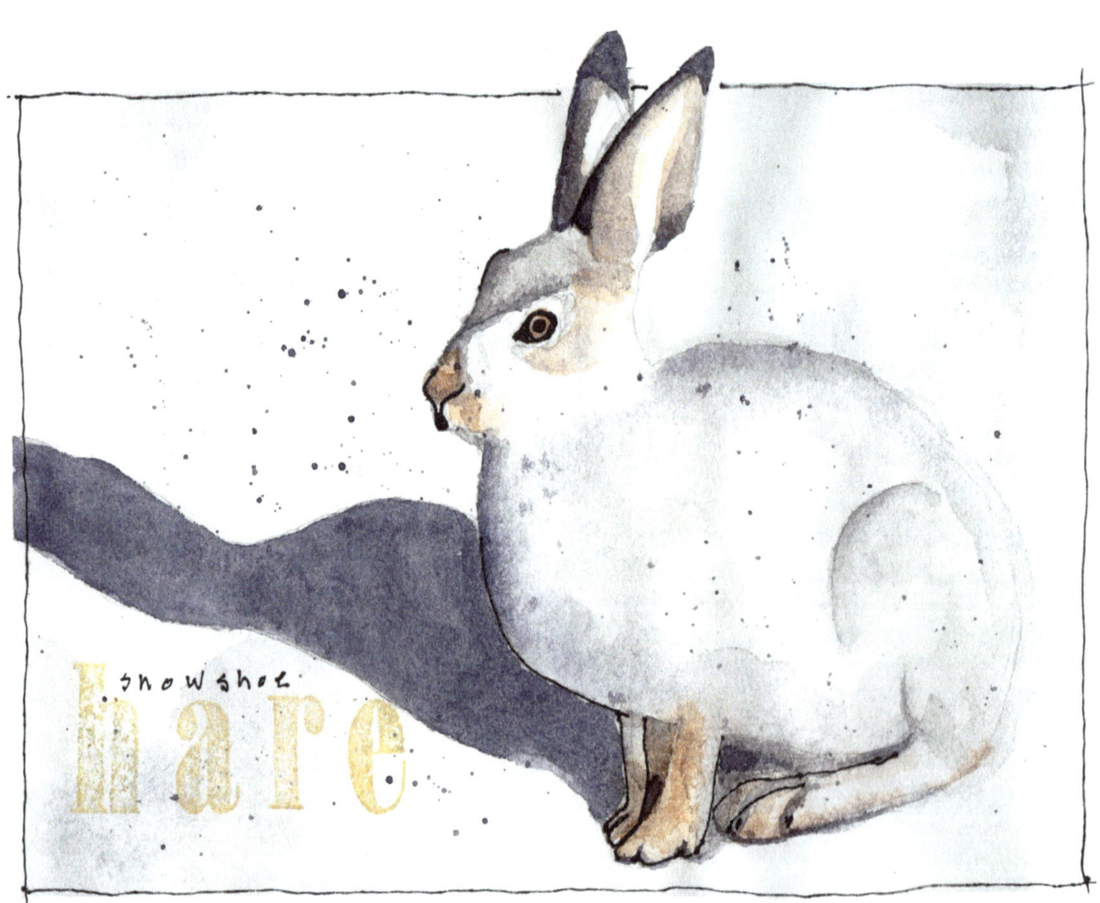

Why a practice works

Regular practice moves you from thinking to doing. Thinking can be a hindrance. At least, I know I can think of everything that could go wrong before I even start. Thinking can stop me from doing things, so I am learning to plunge in instead. When I just do, things often go better or differently than I ever thought they would.

Momentum comes from doing

That momentum comes from doing can seem counterintuitive. It is easy to think that we must feel a certain way before making art or that we need to wait for inspiration or creativity to strike us before creating. In my experience, that is just not how it works. Art gets made when you make the time for it when it is a habit and occupies a regular little corner of your life. If you wait for creativity or inspiration to strike, you may never make much of anything. If, however, you craft a reliable little process for yourself, you will make things. I have read about other people having a little ritual before they begin, and while I might take a moment to center myself or think about where the drawing will go on the page, I just start.

Inspiration comes from doing

You might think that inspiration comes before doing, but a surprising number of artists find that doing itself creates inspiration rather than the other way around. In *Syllabus,* Lynda Barry writes: "We know that athletes, musicians and actors all have to practice, rehearse, repeat things until it gets into the body, the 'muscle memory,' but for some reason, writers and visual artists think they have to be inspired before they make something, not suspecting that the physical act of writing and drawing is what brings that inspiration about." Similarly, in *Making Art a Practice*, the illustrator, author, and teacher Cat Bennett finds, "The more we're engaged with our work, the more momentum we have, the more inspiration will come to us."

Creativity comes from doing

This book is really about ways of bringing creativity into your life without the need to feel creative. I don't think much about creativity; I think more about carving out time to do things. I think very practically about the creative system I can set up and more philosophically about how I can think differently about making art. Creativity, to me, is a little bit of magic, out of my control, that comes to visit when I make space for it.

When practice becomes a habit

The power of just doing is that it begins to transform practice into a habit. At some point, I realized that putting a little something into my journal on most days had become a habit. It felt odd when I didn't do it.

Habits are sneaky things. Because we do them without much effort or conscious awareness, they can shape our lives, almost without us noticing. They influence what we do, how we live our lives, and how we see ourselves. In his book *Atomic Habits*, James Clear explains how this happens: "Each experience in life modifies your self-image, but it's unlikely you would consider yourself a soccer player because you kicked the ball once or an artist because you scribbled a picture. As you repeat these actions, however, the evidence and your self-image begins to change. The effect of a one-off experience tends to fade away while the effect of habits gets reinforced with time, which means your habits contribute most of the evidence that shape your identity."

Setting the self-identity piece aside, the power of habits to shape our lives is enormous. Whatever we hope to do more of, whatever we hope to practice, if we can make it a habit, we will be that much more successful. That sounds like a big, serious thing, but paradoxically, it was making my practice smaller and lowering the bar that was key to transforming it into a habit.

Focusing on process

Creating a practice centered on just doing encourages me to focus on process rather than results. We have all heard the common advice to engage in the process and let go of the outcome. We know this makes sense. Focusing on results can hinder our process; we get so caught up in the destination that we forget to be in the moment and enjoy the process. Prioritizing results can also make starting harder because, suddenly, there is a lot more to think about—we have to know where we want to end up! And that can get complicated because all sorts of expectations can get layered on, and suddenly, we are thinking rather than doing. And while some of what we think may be helpful to starting, it can become a barrier.

That said, as good and sensible as the advice to focus on the process is, it can be hard to do. Part of the difficulty may be that we like finishing more than doing or are dissatisfied with our attempts. We also tend to be impatient to become something or do something. Reminding ourselves that it is always a process can help.

It helps to consider that focusing on process rather than results may be a better way of getting results. In *Atomic Habits*, James Clear suggests that relying on habits is a better way to progress than setting goals, stating, "Goals are at odds with long-term progress." He argues that if you focus on a goal rather than on the process when you reach your goal, you are left somewhat empty-handed. He summarizes the engage-in-the-process advice by saying, "True long-term thinking is goal-less thinking ... Ultimately it is your commitment to the *process* that will determine your *progress*." The trouble with setting goals, Clear says, is that ultimately, goals and results, once achieved, fall by the wayside.

Illustrator Cat Bennett also advises practice over goals in *Making Art a Practice*: "Often we're advised to set goals and follow through, to decide what we want and go for it. But our art practice offers another way. We show up and do the work." Goals or no goals, there is no doubt that regular practice and habits help us progress—without them, progress is much harder to come by.

There is a lot of power in a regular practice. But some days, it can be hard to get started. Having a number of ways to begin, not just relying on one, is helpful. Having a variety of options helps jump-start me on those inevitable hard-to-get-going days. Starting with any one of these methods is just as valuable as starting with drawing because what I am after is simply beginning.

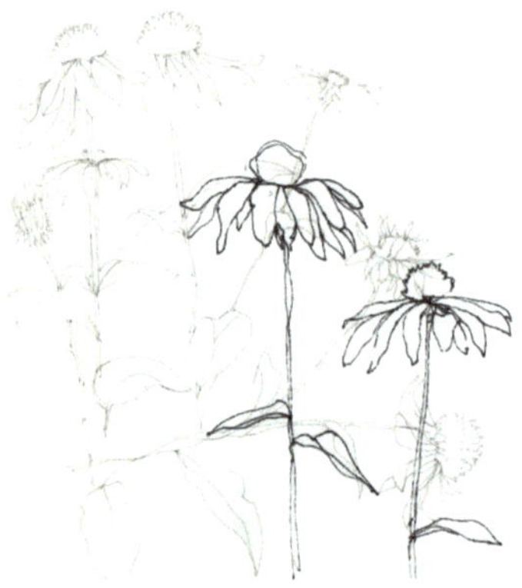

resource

A teacher, illustrator, and author, Cat Bennett offers compassionate, clear-sighted, inspiring advice in her books, *The Confident Creative: Drawing to Free the Hand and Mind* and *Making Art a Practice: How To Be the Artist You Are*, for anyone interested in making art.

Here are some helpful ways to begin

Try blind contour 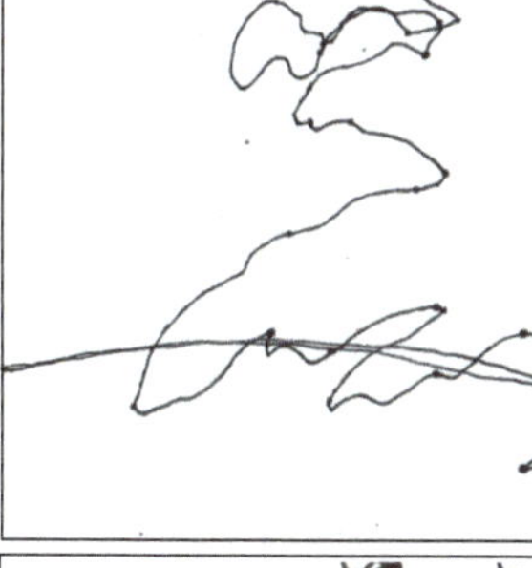

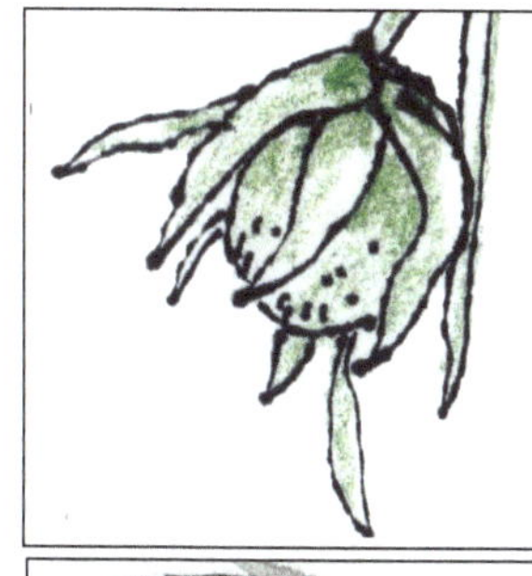 Use gesture

Make marks 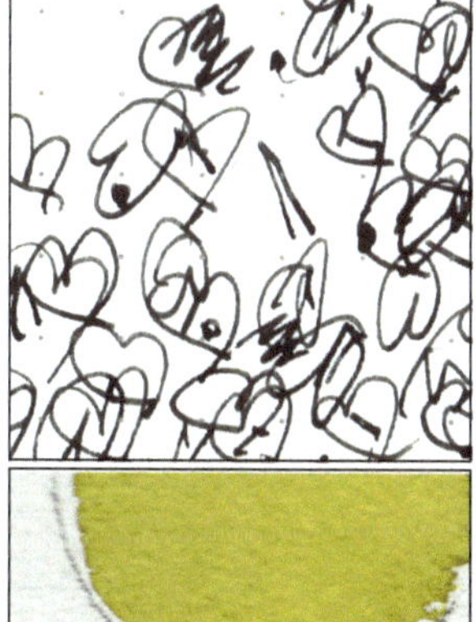

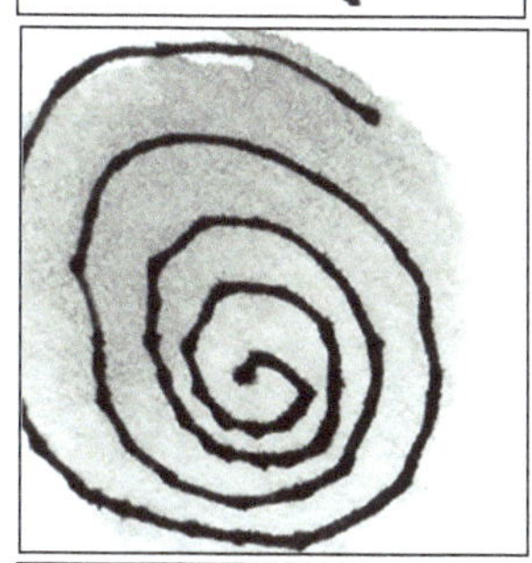 Draw spirals

Play with color 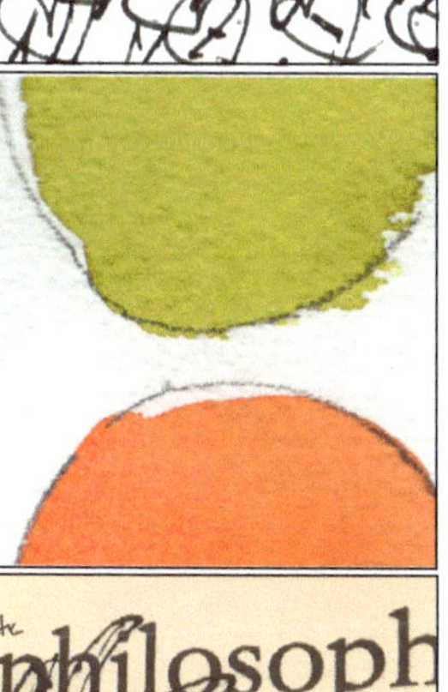

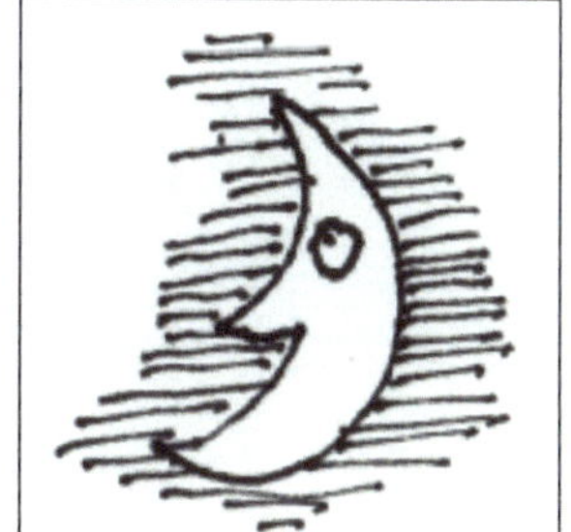 Copy something

Paste stuff in 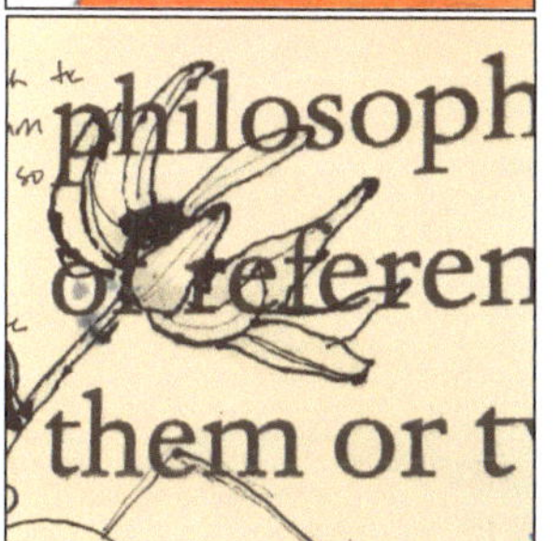

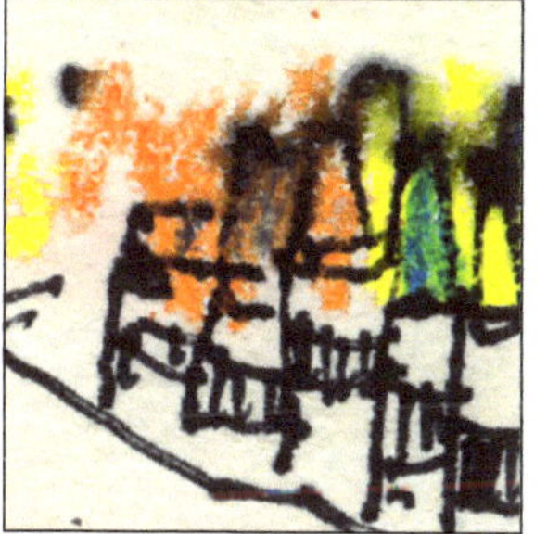 Explore materials

try this

Go ahead and give blind contour drawing a try. Find an object, then draw the contour—the outside edges of the object—without taking your eyes off the object. There is only one rule: don't look at your paper!

Maybe you will want to paint it later with a simple watercolor wash?

resource

Written by artist and teacher Corita Kent and her fellow artist and student Jan Steward, *Learning by Heart: Teachings to free the creative spirit* is a collection of Corita's teaching philosophies and assignments, with further illumination from Jan. Enormously helpful, *Learning by Heart* details inspiring and generative practices of looking and seeing.

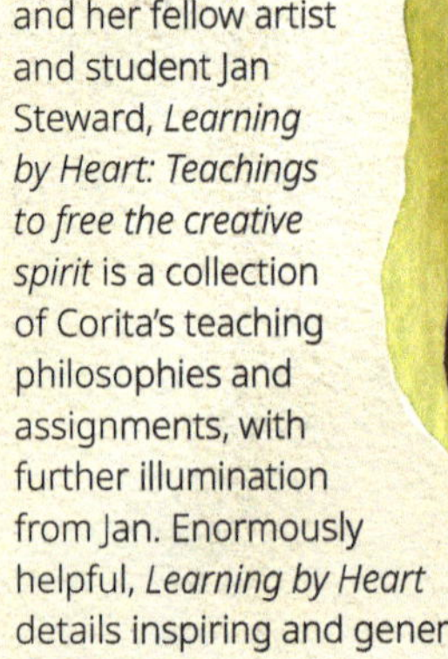

Try blind contour + continuous line drawings

Starting with a blind contour or continuous line drawing is a great way to begin. It is easy to get yourself to start; it can relax your mind and hand, and often, you end up with a surprisingly beautiful image.

Blind contour means drawing the outlines of your subject without looking at your paper. To do this, let your eyes travel around the edges of an object without taking your eyes off it. Let your hand record what your eyes see. You can also draw some interior contour lines and retrace some steps; the only rule is to avoid looking at your paper.

In continuous line drawing, you don't pick your pen or pencil up off the paper. You begin drawing at a single point on your paper and move on from there. The only rule is that you can't pick your pen or pencil off the paper.

You can combine blind contour and continuous line in a single drawing. Blind contour and continuous line drawing can help us sidestep our analytical minds and help us let go. As Jan Steward notes in *Learning by Heart,* "One of the great values of contour drawing is that it makes it very difficult to be judgmental about your work. Contour drawing helps you see things and let your intuition make choices."

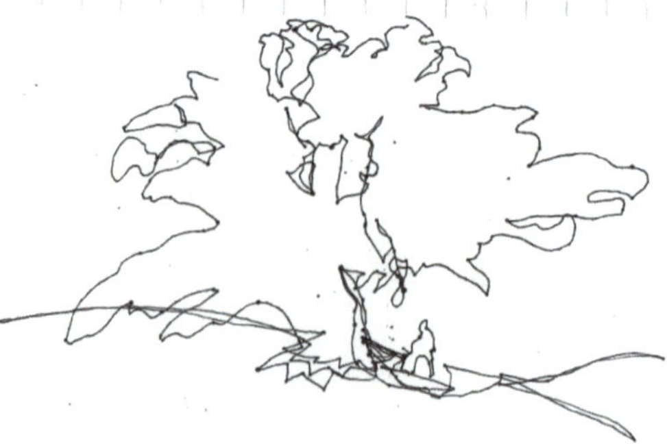

Use gesture

You can free yourself up by following the general movement of whatever you are trying to draw. You can go big: use a big brush, a big pencil, a big sheet of paper. Move your arm and body rather than your fingers and wrist. Be super general about what you see. This is pretty much the opposite of being detailed and specific.

In *Keys to Drawing,* Bert Dodson describes gesture drawing as a way to start: "The gesture is simply capturing the essence of your subject in the quickest and most economical way. Gesture drawing involves a kind of 'scribble' aimed not so much at what your subject *is* but at what it is *doing.*"

When you do this, you start looking less at details and more at movement, which is always interesting to try.

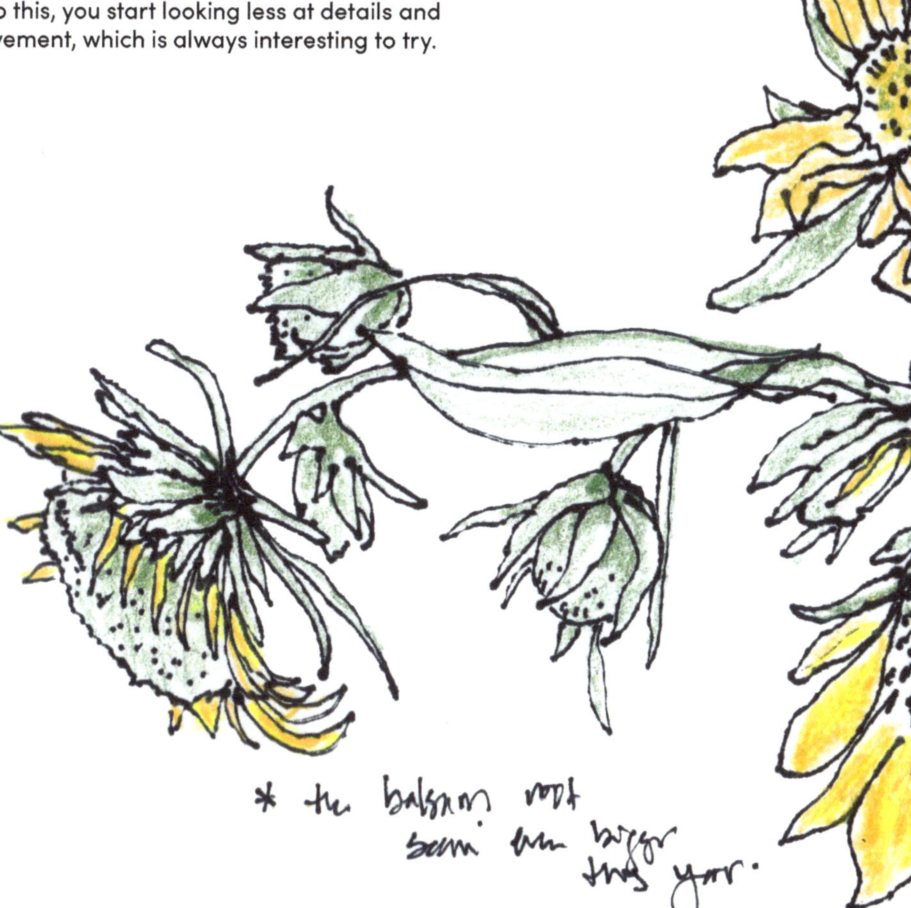

Make marks

We have all doodled. Some of us doodle regularly in meetings, while talking, or waiting on the phone. Call doodling "mark-making," and suddenly, we have elevated our game.

Mark-making is fun on its own. You can draw anything; scribble away! It can be a great way to warm up. Sometimes, it takes a while for my hand and brain to sync up, so drawing random shapes, marks, and lines can get me going. (I have an affinity for dots and circles, so I tend to gravitate toward those.) If I am too tired to draw, mark-making lets me move my hand and have a little fun. It can also get us in the right frame of mind for drawing. As the illustrator Cat Bennett says in *The Confident Creative*, "Making marks frees our hand from the judgments of our mind and catapults us into the space of playfulness and presence. How can the mind complain when we're just fooling around?"

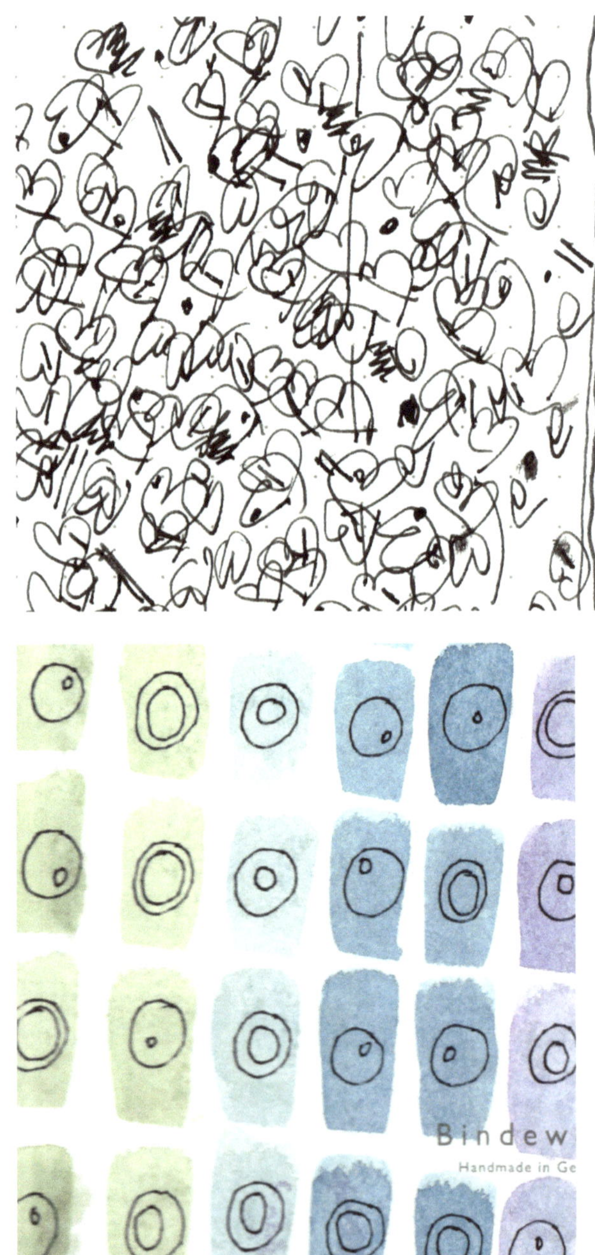

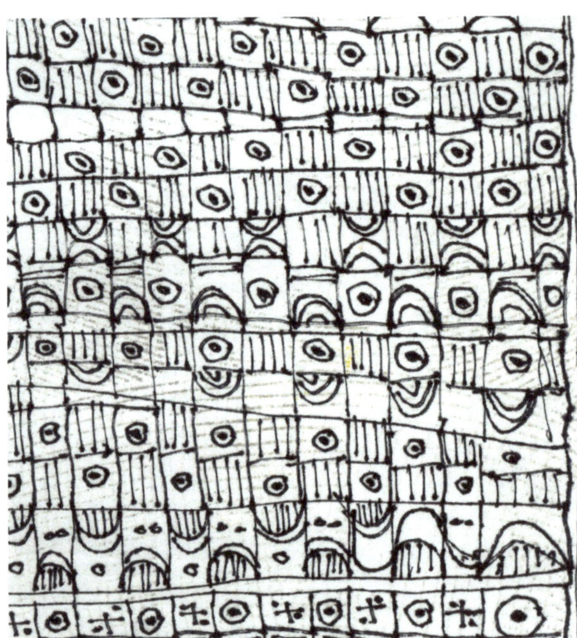

Draw spirals

Drawing spirals can be a great way to loosen up and connect your hand and mind before jumping into drawing. Plus, spirals have universal energy; they appear in nature and in numerous ancient and contemporary cultures. How great to tap into that!

Here are Lynda Barry's suggestions for drawing spirals from *Syllabus*: "Start with a dot. Spiral a line around it. Keep going. It's an exercise in both relaxation and concentration—your task is to get the lines as close together as possible without letting them touch. If they touch, you get electrocuted." Barry suggests doing this while paying attention to the top of the head and then moving your attention down through your body.

Engaging your hand and mind in a relaxed, fun way is what you are after here. Before you know it, your attention will come along too.

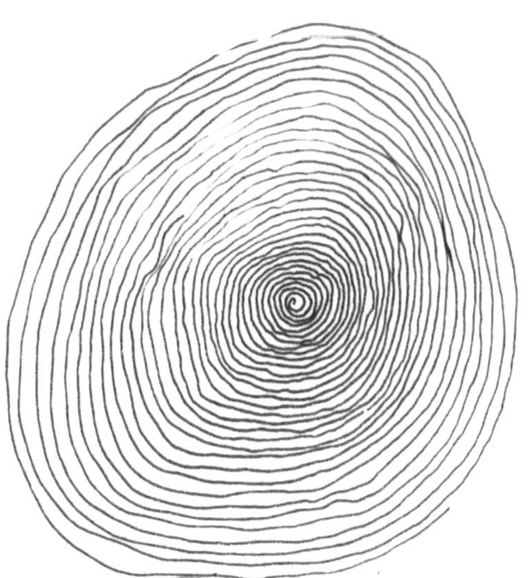

Collect your doodles. Cut them out from your notes and put them in an envelope. Let them collect for a month or so, then take them out and paste them on something. What do you have here? Who knows? But I bet it is interesting.

Color in your doodles. Select three to four colors you like and randomly fill in any shapes you have created.

Fill a whole page with spirals of different sizes and color them in.

Or use spirals to border a page.

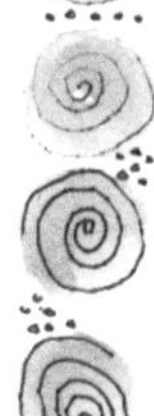
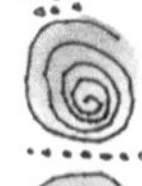
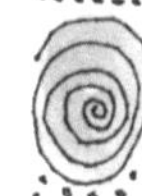
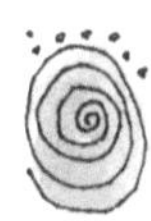
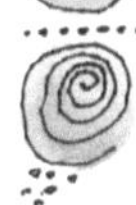
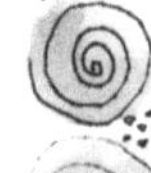
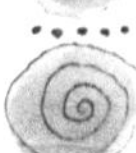
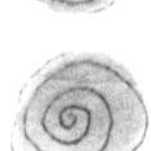
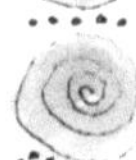
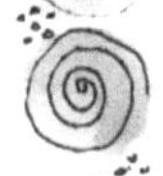
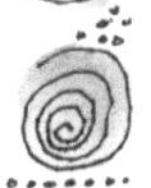
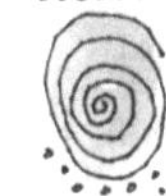
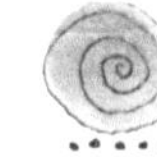
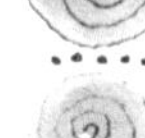
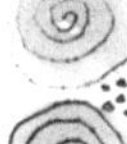
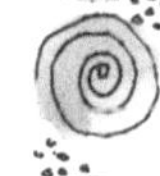
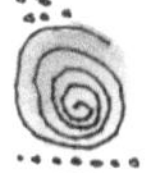
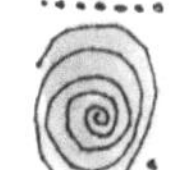

Play with color

If I really can't get myself to draw, I can usually get myself to explore something with color. Color is a marvel, a mystery, and a science, all wrapped up in one beautiful package. There is always something to play with and learn.

Why do I like some colors and not others? It just happens. What is a color anyway?

try this

Look for color combinations in the world around you. I do this frequently when I am out and about. I like to note and collect the color combos in my mind. (One of my favorite sources for color combinations is stacked container boxes on a train.)

try this

Take three colors and mix them together in every way you can think of. Limiting my palette makes me think more carefully about color relationships. It encourages me to mix colors to produce new colors, which is always fun.

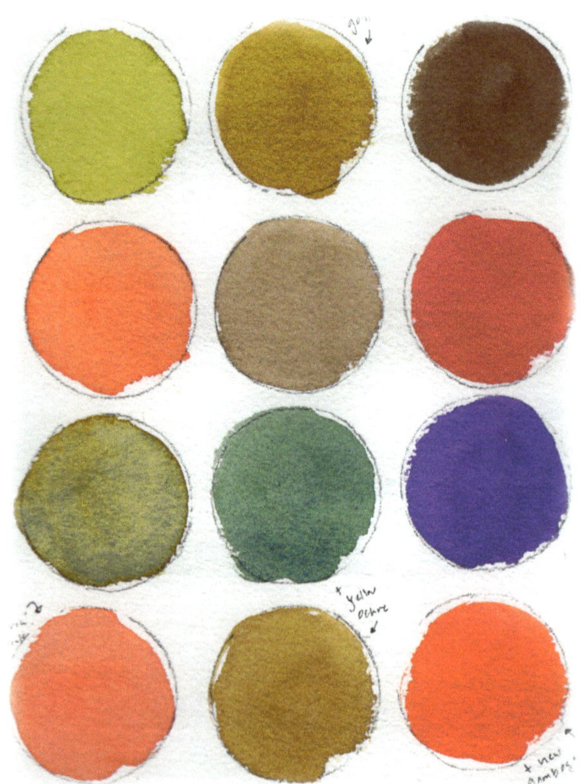

Copy something

If you can't find something to draw, or you don't feel like drawing, copying gets your mind and hand engaged in another way and invites another sort of learning. When I copy something, I always learn more than I think I will.

Copying is good for you because it takes time and it requires a certain sort of sustained concentration that invites a different sort of thinking.

—Lynda Barry

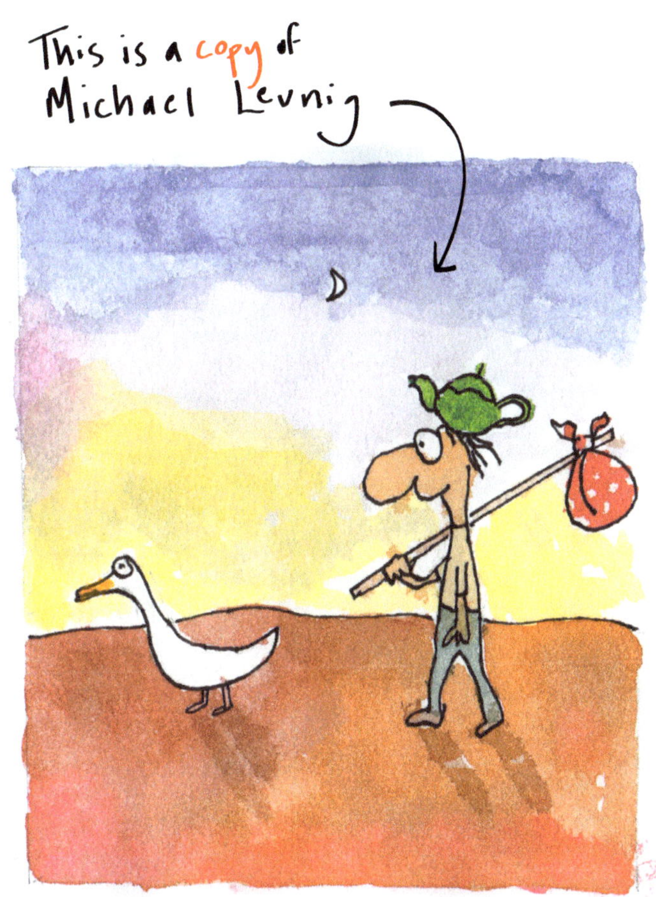

copied M.l.

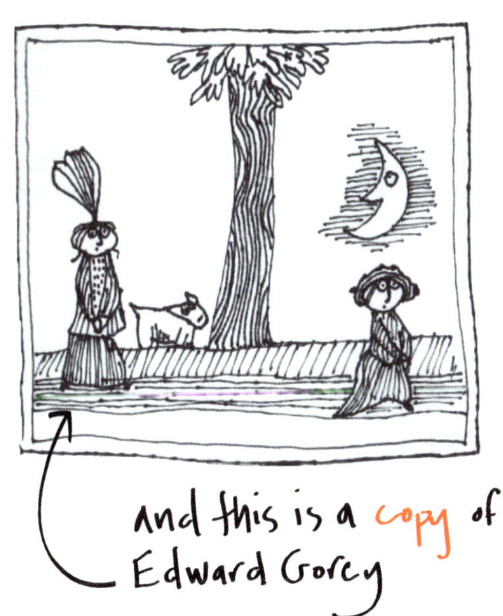

and this is a copy of
Edward Gorey

try this

When you see an illustration you love, save it, cut it out, or take a photo and store it away. Then, when you have one of those moments where you really feel like you can't find anything to draw, pull it out ... and copy away!

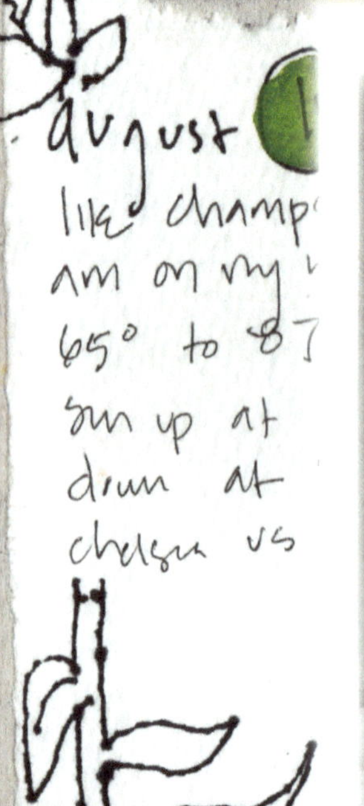

Paste stuff in

If I can't get myself to do anything, I can always paste something in my journal. I don't have to have a reason for pasting something in—I can just do it and then trust that somehow it will work out. Matt medium, a glue stick, and YES paste are all supplies I use to paste things in my journal. Really anything can be pasted in, which makes it considerably easier to find things to paste in.

If you have access to a copier, you can play with resizing images and text and then paste those in. Anything that intrigues you with texture, color, or pattern can be pasted in. Pasting things into a future journal page or paper to work on later provides a fun challenge adding depth and richness, and welcomed chaos to the page.

Pasting in newspaper print can give you a rich background for drawing and be very freeing. Here, I drew over a sticker from a sheet of Ruth Asawa US postage stamps.

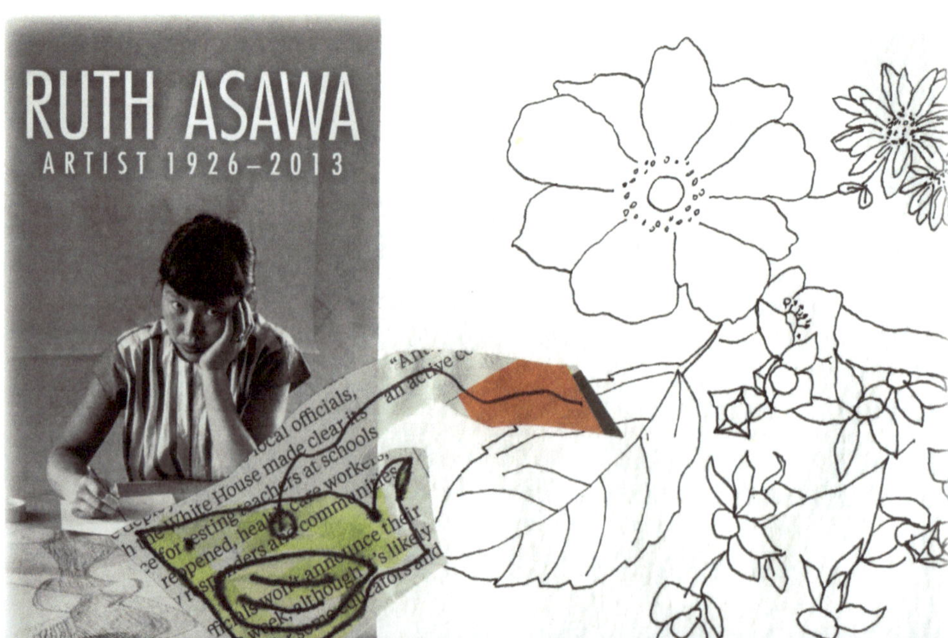

Explore materials

What materials are there in your drawer or on your desk that you could use? Are there crayons left over from school days or some colored pens or pencils you have in a drawer? Old paints? Pastels? Tell yourself you will just see how they work and what they do. Make circles of color with them and blend them together. Make marks. Think of yourself as less of an artist and more of a scientist. It is a great way to just get going.

try this

Become a collector—of interesting colors, textures, images, and papers. File those away!

At some point, take a moment to paste those into a future journal page or a paper to work on later. You can also go back and use them to enliven a page that you worked on earlier.

try this

You don't have to buy a whole set of something to try it out. You can pick just a couple of colors of whatever you are curious about and then see if you like the material and want more. (The colors in the beginners' set often leave me uninspired, so I don't like to get those.)

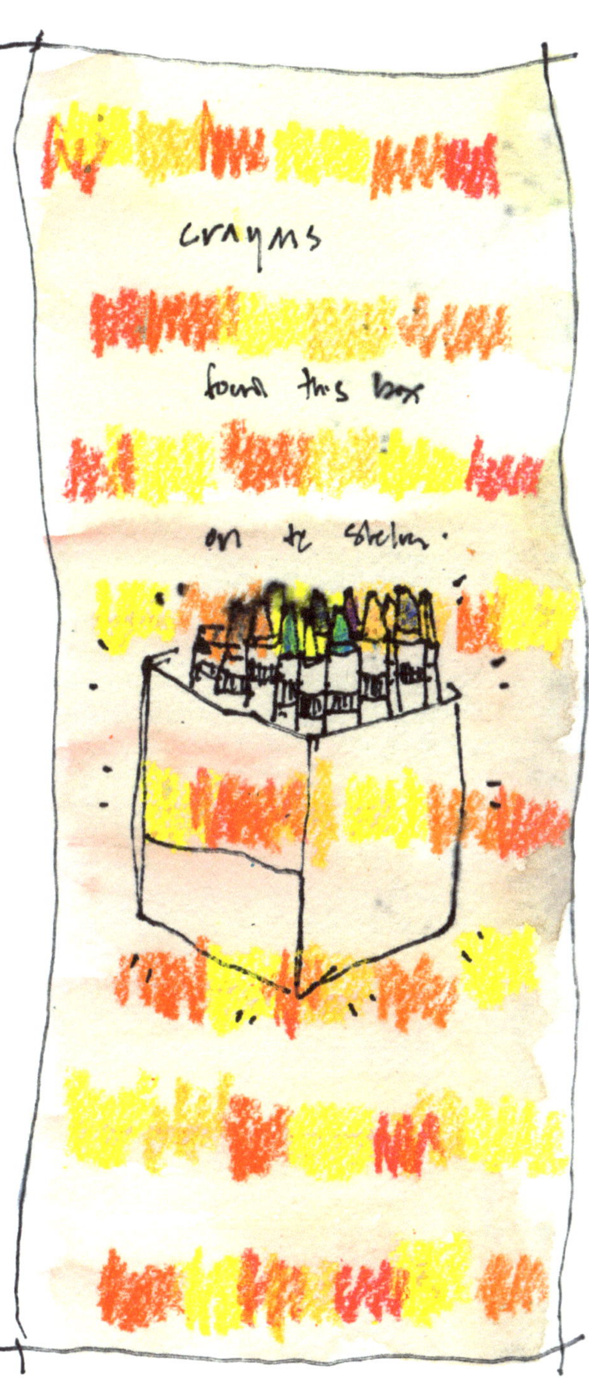

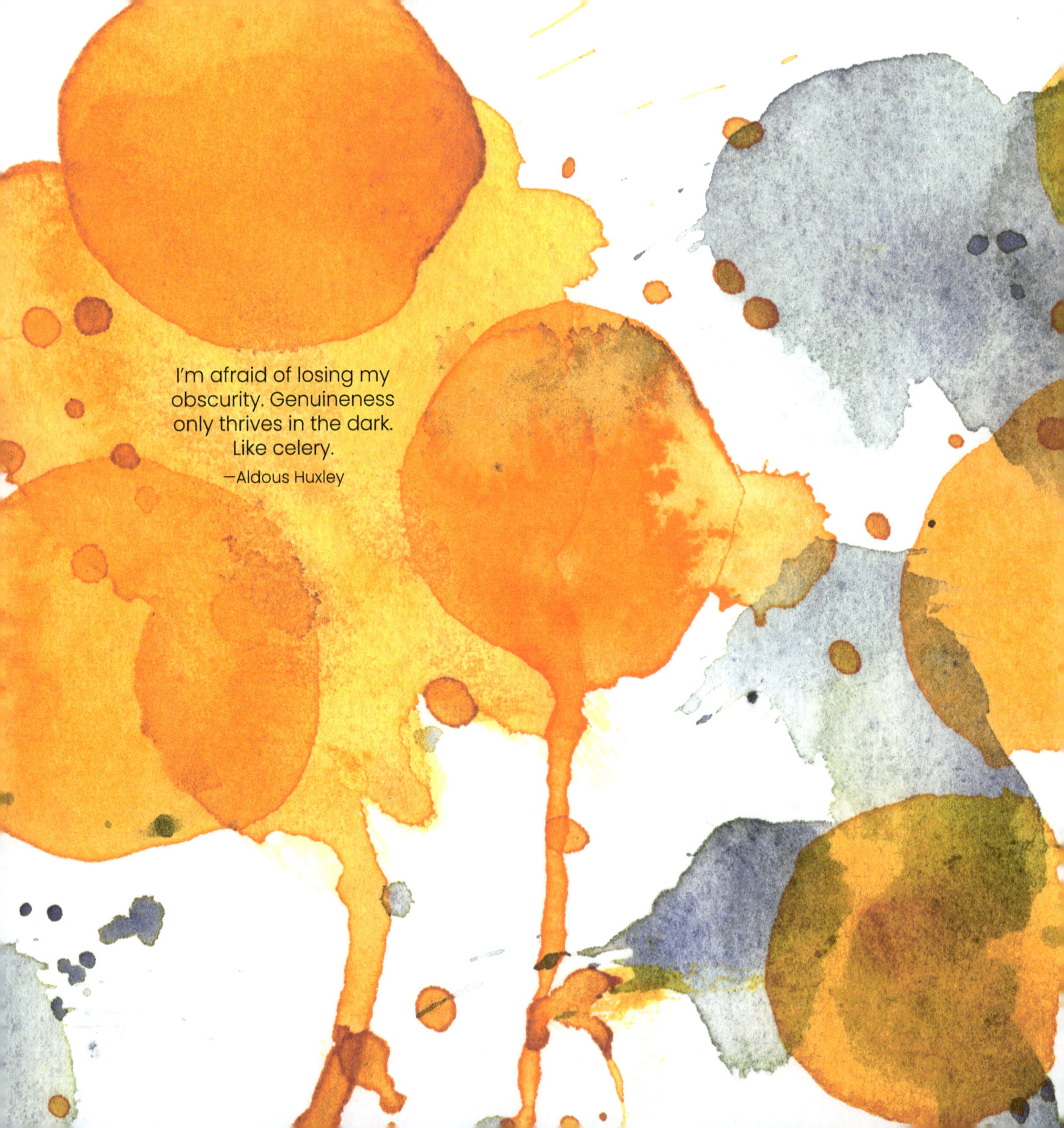
I'm afraid of losing my
obscurity. Genuineness
only thrives in the dark.
Like celery.
—Aldous Huxley

Discomfort

Evaluation

Mistakes

SOS... SOS

Reminding myself of the WHY

Tips for getting out of your head

Other people

Time

Bad days

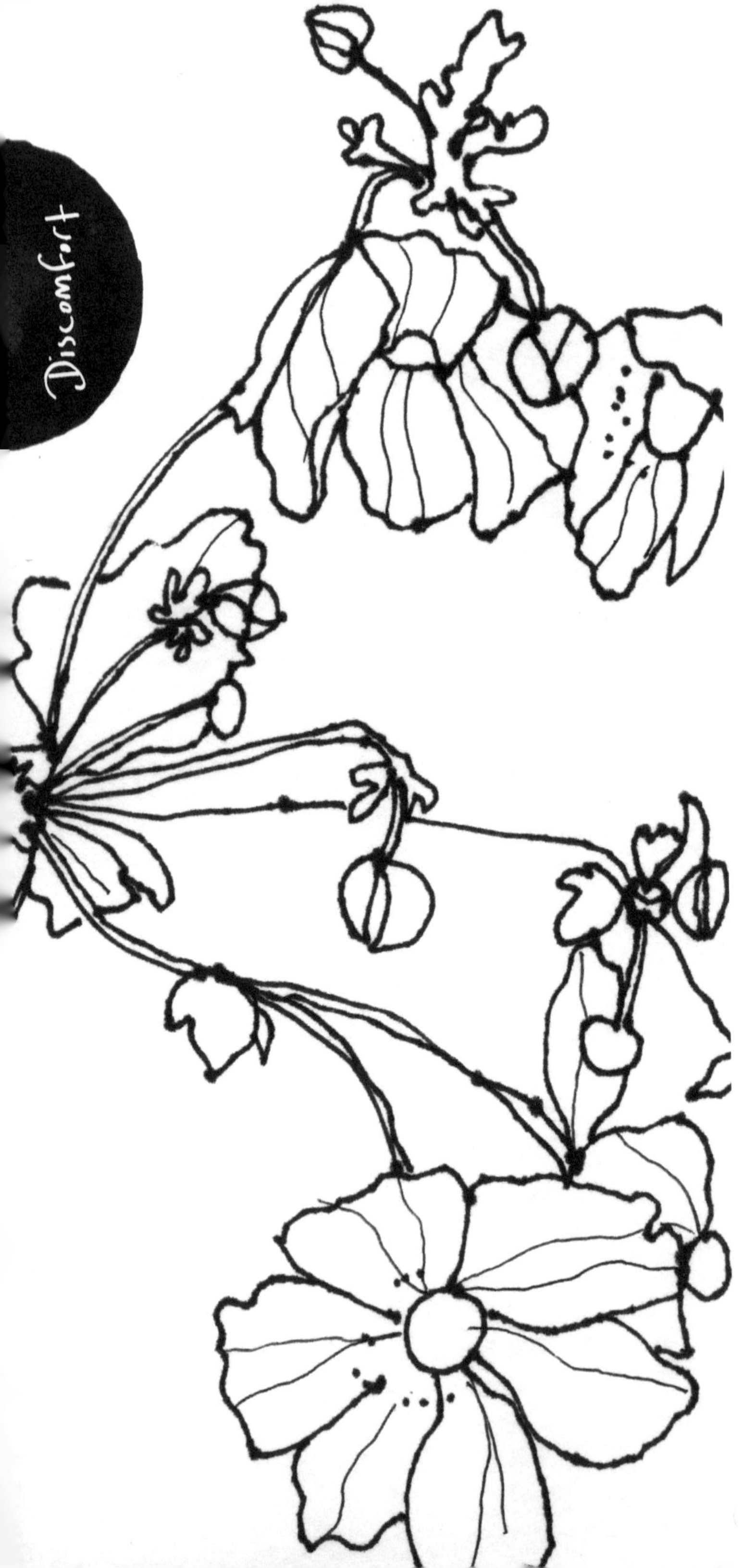

Evaluation

Beginning and continuing a creative practice brings me face-to-face with both fun and discomfort. Frustration, impatience, and dissatisfaction can all accompany art-making.

Examining the varied discomforts art-making can provoke helps me see them more clearly. My goal is not to overcome discomfort but to live with it and see what I can learn from it. Just naming discomfort can be helpful.

One source of discomfort that comes up for me both quickly and frequently is evaluation.

Is it good?

There is a sure way to make drawing, or any sort of art-making, not fun, and it happens quickly and naturally. Just as soon as I make something, and even sometimes while making it, I think: Is it good?

This is a big, loud question. And the answer most frequently is: well, no. But I have come to see this question as lazy—and to wonder instead at all the mini questions nestled inside. So, instead, I ask myself: *What exactly am I asking?*

Am I asking if it is:

Likable?
Realistic?
Technically proficient?
Satisfying?
Expressive?
Unexpected?

Taking a closer look encourages me to use evaluation more skillfully. I can learn more from what I have made and, most importantly, remember to avoid the dead end of unhelpful judgments. Just noticing the emergence of this question can help.

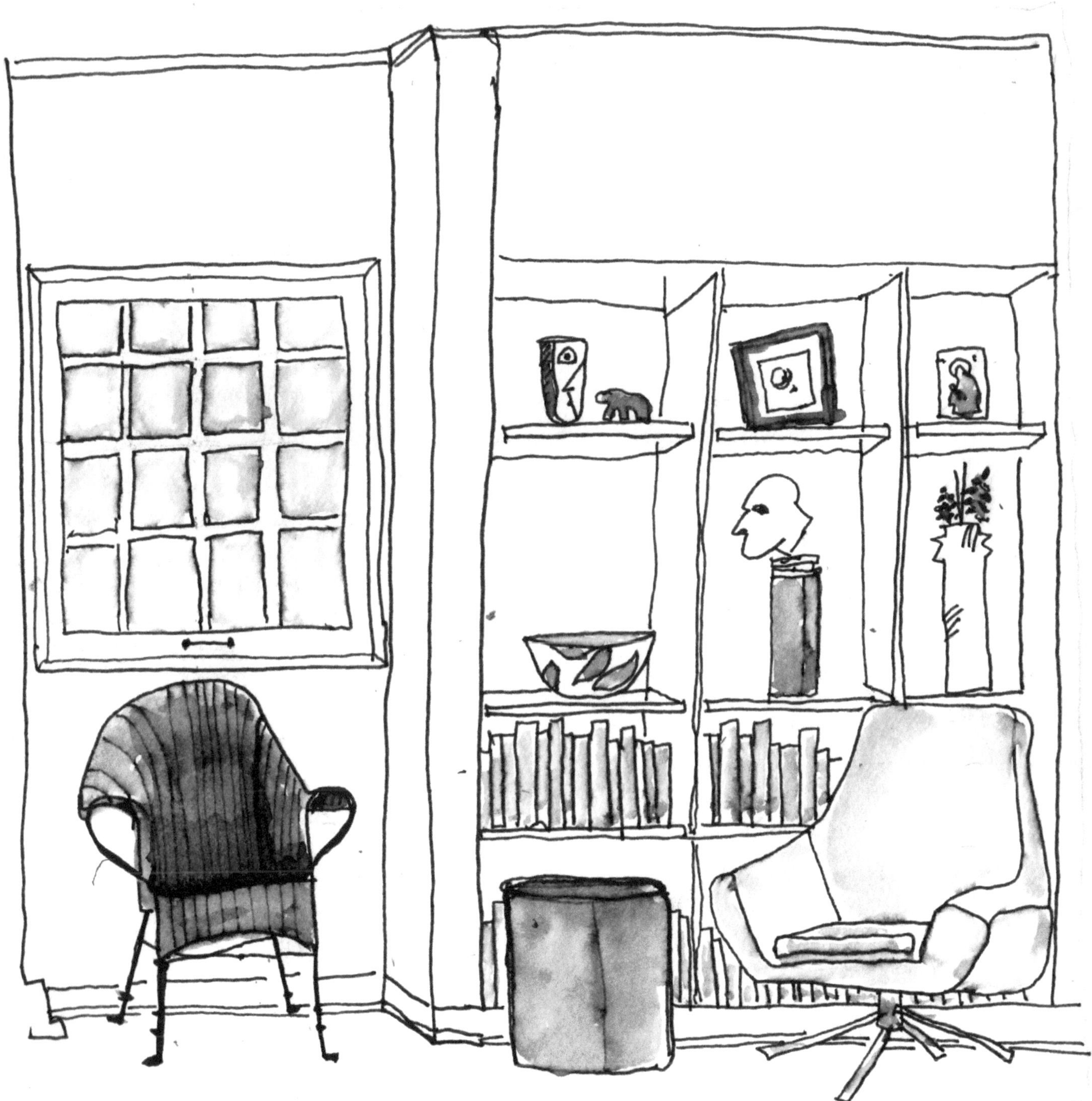

Do I like it?

The answer to this question often comes in a rush and is usually pretty sure of itself, but I am also learning to be wary of this question because it can be blinding and reductive. It often solicits a yes or no answer, overlooking the land of possibility that lies in between.

Often, I will think, *No, I don't like it*, but then if I look a little more closely, there is something I do like. Or sometimes I really don't like it, and later that afternoon, or maybe even later that week, I mysteriously do like it. It makes me want to take a closer look at this liking/not liking business. I have come to believe that this liking/not liking is a formidable gatekeeper that can keep me from the enjoyment and discovery of making art. And while it may be an automatic response, learning to push pause on that response might be the difference between my continuing with art—or giving up.

This is one of those places where art-making coincides with mindfulness because this automatic response to like or dislike whatever I make mirrors my tendency to like or dislike whatever comes up in my experience. In the *Waking Up app*, Sam Harris speaks to this tendency: "One aspect of our experience that is ever-present is the feeling of liking or not liking whatever is arising in consciousness. We find various tasks and sensations and thoughts pleasant or unpleasant and we grasp at those we like and attempt to push those we don't like away. Mindfulness requires that we fully relax this otherwise automatic response and just let our minds stay open and aware, whatever the character of the experience. And in this equanimity, we can find real freedom." The freedom to be found in relaxing this automatic response to whatever we create is the freedom to just stay open-minded and carry on.

The Zen master Seng-ts'an said, "To set up what you like against what you dislike, this is the disease of the mind." I guess because, on some level, it doesn't matter if I like or dislike my art—it just is. Any sort of judgment about it is beside the point. In *Syllabus*, Lynda Barry says it's about "not liking or disliking but learning to pay patient attention to things as they are."

Barry equates liking/not liking to putting blinders on ourselves: "Liking and not liking can make us blind to <u>what's</u> <u>there</u>. In spite of how we feel about it, it is making its way from the unseen to the visible world, one line after the next, bringing with it a kind of aliveness I live for: right here, right. Now." In *Making Comics*, she continues, "In the same way you don't have to like the way your liver looks for it to be able to function, you don't have to like the way your drawings look for them to start to work."

Sometimes, after I make something, I am struck by its emergence. In some crazy way, this just thrills me. Where did it come from? It seems like a pretty big mystery. And then suddenly, this liking/not liking business becomes almost a trivial consideration, which is weird because it seemed so very important before.

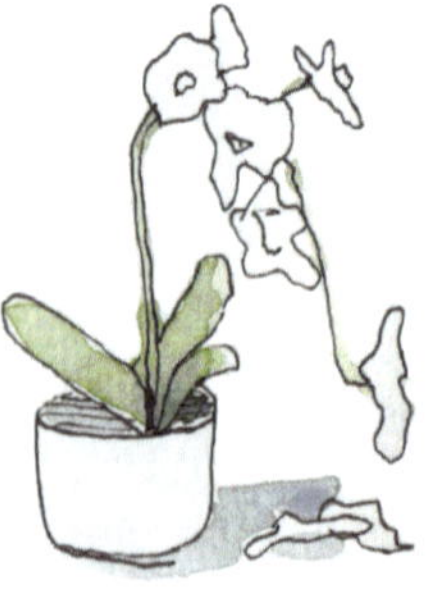

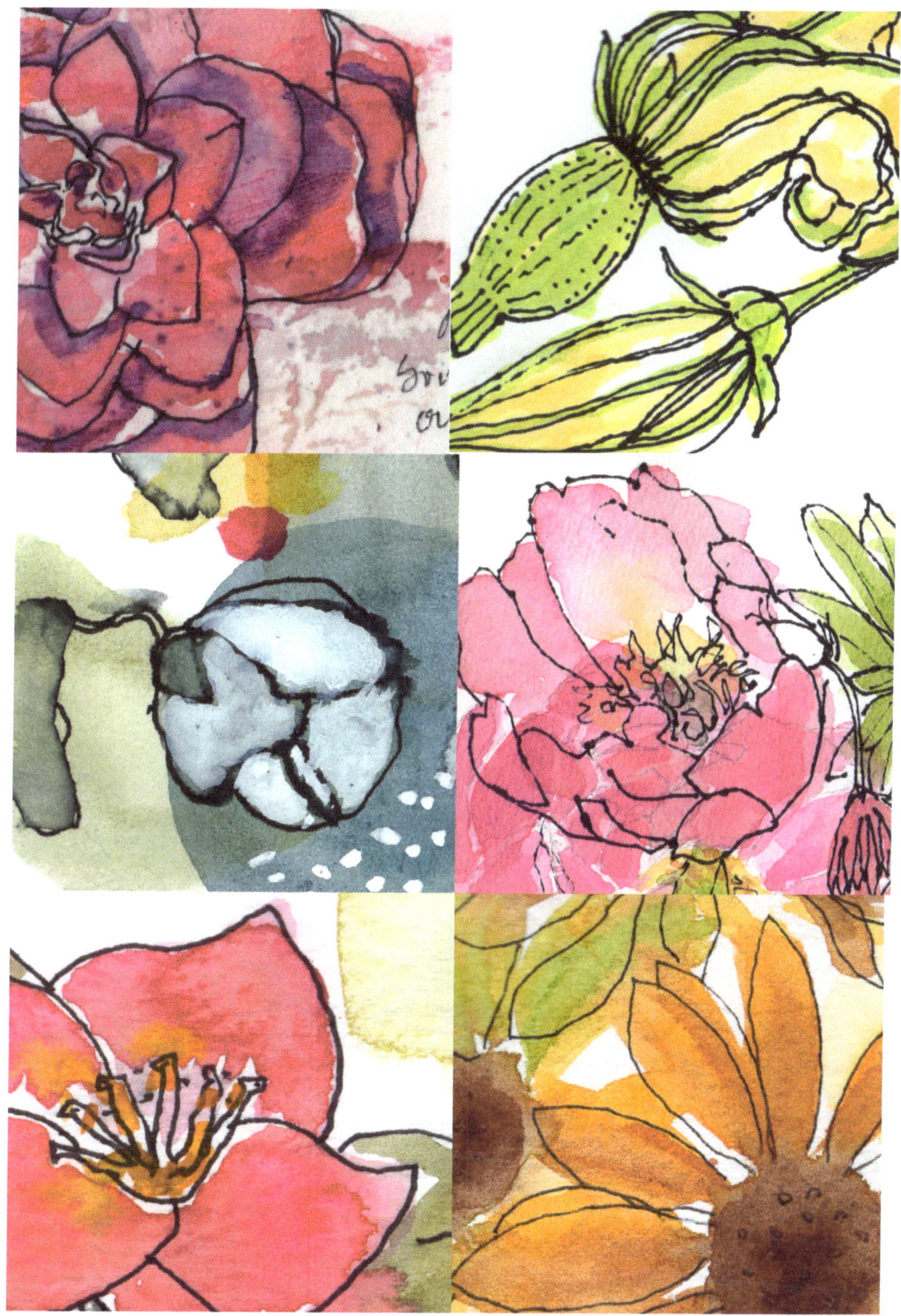

try this

Try keeping your journal/notebook, whatever you are working on, open and available.

This allows you to take a glance at what you did earlier when you walk by.

It astonishes me how I can see things later that I didn't see in the moment of doing. When you come back to something, you often have fresh eyes.

Is it realistic?

If you draw a chair and it looks like a chair, then it is good. If the proportions are off and it looks like a seven-year-old drew it, then it's bad. That is how evaluation often goes. It is pretty simple.

And while I like to end up with a drawing that mostly resembles the subject I am drawing (and don't always), I don't think it is that simple.

There are all kinds of reasons a chair can end up not looking like a chair. Maybe I have never drawn that chair before, maybe I am still working out perspective, maybe I am just tired, or maybe that is actually the true nature of the chair?

Realism is often related to technical proficiency. And it turns out that if you didn't make art for fifty years and didn't go to art school, there is a lot of practice and how-to's you miss out on compared to someone who did. And a lot of art is made by people who have spent a lot of time making art. They simply know stuff that I don't.

There is a challenge here. I know I will improve at what I spend my time on, but if feeling bad because my art isn't technically proficient or realistic keeps me from making art, I will never become more technically proficient.

And it is not always realism that makes art interesting. The wonky line can be far more interesting than the straight line. It's the interpretation that catches our hearts.

At any rate, I think the thing to wonder about is how did we ever decide realistic = good and unrealistic = bad? After all, abstract art isn't realistic, and it is pretty awesome. And even more importantly, what about this bad versus good thing?

The illustrator Cat Bennett in *The Confident Creative* offers a helpful way to approach assessing work when she points to the difference between judging our abilities versus taking a clear look at our work: "If we're approaching what we do with any degree of seriousness, we do need to take a good hard look to see where our work is unclear and why ... Yes, that forehead is too large. The thing to remember is this: it only means the forehead is too large; it doesn't mean that mistakes are bad or that you, as an artist, are hopeless. Far from it. We just need to notice what's there. We can't grow without honest assessment." What Cat is highlighting here is the difference between discerning versus judging.

Discerning versus judging

I often fall quickly into judgment and have to nudge myself to be discerning instead. Judgment, for me, shows up as a simple bad or good declaration, while discernment prompts me to ask questions. Cat talks about discerning what is working in a drawing and building on that: "Even if the artist fails to make an accurate observational drawing, there is nothing 'wrong.' Everything is part of the journey of discovery. What's helpful is to notice what's working, so the artist can build on that. The idea is that building strength overcomes all weakness."

"Is it bad or good?" is an entirely different question from "What is working here?"

Asking if it is bad or good makes my mind contract; asking what is working and/or not working opens my mind up. This is something essential that I often have to remind myself of.

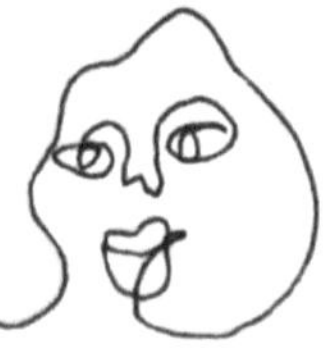

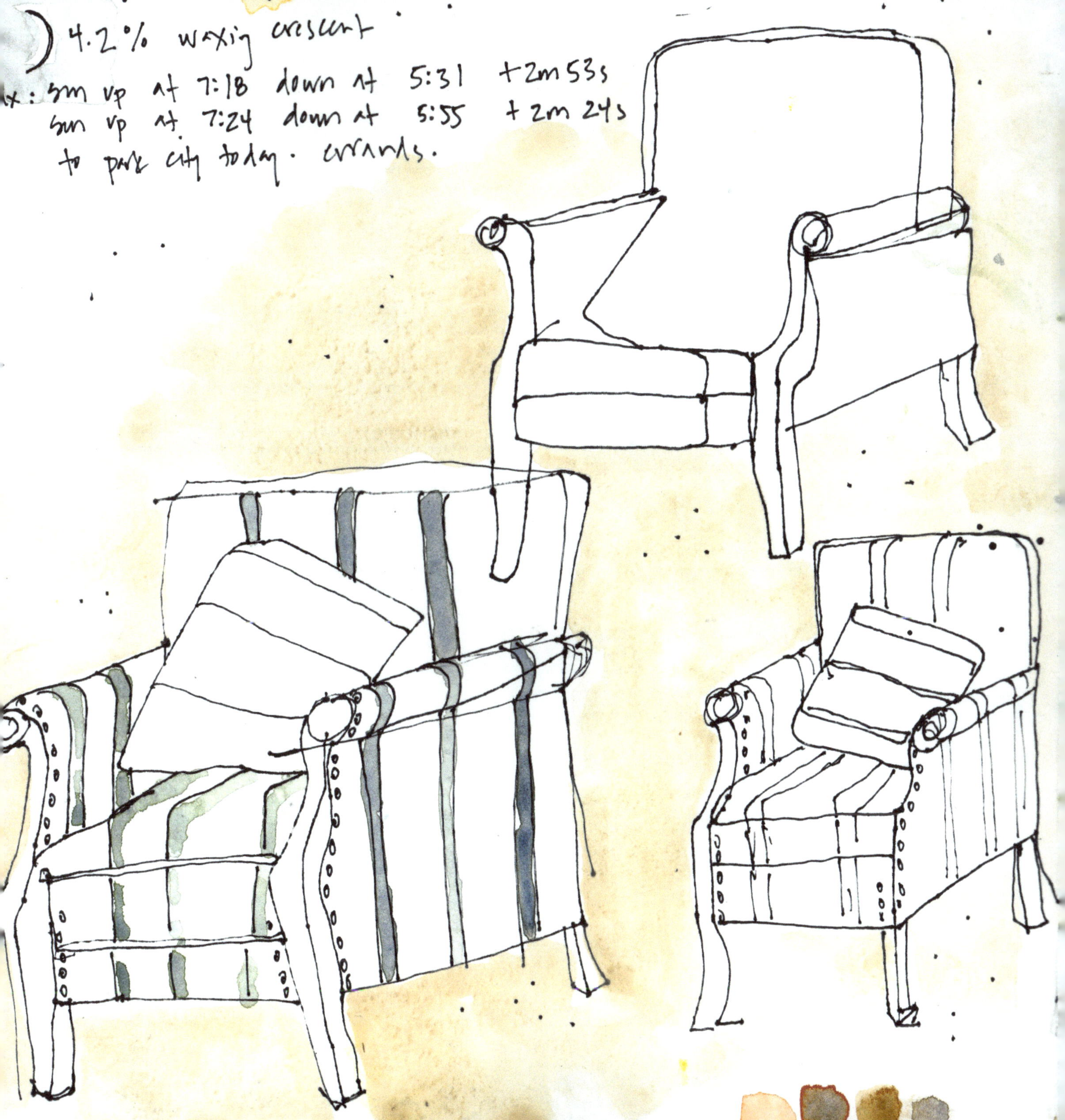

4.2% waxing crescent
x: sun up at 7:18 down at 5:31 +2m53s
sun up at 7:24 down at 5:55 +2m24s
to park city today. errands.

Is it satisfying?

Sometimes making art is very satisfying, but often it just isn't. Martha Graham acknowledged many artists' ever-present dissatisfaction when she said: "No artist is pleased ... There is no satisfaction whatever at any time ..."

I can't help but be dissatisfied with much of my work. I can see how it could be better. I don't think the answer is to pretend those feelings don't exist or to pretend that my art is just what I want it to be.

Diana Winston, in her book *The Little Book of Being,* talks about "bliss ninnies"—those who ignore the state of the world and walk around all the time feeling blissed out despite the many real problems all around us. I don't want to be a bliss ninny in life or in how I think about my art.

Other artists advise not to overlook the disappointment that is part of creating. Danny Gregory says, "Honor your work. Don't make excuses. Don't make apologies. Do your best and stand behind it."

Cat Bennett says, "Be Honest. We don't need to puff ourselves up or tear ourselves down; we just tell the truth and show up as we are. When we look at our work, we can describe how we feel about it in an honest way. If we are disappointed, we can say we're disappointed and why. If we love what we see, we can say we love what we see and why ... We're big enough to take it."

It doesn't always feel good. Discomfort is uncomfortable. And the point isn't to make it comfortable but to learn to accept it. This sounds simple, but I spend a lot of time unconsciously trying to fix my discomfort even though my wiser self knows that's not really what I am after. If, instead, I accept that being dissatisfied or frustrated is part of the territory and not something wrong or that I have to avoid, then paradoxically, it becomes much easier to accept. I try to remember what mindfulness teachers suggest, that it is by accepting and being curious about our emotions that we create some space around them.

Not being satisfied also pushes us forward. Corita Kent noted this in *Learning by Heart*: "I think what contributes most in my life to allow me to open to new experiences is a sort of sheer frustration with where I am, and I try to move out of that place, and that can lead to new experiences."

I am learning to perceive dissatisfaction not as a problem but simply as an inevitable part of the process and perhaps even as an invitation.

resource

Danny Gregory has published several books encouraging drawing, painting, and creative work. Two of my favorites are *Everyday Matters* and *The Creative License.*

Danny also started an online classroom, Sketchbook Skool, that offers numerous courses. He encourages art-making through newsletters, draw-alongs, and art communities.

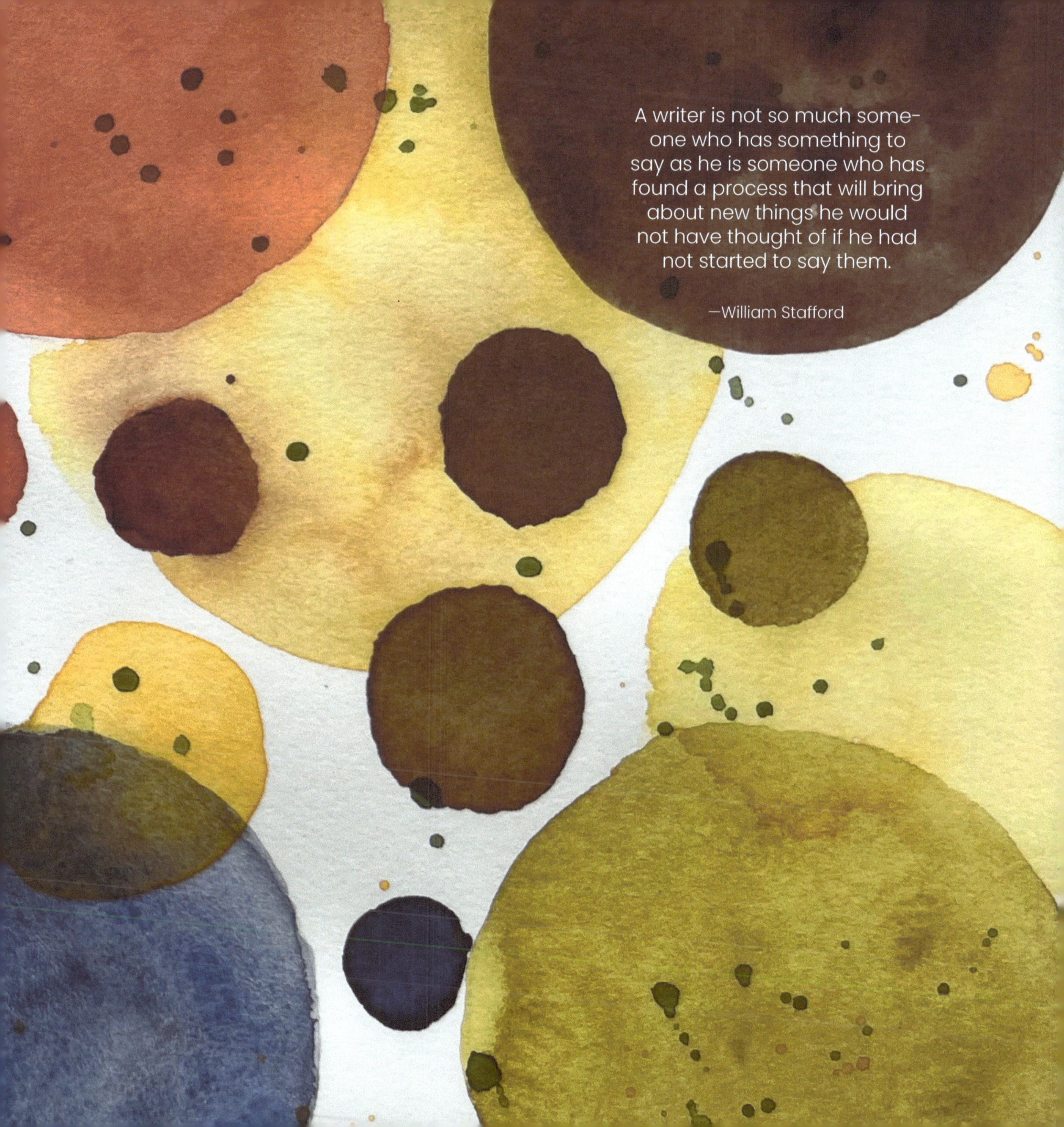
A writer is not so much some-
one who has something to
say as he is someone who has
found a process that will bring
about new things he would
not have thought of if he had
not started to say them.

—William Stafford

Mistakes

Mistakes feel bad; they feel like problems. I don't like making them. But while they feel like failures, I know they can also serve a greater purpose.

Working with mistakes is part of any creative endeavor. The only way to stop making mistakes is to stop making things, so rather than being discouraged by mistakes, learning from them and even ingeniously using them seems like a good way to go.

In *The Confident Creative,* Cat Bennett asserts that there is something genuinely generative in mistakes: "Mistakes look like a mess, like failure, but they open the gate to possibility. We need only take the time to look, give them our full appreciation, and whisper a humble word of thanks. They have genius in them."

She is right: There is genius in mistakes if we can learn to accept them, look at them, and stay curious. What is really there? What can I learn?

And if I really can't stand something, I follow my art teacher Jude's advice to paste over it or cut it out. Instead of feeling discouraged, I ask: *What can I paste it over with?* My mind stops being stymied by the mistake and starts looking around. Now I have a lovely new creative problem to solve. Eventually, I end up with something completely different from what I intended—and I love that.

Making a mistake also humbles me and reminds me of my essential shared human fallibility. As Cat Bennett says, knowing everyone makes mistakes helps everyone feel a little better: "Not only do we learn most from our mistakes, they can make other people feel good!"

And then, I can always ask: What is a mistake, anyway? Does considering something a mistake mean there was a "right way" to do it? If it showed up, is it a mistake? It's kind of fun to think about.

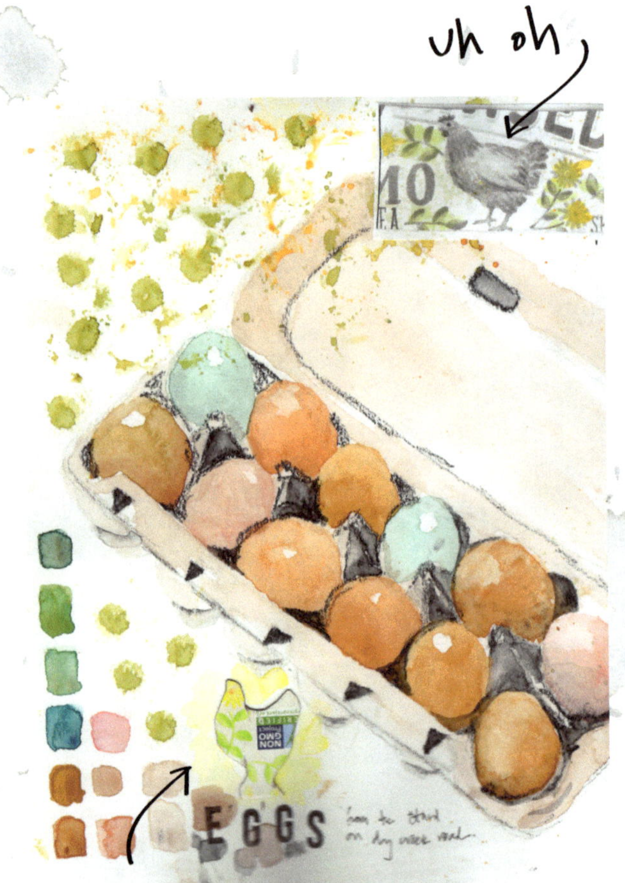

I pasted over two mistakes here. I can't remember what they were, but I cut out a piece of the egg carton (that I was drawing) and pasted that in the upper right. I also cut out a little chicken shape from the carton and pasted it above the word "eggs" to cover something up.

SOS...SOS

There are times when I make something and think it is so bad that I am almost embarrassed to have made it; it makes me feel like I should give up. But if I can hold off long enough from ripping it out or pasting it over and somehow manage to pause my automatic liking/disliking reaction, I usually can find something interesting.

My SOS practices

1. I look for a little area to love

Sometimes, I will make a little frame to look through to help me narrow my focus.

2. I look for the unexpected

What surprises me? Is it expressive in a way I wasn't expecting? Is there maybe just a small area that surprises me?

3. I look for just one thing

There is so much to look at—line, form, color, composition, to name just a few. Is anything working?

If I find an interesting little area, I can cut it out, frame it, or highlight it. There is always a little something to love, even if it is just a wee little bit.

Make a viewfinder with your hands, or make a little frame out of paper.

Look through it at different parts of your creation. If you can't find something interesting, make the viewfinder a different size or shape. Sometimes, making the viewfinder smaller can help.

Instead of tearing out, crumbling up, or pasting over a "mistake," consider the ways you might evolve your wayward creation.

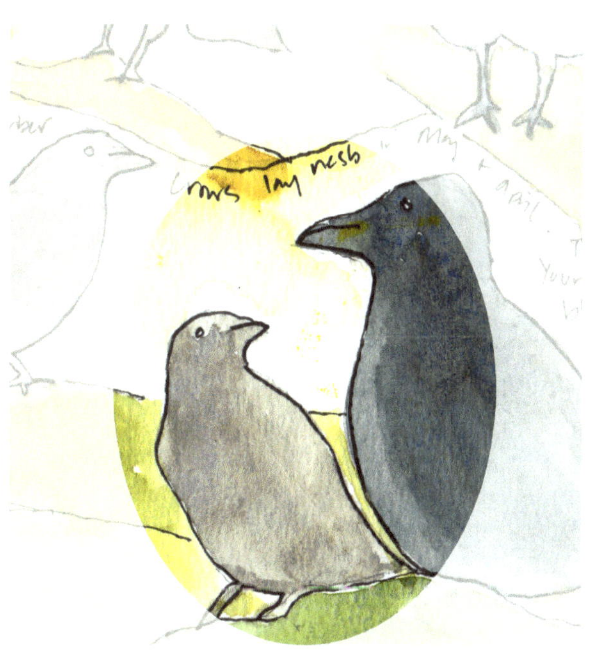

What interests me here is the simple shapes, the turn of the head, and the upward gaze of the little crow.

Reminding myself of the Why

Moving from the little details to the big picture can also be helpful. I can remind myself WHY I am doing art. How does going back to the WHY help with evaluation? If I don't know why I am doing something, it can be hard to evaluate my work honestly.

If my WHY is to create technically proficient, accurate representations, then my assessment of my efforts will be different than if my WHY is simply to try to see better and become more aware.

I remind myself that what I am after is the practice, not the result. If I have gotten myself to draw, that itself is a victory. And most likely, I have learned a little something, even if that isn't showing up on the page.

I remind myself that part of my WHY is to practice letting go, to enjoy and trust whatever happens, and to be kind to myself. I can remind myself that I actually want to have fun.

You might even say that my most frustrating moments are also my greatest teachers. If I can remember to not get sucked into reacting and instead return to my WHY.

try this

Leave a piece of paper or your journal open and ready to be worked on whenever even a few minutes present themselves.

The idea of "radical incrementalism" encourages working for a smaller part of each day in brief daily sessions. This is how I do a lot of my art.

Never underestimate the power of having materials readily at hand and a place to use them.

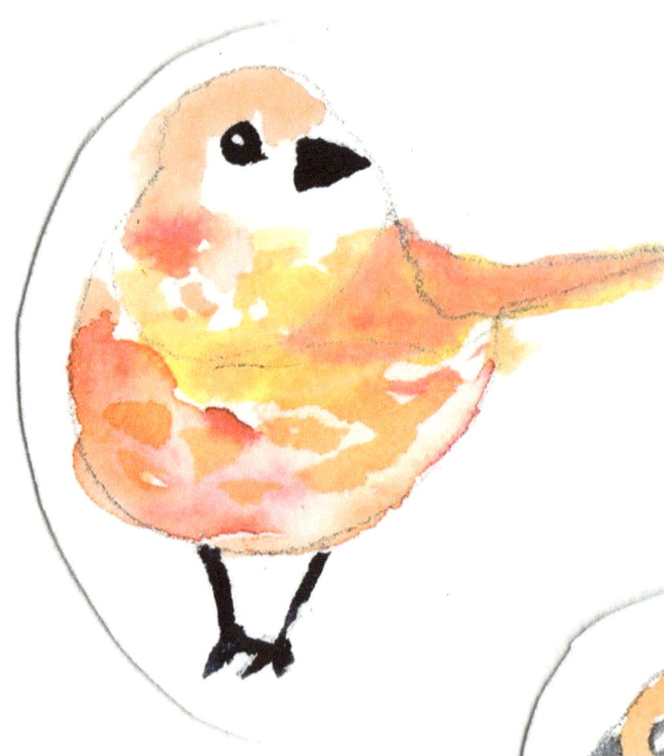

Tips for getting out of your head

Sometimes it is very hard to get out of my head.
Here are eight techniques you might try if the same happens to you:

1. Talk

There are times when I sit down to sketch, and a voice immediately starts up: *Is this going to be good? Are you getting any better? What would others think?* Etc, etc, etc. It's annoying and distracting. Somewhere, I read that while you may be unable to stop that voice in your head, you can choose not to listen. But it is hard not to listen.

If I am alone, I can start describing what I am drawing aloud. As I draw, I will talk to myself: "You see that curve of the leaf there, how it bends down and intersects with the broad section of that other leaf? Isn't that a lovely little section there where the line of the bud gets absorbed into the line of the branch?" It brings my focus away from the neurotic voice in my head and back to whatever I am drawing. I do the same thing when others are around but in my head.

2. Add Music

Some music is distracting, and other music helps me relax. Deciding what kind of music works has to be one of the most personal things in the world.

3. Hum

The little vibrations your vocal cords create when you hum somehow travel down your vagus nerve, and then your vagus nerve somehow signals to your mind and body that it can relax. I don't exactly know why or how it works—but it works.

4. Keep it simple

It is easy to get bogged down by complexity. Ask yourself how you can simplify whatever it is you are trying to do.

5. Relax

If you worry that you will draw something ridiculous or that your line might wobble or your color will be off, gently remind yourself that the universe won't mind a bit.

6. Get silly

Do something goofy or ridiculous. It might lead you somewhere unexpected.

7. Be kind

Self-compassion for yourself and your efforts will not only keep you going but also extend well beyond yourself.

8. Really stuck?

When I get stuck, it usually signals that I am thinking too much about the end result. The remedy is to go back to process and let go of the outcome. (Doing a blind contour drawing can be a quick, fun way to get unstuck.)

Other people

Up to this point, we have looked at the discomfort that comes directly from the act of making things. Other sources of discomfort frequently come up for me. One, not too surprisingly, I guess, is other people. As soon as you make something, people will have their own ideas about it.

If you are lucky, you will have supportive people in your life urging you on. But chances are, if you are finding your way to art, other people won't be able to see all that is invisible within you and where you are headed. Instead, they view what you have made, and most likely, they will make a judgment about it.

This is hard. Especially when we are beginners and not very confident.

When people comment on my art, they often say what they like, which makes perfect sense. We almost all have this automatic response of liking/not liking. And they are most likely judging if what I have made is "good." I can't expect others to have traveled the same journey I have, so it is good to have some way to deal with their response. If I feel like sharing, I can tell them what I was working on, what I saw, and what I am trying to do.

But I still don't do this well. Someday, I would like to feel free enough to take my sketchbook anywhere and sketch in front of anyone! I do hope that moment arrives for me. In the meantime, I will keep working on accepting the discomfort I feel while working where others can see me.

After all, I remind myself that my art is not about pleasing anyone; it is only an artifact of a process. I also know other people actually care far less about what I do than I think they do, so rationally, it just doesn't make sense to make them the arbiter of my experience.

Whatever someone's reaction is to my work, I try to hold it lightly.

However, the need for external validation can be strong. We habitually want others to value and appreciate our work. This is why I need my third permission: to allow myself to be an audience of one.

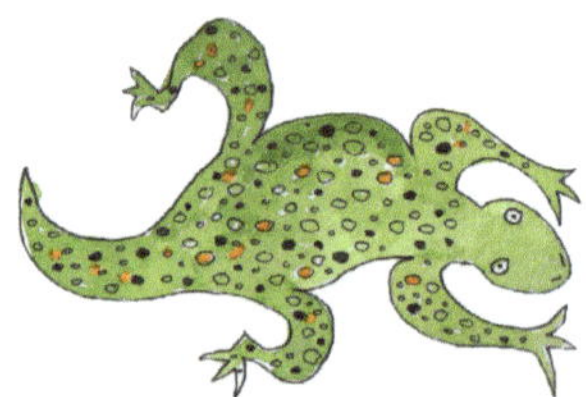

Letting go of outside validation

When I can let go of the desire for outside validation and tune in instead to my own curiosities and interests, there is immense freedom. I no longer have to consider what the outside world might like; instead, I can place my attention on what interests me.

In his book *4,000 Weeks: Time Management for Mortals*, Oliver Burkeman suggests that this desire for validation is, in part, a need to feel secure. Burkeman writes: "The attempt to attain security by justifying your existence, it turns out, was both futile and unnecessary all along. Futile because life will always feel uncertain and out of your control. And unnecessary because, in consequence, there's no point in waiting to live until you have achieved validation from someone or something else. Peace of mind, and an exhilarating sense of freedom, comes not from achieving the validation but from yielding to the reality that it wouldn't bring security if you got it."

I remind myself that the trouble with wanting and waiting for validation from outside sources is that it means I am handing over the reins to someone or something that is not me. That just doesn't make sense when it comes to personal creative work.

When I think of someone who truly understood an audience of one, I think of a story that has stayed with me ever since I read it. In *Drawing from Life: The Journal as Art,* Jennifer New tells the story of Masayoshi Nakano.

After retiring at age seventy, Nakano walked through his home region of Musashino, Japan, for twenty-three years, filling journals with maps and photos. New includes pages from one of Nakano's journals. They are exquisitely detailed and complex. He completed forty journals, but only one exists today. New writes, "Finding little value in them beyond their making, he burned all of them except one completed book. It is hard to imagine the destruction of all the intricate maps, the years of work, the complex memories and knowledge he surely built up during that time."

I often think about Nakano and his journals.

Time

It is easy to feel trapped by time. Time itself is a mystery, but one thing we often feel about it is that we don't have enough of it. Because our time is truly finite, struggles with time are ever-present for many of us.

"You have twenty-four hours a day like everyone else," my dad would say. It was his way of saying that my problem was not with time itself but with how I was prioritizing and managing my time. While I don't think that is true, as some of us have far more unyielding demands on our time and pressures on our lives than others, I think he was trying to point out that I have a choice in how I spend my time—and having too little time is not a unique dilemma. Not having enough time to sweep the deck wasn't a valid excuse for not doing it. And if sweeping the deck meant I didn't have time to do something else, well, that was just the way it was.

Choosing to do anything means not choosing to do an infinite number of other things. Making decisions about how we spend our time, either consciously or unconsciously, is part of life. And while we may not have unlimited choices about how we spend our time, and some of us have far more freedom to make choices than others, even those of us with more available time feel a sense of time scarcity. It comes, I think, from being aware of the unlimited options for how we could spend that time. We can see all the good and important things that could be done if only we had the time. I can think of more things to do before breakfast than I could complete in years. Add to that the stark reality that life is comprised of unending problems to solve and tasks to complete, and it can seem like there is never enough time to do what we want or need to do.

Actual and perceived time scarcity is a big part of the issue, but so are ideas or stories we commonly hear about time: time is money; time is the most important resource we have; we're wasting time if we're not getting something done; the more efficient you are with your time, the better. And then there is the issue of our mortality, which is what makes all this matter oh so very much.

Implied in all of these ideas and stories is that how I spend my time matters a lot. So, how can I justify time spent scribbling away while the world burns? For me, it comes down to remembering three things:

1. What is important to me matters. And if I don't make time for it—it will never happen.
2. A few minutes is enough. It is not about spending hours and hours doing something.
3. I will always have to leave things undone.

These acknowledgments help me avoid the time traps I frequently encounter: believing that what I do always has to be seen as useful by others, that it's not worth doing something if I don't have lots of time for it, and that I can only engage in what matters to me once I have taken care of everything else.

There is a lot here. After all, how we spend our time ends up being how we live our lives. Ideas about time and how we should spend it permeate our culture. Because it is so ever-present for so many of us, there are more explorations of time ahead.

Three time reminders

1. What is **important** to me matters. And if I don't make time for it—it will never happen.

2. A few **minutes** is enough. It is not about spending hours and hours doing something.

3. I will **always** have to leave things undone.

try this

Go forward to work on pages, go backward to work on pages. If you think of what you are working on as a conversation, you might find there is a past conversation you want to pick up later. Or something to paste on a page or paper that will jumpstart a future conversation.

When is the conversation over? That is always an interesting thing to think about. Sometimes I find I overwork a page, other times I wonder if I have left something unsaid.

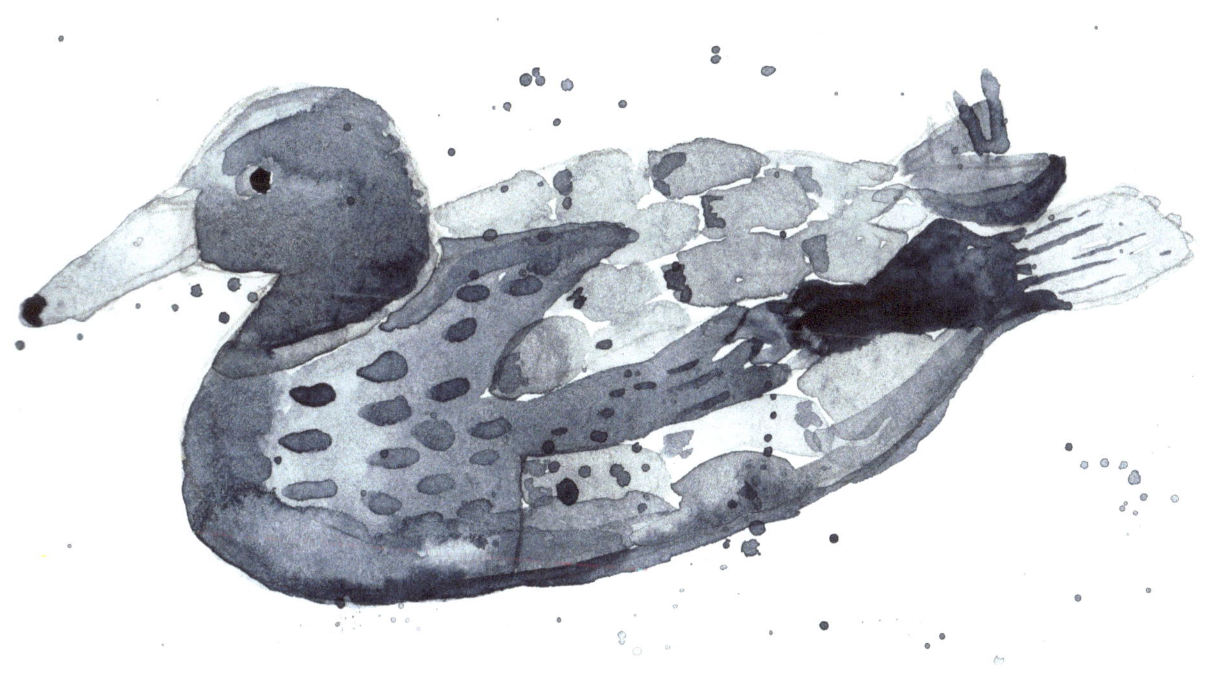

Bad days

I am not talking about really bad days here—those times when life becomes hard and traumatic—but the kind of bad days that crop up when life seems to be, well, pretty normal.

I can't expect every day to be the same. Some days are just busy, and others, I don't feel well. It is just not possible to draw or write on these days. It is hard for me to not panic when I feel down or sick or have low energy, but I am learning to respect that I am not a machine, and there is no sense in resisting it. And being aware means being aware of challenging and difficult things, not just the good stuff. Not every day sparkles.

Accepting the situation, allowing the situation, and resisting the urge to tell myself a story about the day or the future helps. I can try to let the day unfold on its own, as it will, knowing that there may be some-thing in the day for me to see if I let it be.

Many mindfulness experts believe that seeing the impermanence of our lives helps alleviate suffering. Recognizing that everything that comes will also pass away allows me to stay right where I am, over my feet, and not overthink it.

And I can remind myself that there may be bigger forces at play here and that this day that seems so barren may be just what I need to carry myself to the other shore.

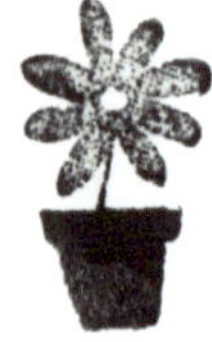

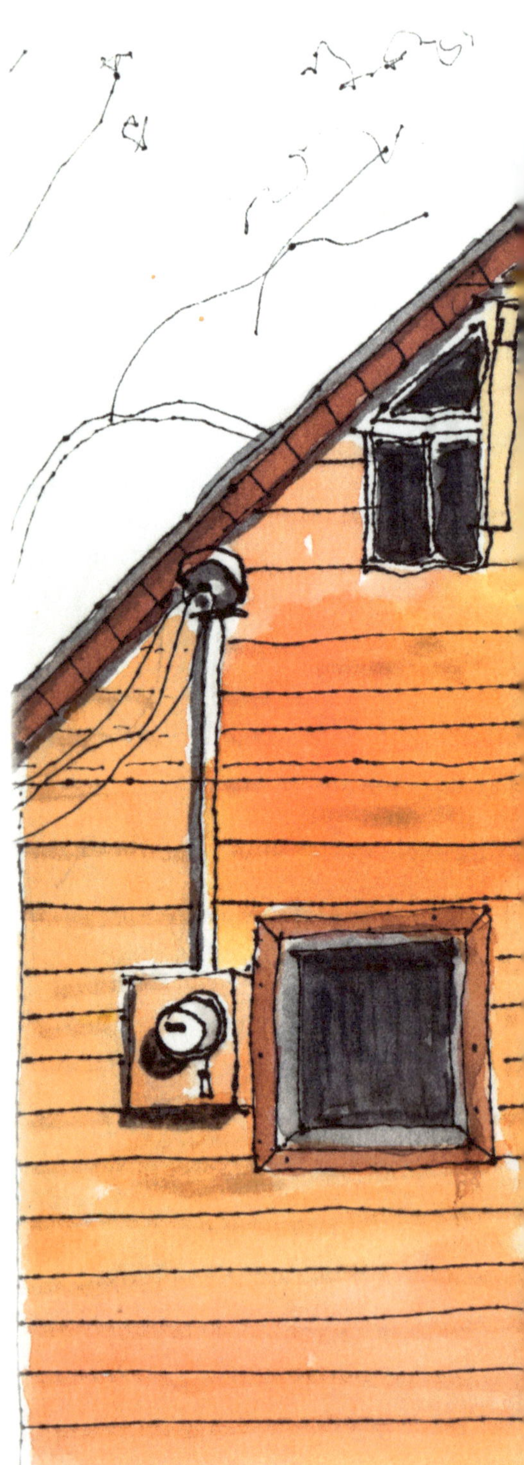

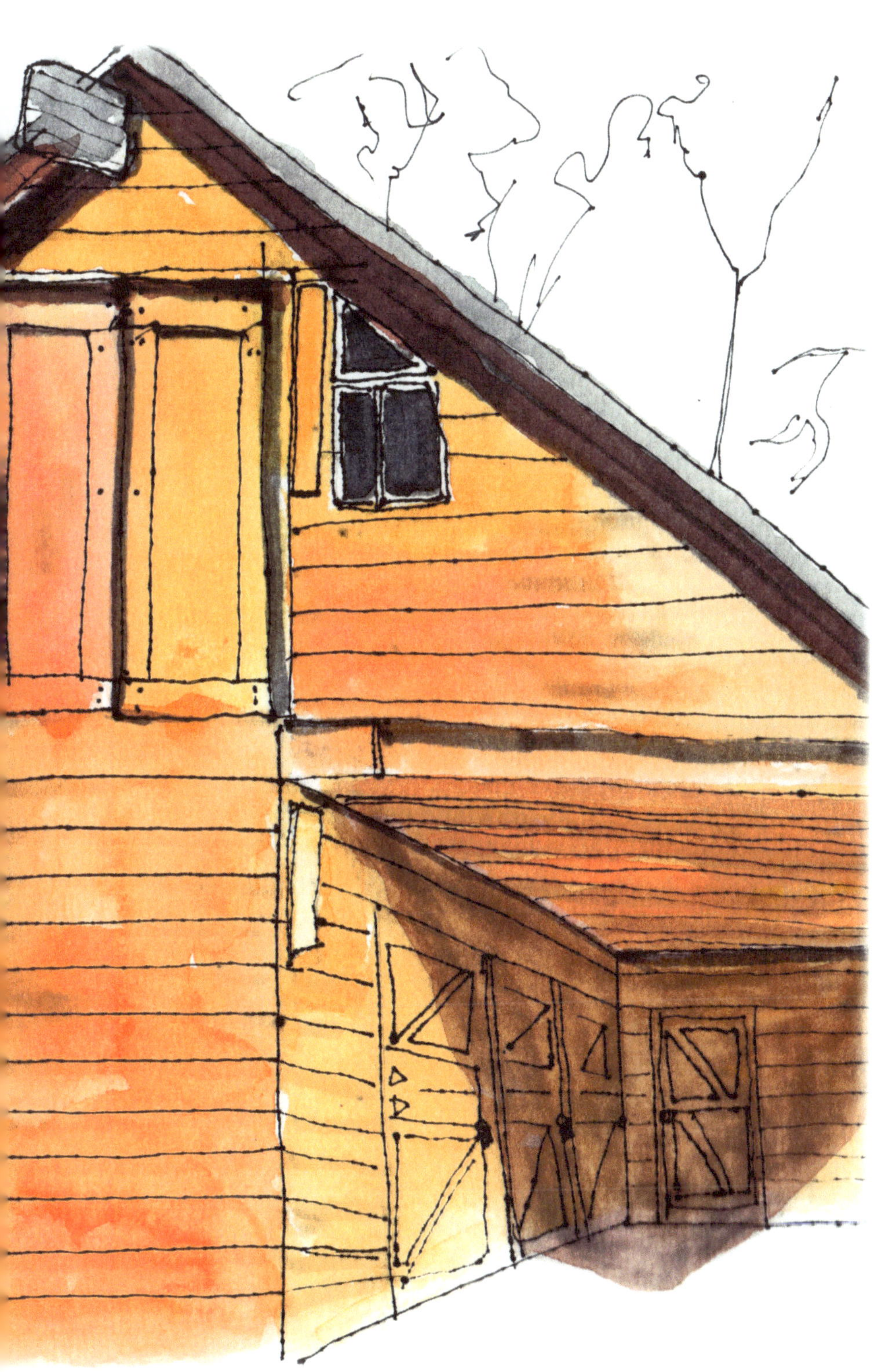

There are moments when I am overflowing with ideas of things I want to try, and then there are moments when I am not.

You can't do everything you think of at once, but you can make a list and keep it handy for when you can't think of anything you want to do.

Don't think of it as a to-do list with an implied need for completion; instead, think of it as a sort of delightful menu of things to pick and choose from. A kind of remember-you-wanted-to-try-this list.

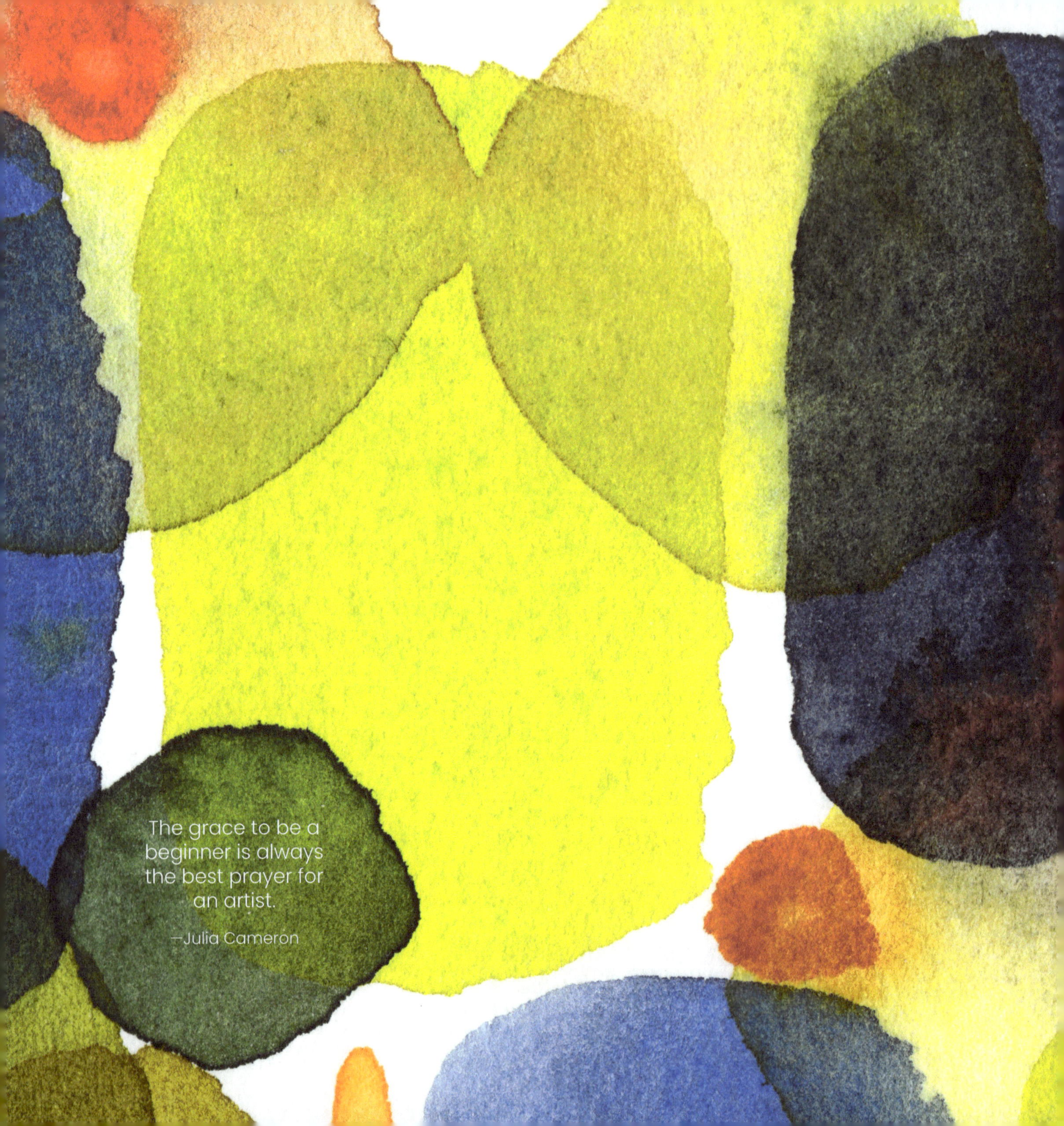
The grace to be a
beginner is always
the best prayer for
an artist.

—Julia Cameron

Working with discomfort

Always a beginner

Accepting

Cultivating patience

Self compassion

Working with discomfort

Thinking more philosophically and generally about discomfort can help me tolerate, accept, and even appreciate discomfort. I am talking here specifically about the discomfort that can accompany both art-making and being a beginner.

To begin with, I know I can tolerate discomfort because I do it regularly. It is a rare day that goes by without any sort of discomfort. For example, getting exercise is often uncomfortable in one way or another, but we tolerate (and sometimes even welcome) the discomfort because we believe it is good for us.

I remind myself that discomfort is a natural part of life rather than a signal that something is wrong. Life is filled with all sorts of discomforts. Expecting my life to always be comfortable is unrealistic and limiting. Avoiding discomfort would make my life quite small. Conversely, if I learn to tolerate discomfort, it means I can learn and do more.

This entails learning to accept rather than resist unpleasant feelings. Mindfulness experts advise us to experiment with being present with whatever feeling is coming up instead of thinking about it, fixing it, or solving it. Sitting with the feeling often allows it to go the same way it came. I have always liked envisioning difficult emotions as prickly animals that I simply need to let rest in my lap.

Ironically, the idea of discomfort is often greater than the actual discomfort itself. If I just get myself to do something without worrying about it, it often turns out better, or at least differently, than I envisioned.

Not much is at stake here; I am not working myself up to jump out of an airplane or navigate a complex surgery. How terribly can things go wrong with a pen and paper? It is only my ego that gets bruised by a wayward drawing. And yet, this sort of discomfort can keep us from trying things we actually would like to try.

In his book *Four Thousand Weeks*, Oliver Burkeman suggests that an essential part of productivity is learning to tolerate the discomfort of not getting everything done. I think there is a parallel anti-skill worth developing in art-making: the ability to tolerate the discomfort of making unskilled art. I spoke with a friend the other day who is taking an art journal class. When I asked how it was going, she said she hadn't started a journal because she was waiting until she had more skills. If my friend had developed an anti-skill, would she draw more and have already started a journal? I don't know, but I like the idea of anti-skill here too.

Maybe I can even learn to see the appearance of discomfort as a sign—not that things are going wrong but as a welcome part of the process.

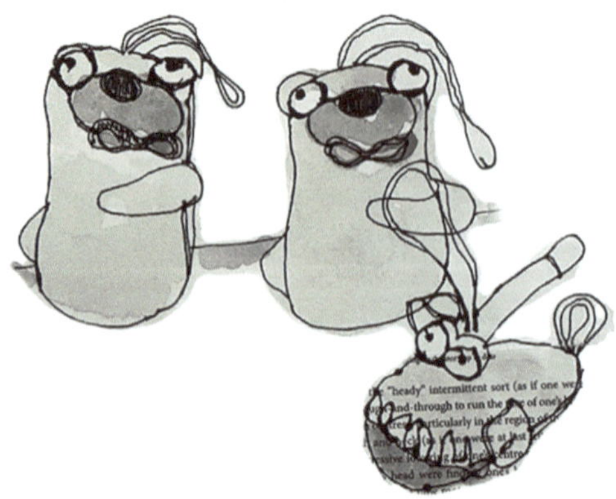

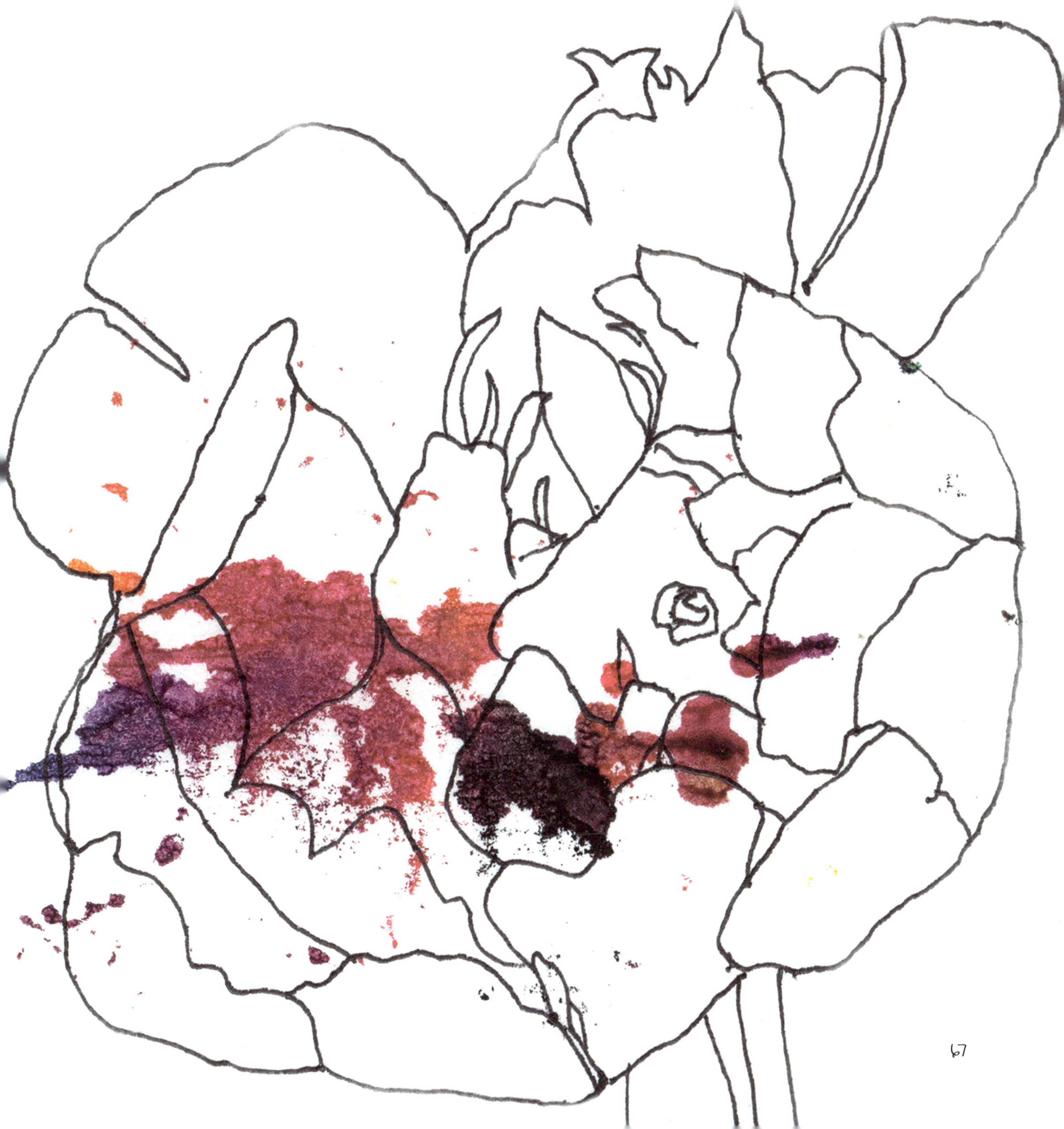

always a beginner

If both art-making (and particularly) being a beginner at art-making brings discomfort, wouldn't I rather be an accomplished artist than a beginner? Well, maybe yes, but maybe no. The lure of accomplishment, recognition, and confidence in being an accomplished artist is clearly enticing. Sometimes, I just ache when I think of what I would have learned in art school. The benefits of being a recognized artist are apparent and rarely questioned. Still, I wonder: What does it mean if I think of myself as always a beginner?

There is a fundamental freedom in thinking of myself as a beginner; I can just try things. If I shade in an area with my watercolor pencil, I wonder: *Should I blend it in or just leave it?* I really don't know. Then, if I blend it in and it turns into a muddy mess, well, I just learned something.

Seeing myself as a beginner allows me to make mistakes, be curious, and try new things. Seeing it that way turns what could be seen as a lack (of experience or competence) into an endlessly unfolding opportunity. As the Zen monk Shunryu Suzuki famously said, "In the beginner's mind, there are many possibilities; in the expert's mind, there are few."

Jan Steward speaks to the openness of being an amateur in *Learning by Heart:* "A tremendously constricting force on our contemporary society is the concept of the professional or specialist, who deals for the most part with what has already been done and builds on his own limits. To the extent we can approach our job as an amateur (from the Latin *amare*, meaning "to *love*"), we will be successful in our work. When we pursue a thing for love, we are free to fumble and make mistakes. The course of our work may not run smoothly, but we are open to possibilities, embracing everything we have contact with."

If you aren't a "professional," you can be free to do things a new way. There can be vibrant originality in the work of people who haven't been taught to draw—being an experienced artist can get in the way. In *Making Comics*, Lynda Barry writes: "A certain sort of unlearning has to take place before a practicing artist can get to the place where this kind of drawing can take you. It's hard for something original to make it past 'already knowing how.' Being good at something is its own curse, sometimes. Because a non-artist can't control his line, he can't interfere with what is showing up, he can't stop the mood his character is in because of the way he drew on the eyebrows, and so the original has a chance."

I once heard an artist say that it is apparent from some artists' work that they are unaware of conventions. (He cited the lack of European perspective in the work of Giotto, the Florentine painter.) So, art has conventions like everything else. Do I want to learn these conventions? Or do I want to explore on my own? Or is it some combination of both? I don't know, but I do know the great thing about seeing myself as always a beginner is that there is just all sorts of learning ahead.

Two concepts from mindfulness remind me to approach art-making as a beginner. The first is the Zen concept of "beginner's mind," which asks me to let go of my preconceived ideas of how things will or should be and be freshly aware of what is. To me, beginner's mind means approaching something as if you were doing it or seeing it for the first time. This is hard. It is a challenge to resist letting what I anticipate become the reality and just let things be as they are. But when I can adopt a beginner's mind, I look at the world with new eyes rather than just assuming I know what is, or what should be, there. This is easier to do when you are truly a beginner. It becomes more challenging when I think I know how something should go.

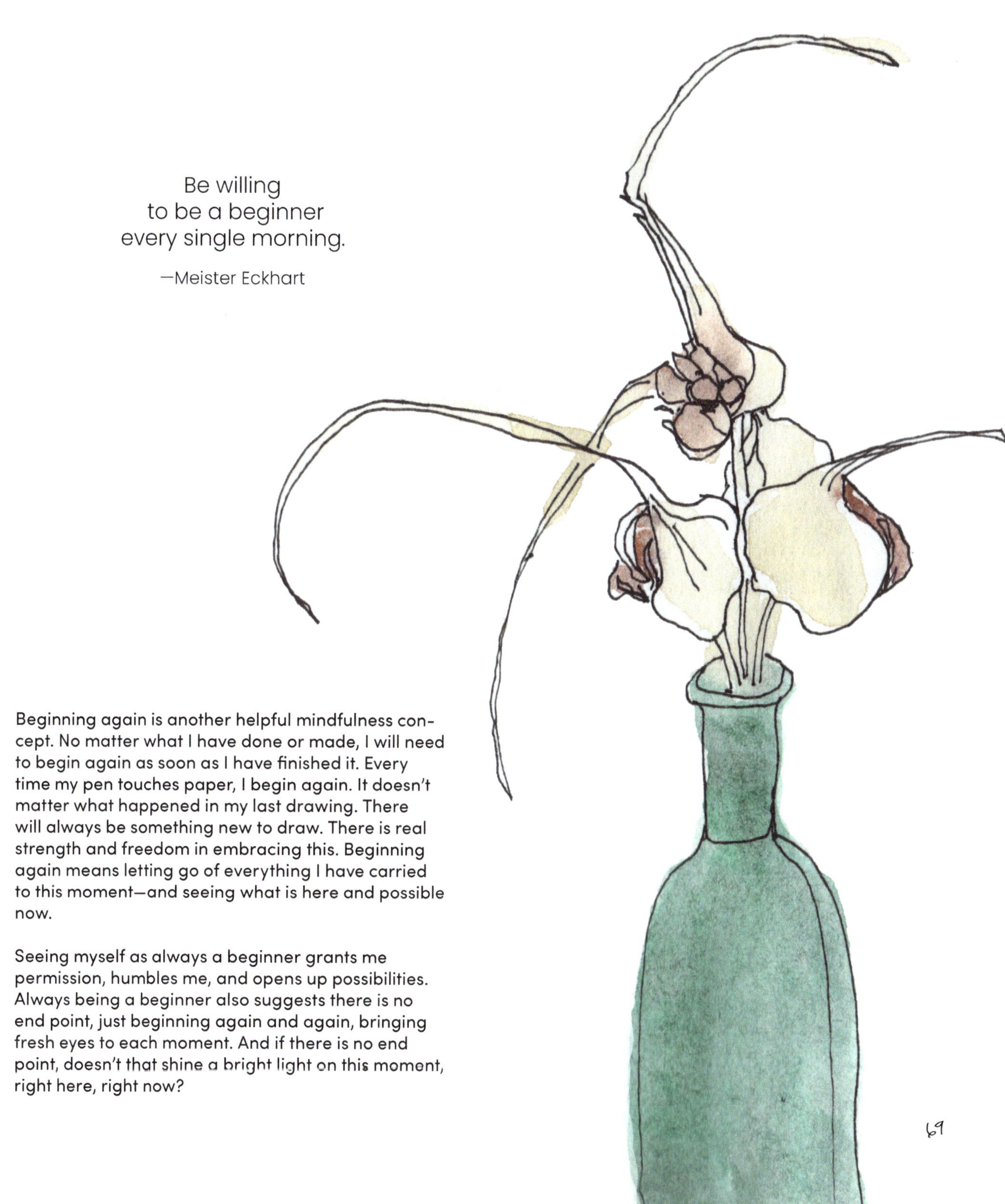

Be willing
to be a beginner
every single morning.

—Meister Eckhart

Beginning again is another helpful mindfulness concept. No matter what I have done or made, I will need
to begin again as soon as I have finished it. Every
time my pen touches paper, I begin again. It doesn't
matter what happened in my last drawing. There
will always be something new to draw. There is real
strength and freedom in embracing this. Beginning
again means letting go of everything I have carried
to this moment—and seeing what is here and possible
now.

Seeing myself as always a beginner grants me
permission, humbles me, and opens up possibilities.
Always being a beginner also suggests there is no
end point, just beginning again and again, bringing
fresh eyes to each moment. And if there is no end
point, doesn't that shine a bright light on this moment,
right here, right now?

accepting

Approaching art-making as always a beginner is part of a greater practice of acceptance. While it seems paradoxical, I have learned that by accepting where I am, even if it is not where I want to be, I can keep going.

I have had some genuinely hilarious moments trying to draw something that even slightly resembles my subject. And I would be lying to you if I said I don't want to get better. I do want to get better at drawing, painting, and creating. Would I keep drawing if I thought I would never get any better? Well, yes, I guess so, though part of what I enjoy is learning. Can I accept where I am now? Well, yes, mostly.

I have to accept what I create—I would say even enjoy it—while working toward improving. If I can't accept what I am able to create right now, I will get discouraged and stop creating. And if I stop trying, it truly is impossible to get better. Trying to navigate acceptance and improvement is a continual paradox.

Acceptance doesn't signal approval. For example, I can accept that the perspective in my current drawing is way off without disparaging where I am now.

Zen teacher Henry Shukman uses a garden metaphor to illustrate accepting the moment while planning for the future. When speaking of the path to enlightenment, he describes moments of meditation as tilling the earth or putting down compost. Just as we don't expect our garden to grow overnight, so it is with enlightenment. We nurture our garden, we are patient, and we take care of it. I like to think of my regular practice as a garden where I plant who knows what. But whatever it is, I don't expect it to grow overnight.

Sam Harris often speaks about living this paradox of accepting the moment just as it is while simultaneously working to make life better. "Most of what we do in life is try to change what is into what should be. But the paradox is that truly accepting what is is often the best way to do that."

"It's a simple and generous rule of life that whatever you practice, you will improve at."
—Elizabeth Gilbert

Acceptance involves wisdom, compassion, and patience. Much of what I have written about in this book is about learning to accept and enjoy work that could be improved upon. Acceptance, bolstered by love and patience, is perhaps what we all need to grow.

And I will get better.

Here is the thing I know: if I can keep going—just keep going—I will get better.

I know this is true because if I draw the same object three times in one afternoon, it usually gets better. And what do I mean by better? I am not sure, but somehow, what I have created just feels more right to me. I can also look back at work I did months before, and while I can still spy the wild and untamed bits that spurred me on, I can also see that I have learned a thing or two since then.

Generally speaking, the more we do something, the better we get at it. The magic is in the practice.

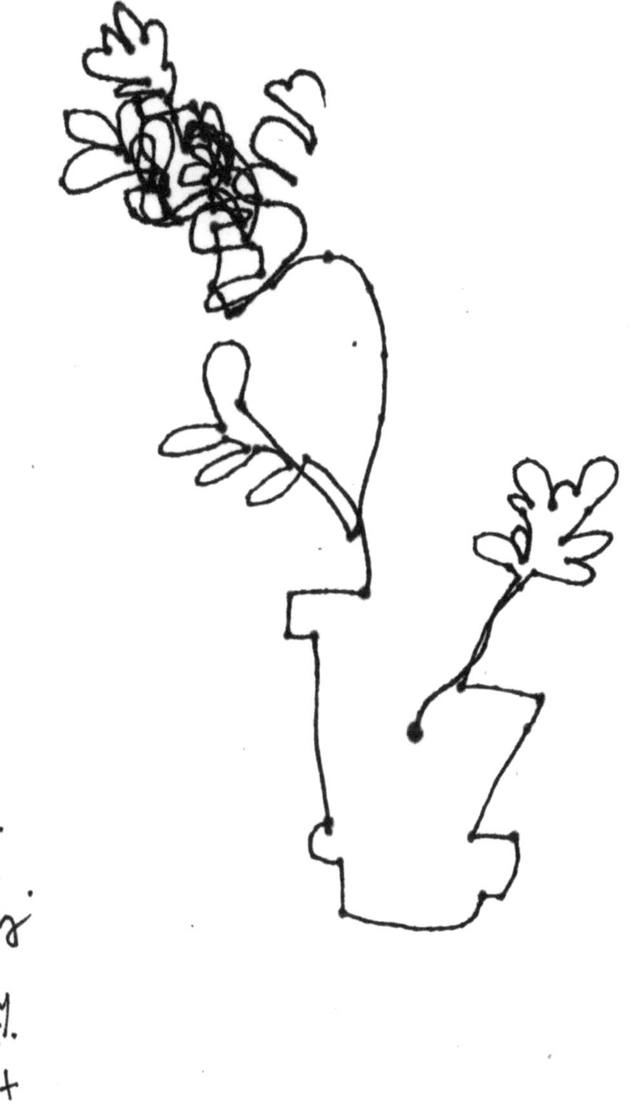

do blind contour
every day to get
better at drawing

good creative way
to start somethin'.
to connect brain +
your eyes.

everything
is practice .

Cultivating patience

It is very ironic for me to write something about patience since being patient is hard for me. I recently took an online workshop with Oliver Burkeman, and he said, "We advise and talk about the topics we struggle with. There is a form of wisdom that comes from the struggle." So maybe in that way, it makes sense that I think about patience.

Patience comes in different flavors, but I would like to look closer at a couple. The first sort of patience is about accepting that things will take the time they take and that I can't hurry things along or find a shortcut. It takes me, oh, I don't know, five minutes to unload the dishwasher, and trying to do it in three will just make me jumpy and slightly miserable. This impatience comes from wanting to do more in any given time period than is possible.

Conversely, a marvelous relief happens when I can find more patience with tasks. Once I recognize that things will just take the time they take, I can relax into that. I can't really fight that, so why try? Patience here manifests a bit of kindness, a nod to the everyday realities of life.

Ironically, I have learned that it doesn't work to get impatient with my impatience; instead, I have to acknowledge it and thank it for trying to get me prepared for the next thing right now and reassure it that it is actually okay for me just to relax and do one thing at a time. I wish I could say this makes my impatience go away (it doesn't). Still, if I continue to recognize it and focus on the task at hand, it fades for a while before jumping up again and asking to be recognized, which I do and start again.

A second type of patience is one that drawing and meditation encourage. Drawing requires me to slow down and allows me to see things I otherwise would miss. It is about giving myself the time and space to notice things I overlook when I move too quickly.

Another sort of patience is about allowing myself to rest in the moment without having a specific plan or idea of how things should go; if I don't rush into action and instead just pay attention, something is there. Patience is a friend of uncertainty. Often, if I allow myself to remain uncertain and don't try to rush into action, solutions will eventually appear. Or I will learn that given patience, uncertainty no longer seems like a problem to be solved but rather an opportunity to soften into not knowing.

We can be impatient with being a beginner, impatient to finish a journal, a book, or a drawing, but if it is really the journey that is important, that just doesn't make sense. Accepting that things will take the time they take means accepting things as they are, which somehow helps ease my always-doing, always-fixing self. When I can find patience, it allows me to see the world more clearly and relax into it just a bit more.

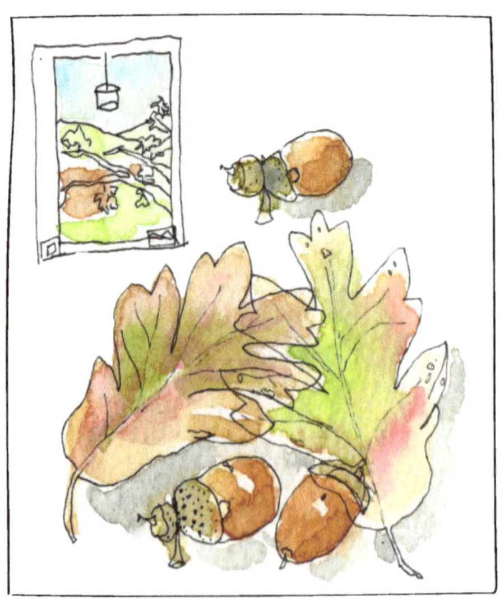

Patience is a form of wisdom. It demonstrates
that we understand and accept the fact that
sometimes things must unfold in their own time.

—Jon Kabat-Zinn

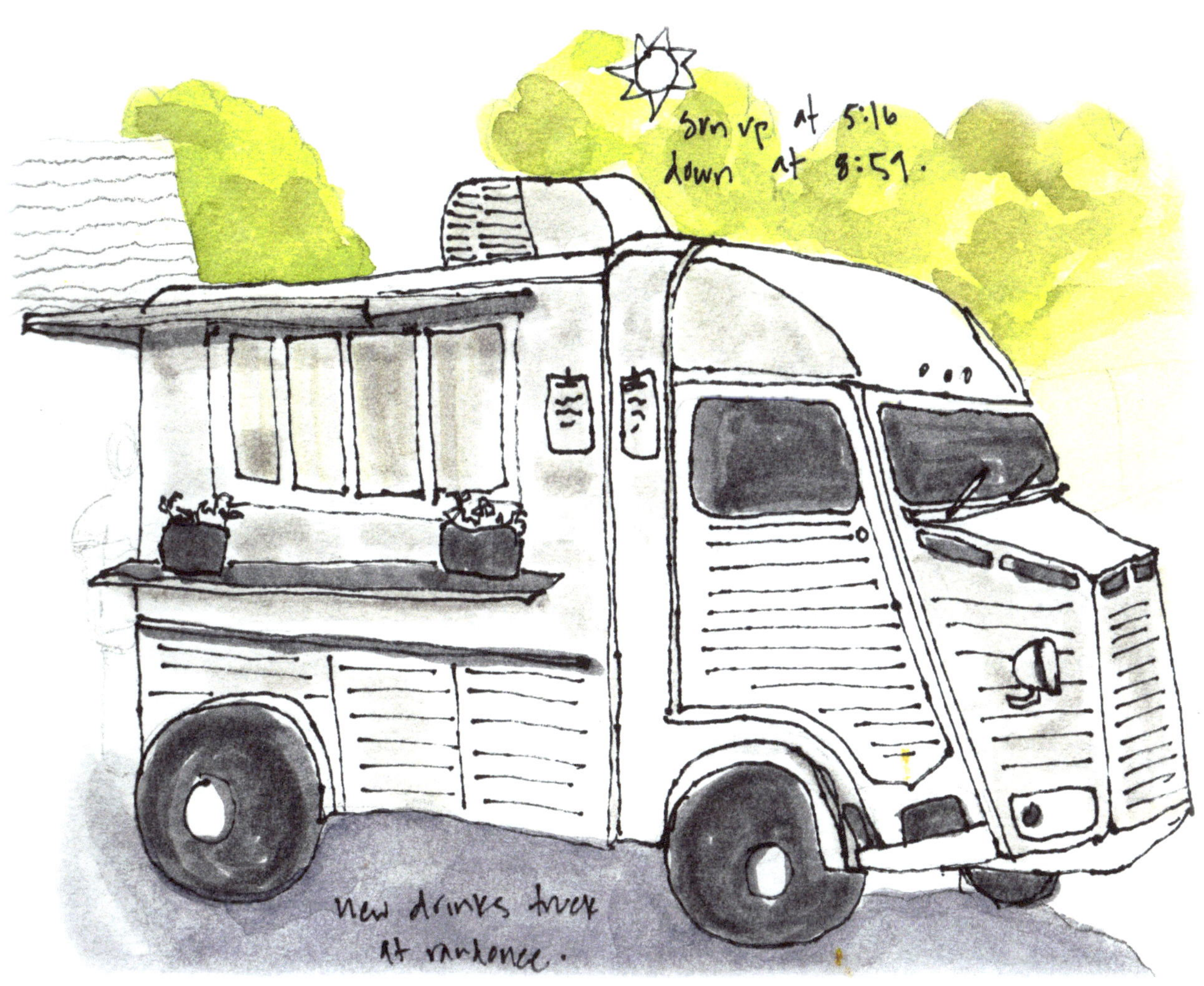

Finding Self-compassion

Oh, that elusive self-compassion! My friend Lisa's therapist is helping her work on cultivating self-compassion. When I ask her how it is going, we both just giggle. I think we giggle at the irony of thinking it should be simple and accessible despite knowing it can be so hard to find. We also giggle because we know that self-compassion brings many gifts, both to ourselves and others. Yet it sounds vaguely superficial, like something you might read on a Hallmark card.

For me, making art and practicing mindfulness continually call out for self-kindness because it is so easy to see where I fall short. I am presented over and over again with both the need for self-compassion and the chance to actively practice it. Accepting discomfort doesn't mean being hard on myself. I can find a place where I accept discomfort while simultaneously being kind to myself. Maybe even in acknowledging discomfort, there is a simultaneous call for self-compassion if I listen for it.

I know self-compassion is essential to my practice—it is often what allows me to keep going. So, where do I find that mysterious self-compassion? I remind myself of a couple of things:

I am always a beginner.

There is no need to take myself so seriously.

It is okay to fall short—a notion that encompasses acceptance and allowance into a sweet little bundle.

Awareness is also essential to self-compassion. Without awareness, I wouldn't be able to see where my thinking trips me up. I wouldn't notice when I put labels on things and put myself, others, and experiences into boxes. I wouldn't see when I stopped looking and started making judgments. I also wouldn't see when I was being hampered by old stories.

Awareness helps me to consider that somewhere, there is an unhelpful, unvoiced, abstract idea of what I am supposed to be and be doing. Self-compassion suggests that maybe I should just go with what is.

Awareness also helps with my growing understanding that the story is not as simple as me being a lone entity making something. Life is more about co-emergence and co-creation than it first appears. Awareness allows me to see that the situation is far more fluid and mysterious. Staying open to that possibility softens my heart.

I know that lack of compassion is a showstopper. It is a quick way to make my world and my heart small. A lack of compassion puts my blinders on. When I find myself judging something I have made as falling short, when I feel discouraged or frustrated, the remedy is to be kind, let go, and lighten up.

Self-kindness is the magic fairy dust I need to keep my creative self going. If I want to keep making things and having fun, I know I have to cultivate self-compassion. It is as essential as paper and pen.

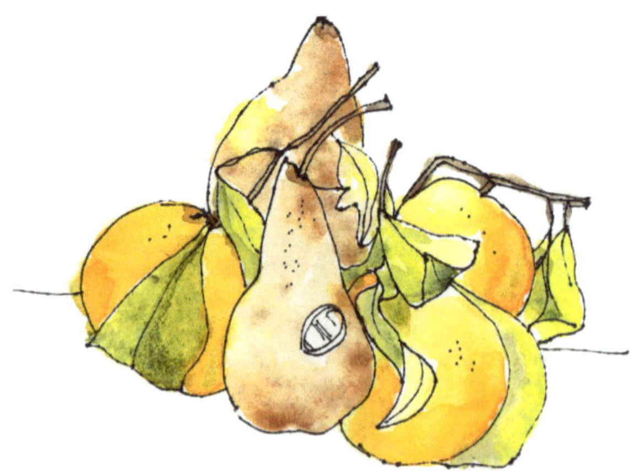

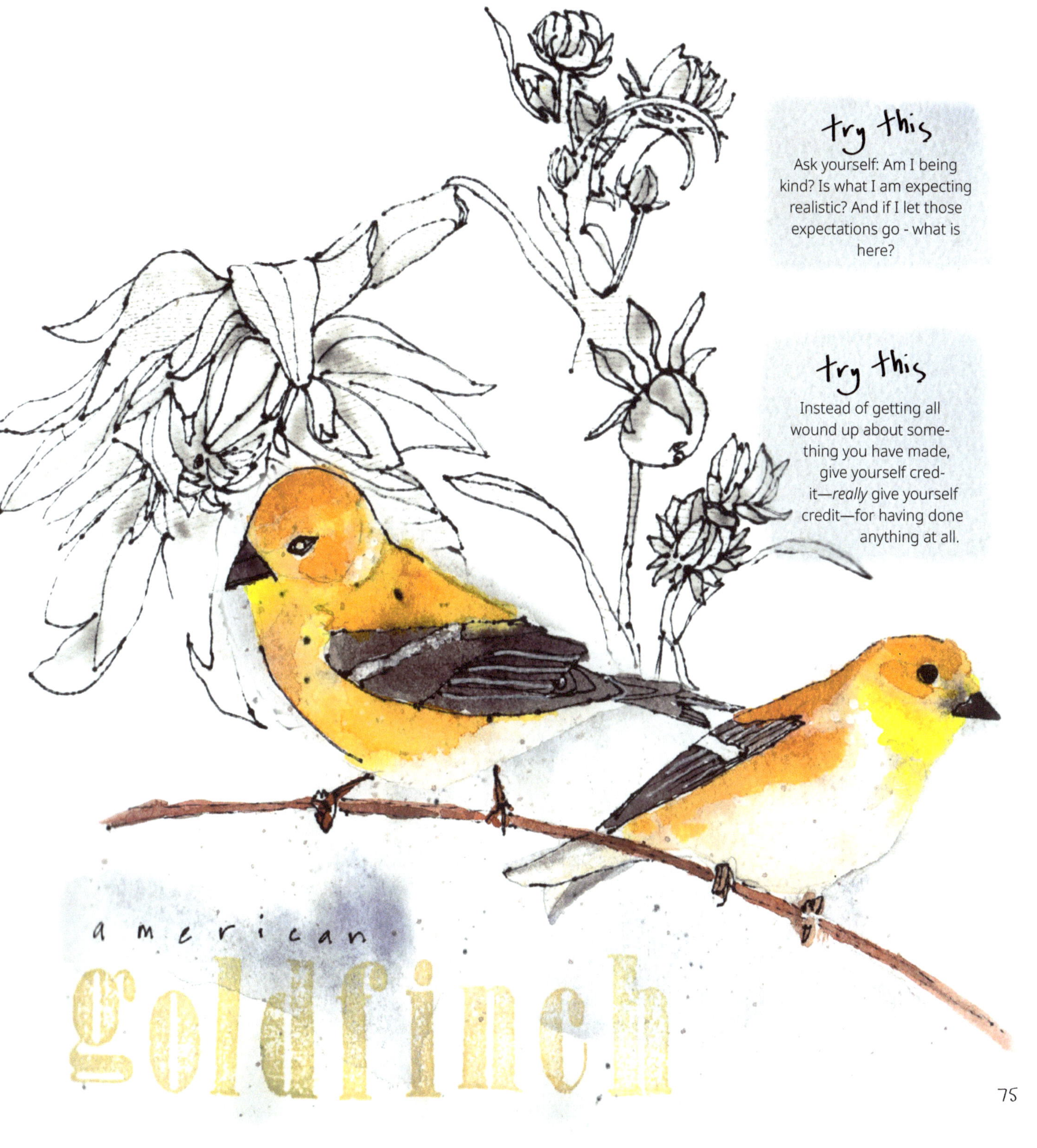

try this

Ask yourself: Am I being kind? Is what I am expecting realistic? And if I let those expectations go - what is here?

try this

Instead of getting all wound up about something you have made, give yourself credit—*really* give yourself credit—for having done anything at all.

a m e r i c a n

goldfinch

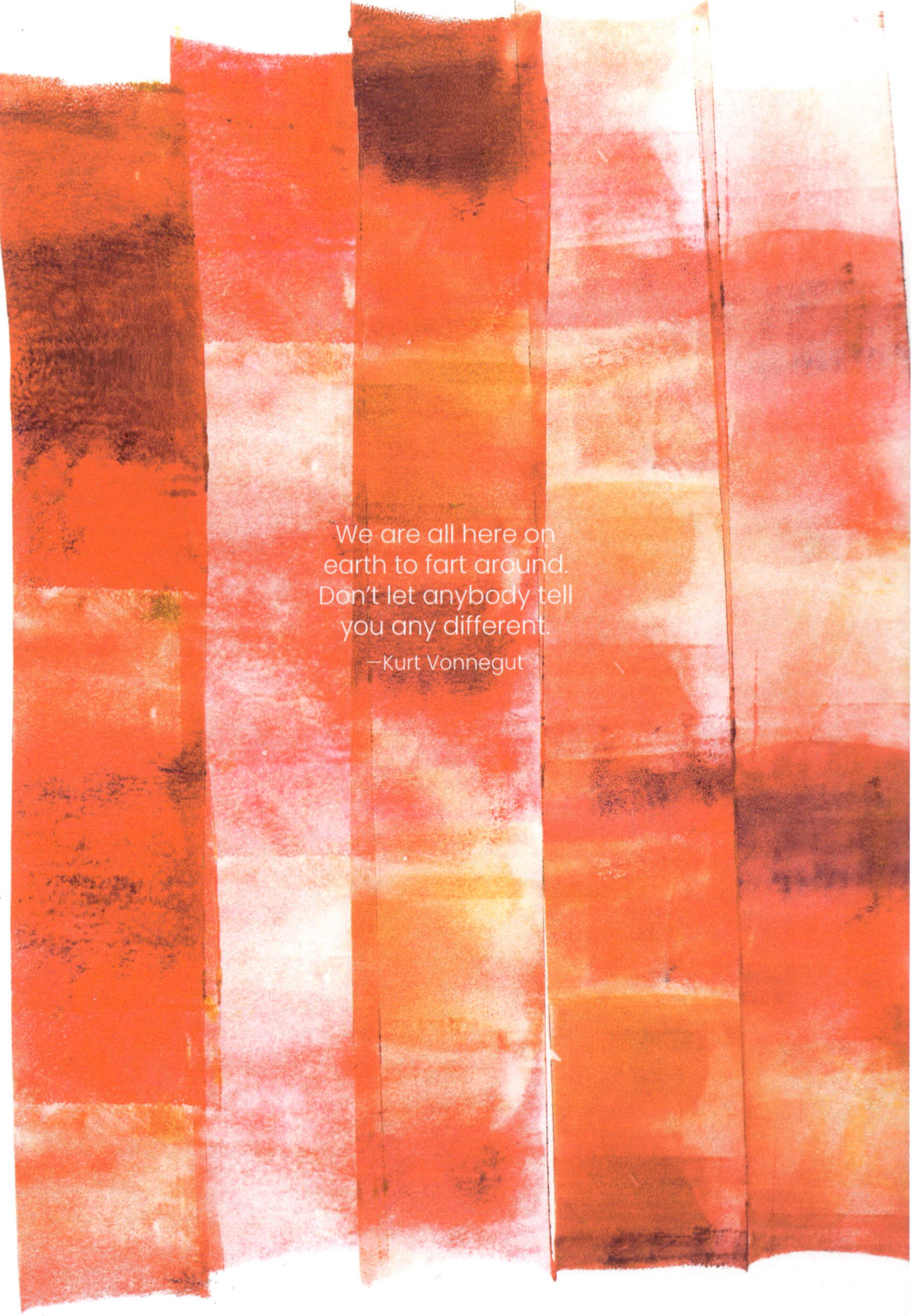
We are all here on
earth to fart around.
Don't let anybody tell
you any different.
—Kurt Vonnegut

Play

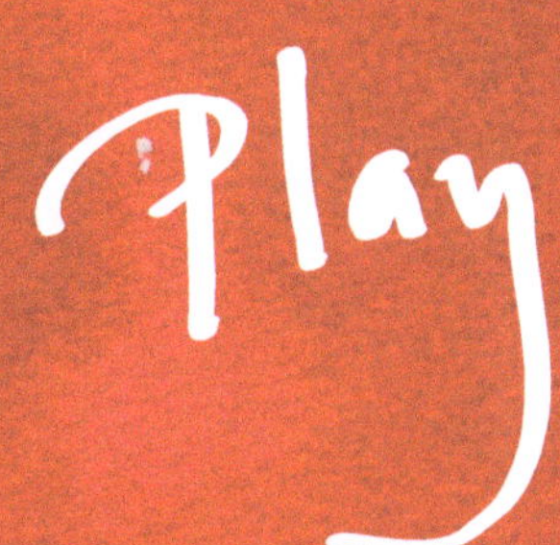

You get to play

Atelic or telic?

Wait to play?

Too important to play?

Play matters

A hobby?

You get to play

When my son, Walker, was young, he said, "Adults can take the fun out of anything." He was talking about playing soccer and how the fun disappeared when he was on a team playing in a tournament rather than just playing soccer with friends. Similarly, I wonder if adults have taken the fun out of art. Of course, art can be serious, but it doesn't have to be.

At some point, I stumbled my way into an art playland. It seems like it should be an easy place to find because there are so many enjoyable possibilities out there, but it took both curiosity and letting go of old ideas to get there. Play is fun and can be wildly generative, but to get myself to play, I first have to leave some things behind.

First, I must leave behind a sense of purpose or any expectation of the outcome. When kids play, it is open-ended. They don't have a result in mind. They don't have a purpose to their play—they are just doing and enjoying the doing. Kids naturally do this. Adults tend to be more focused on the purpose or end product of any activity. As a result, a measure of freedom, exploration, and enjoyment is lost.

atelic or telic?

Exploring the difference between doing things just for the pleasure of doing them versus doing something with an outcome in mind reminds me of a discussion about the difference between atelic and telic activities. In his book *Midlife: A Philosophical Guide*, philosopher Kieran Setiya explains that telic activities are ones that can be finished and have an end. In contrast, atelic activities are ones you never complete. "Driving home is telic: it is done when you get home. So are projects like getting married or writing a book. These are things you can complete. Other activities are 'atelic': they do not aim at a point of termination or exhaustion, a final state in which they have been achieved."

Kids' play is atelic; play is atelic. But the world seems more oriented toward rewarding telic activities. At least, it is easy for me to get sucked into a telic mindset, where I value only the finishing of projects, the final completion of tasks. Somehow, it can seem that finishing is the thing that matters, that the rest is somehow just fluff, only important in the service of finishing. This, of course, backfires because the moment of satisfaction derived from completing anything quickly passes, but still, it can feel like I am only valuing the completion of an activity.

Setiya suggests a remedy: "If my problem is an excessive investment in telic activities, the solution is to love their atelic counterparts, to find meaning in the process, not the project."

Making art can either be telic or atelic. If you identify with the finished product, it becomes more telic; if you focus on the continual making instead, then it becomes atelic. Viewing art making as an atelic activity rather than a telic one means there is no end point; it becomes more like play. This may sound like common sense, but it changes my approach to making art. It is the difference between thinking *Oh, I need to finish that painting versus I am just going to sit down and do.* One is goal-oriented, the other more open-ended. Taking an atelic approach invites play.

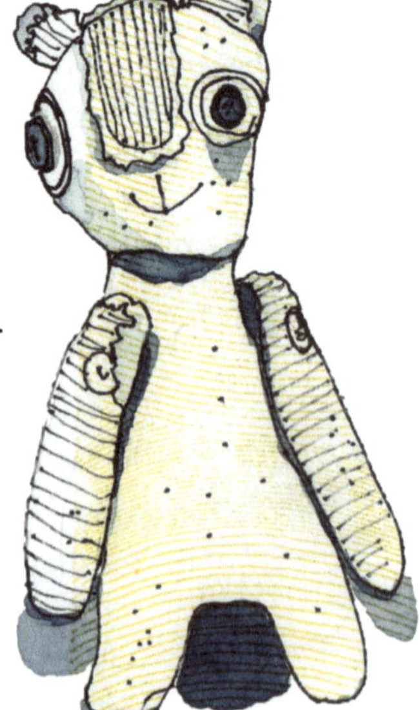

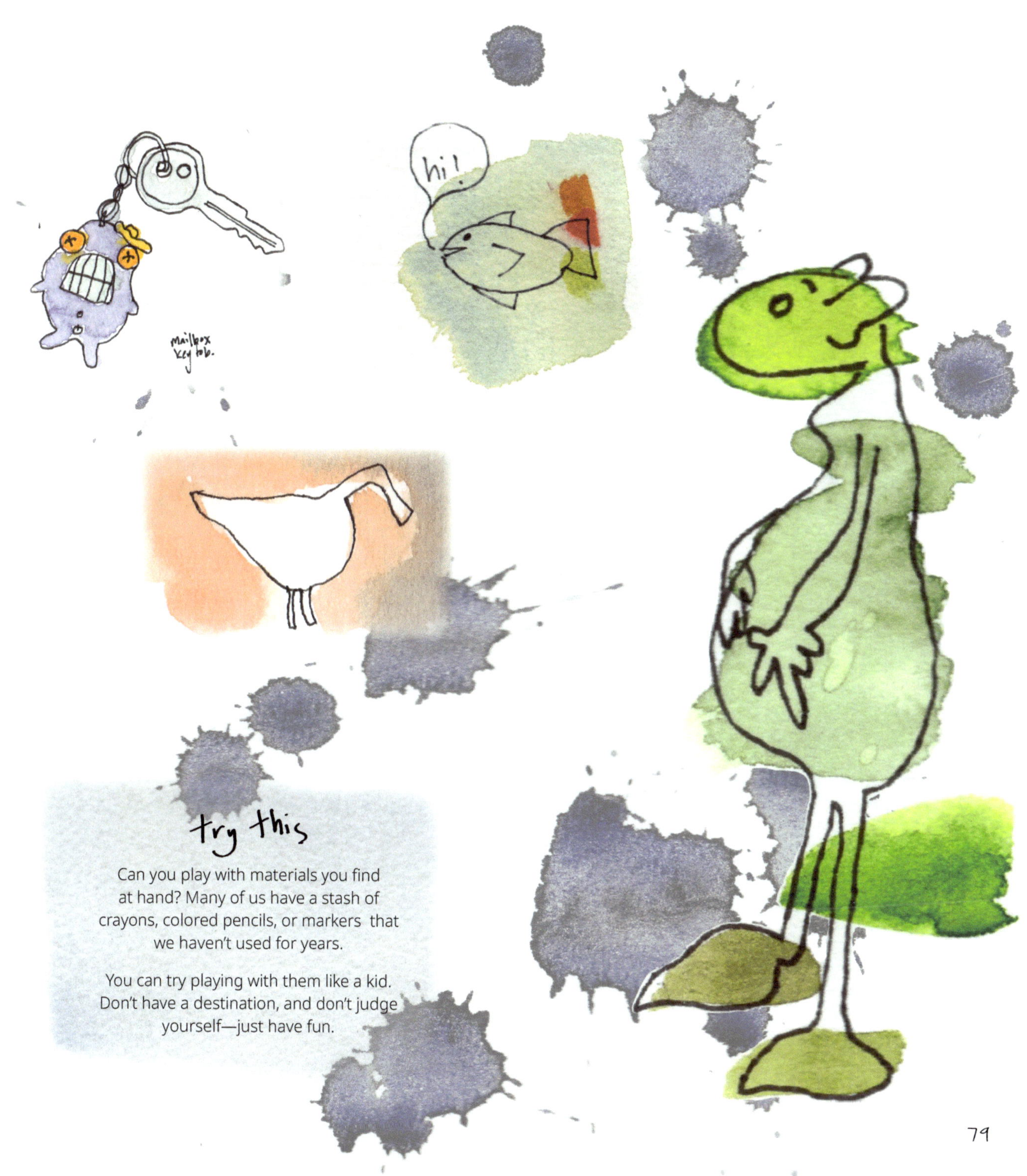

try this

Can you play with materials you find
at hand? Many of us have a stash of
crayons, colored pencils, or markers that
we haven't used for years.

You can try playing with them like a kid.
Don't have a destination, and don't judge
yourself—just have fun.

Wait to play?

There is play land, and then there is task land. We all spend a lot of time in task land. And while I know some people have no trouble playing, for some of us, it can be a struggle because our to-dos are forever looming.

Not getting to tasks makes me anxious; running around and getting things done relieves some of that anxiety and makes me feel useful, even if it means not getting to play. Who has time to goof off and do something just for the fun of it?

I often find that planning ahead and completing tasks promises a sort of control over my life, leading me to lean forward into the future, deferring my happiness to a later date. Unfortunately, this can lead me to think my real life is in the future and cause me to overlook the current moment. As Oliver Burkeman points out, this is all too common: "To treat all these moments solely as stepping-stones to some future moment is to demonstrate a level of obliviousness to our real situation that would be jaw-dropping if it weren't for the fact that we all do it, all the time."

Of course, my actual situation is that I am mortal and have limited time on earth. So, while getting tasks completed brings me a sense of usefulness and lessens my anxiety, that list will never be completed. If I wait until everything is checked off to play, play will never happen. Learning to tolerate the anxiety of not getting everything done is part of what Oliver Burkeman suggests we need to do in order to spend time doing other activities that pull at our hearts.

Sam Harris bluntly reminds me that this is actually my life right now—it doesn't happen at a better future date. "It has often been said that how you spend your days is how you spend your life—and like many cliches—this is true. See if you can absorb this truth. Take a moment to think about how you have spent this day so far—and what you have planned next—and recognize that this isn't a dress rehearsal for some future life; this is the show."

Time scarcity is a reality; I can't ignore that. I remember long stretches of my life when I couldn't even catch my breath.

But now I also know that I have to abandon the idea that while I have too much to do now, later I can play because that time may never come.

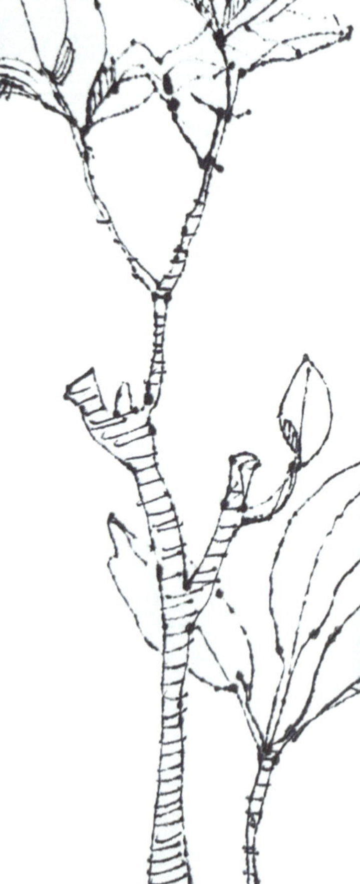

Too important to play?

Another idea I have to leave behind is that I am too important to the universe to play.

I was chatting with an old college friend at a wedding the other day. We are both retired, but she is on the board of a local museum and is developing a nonprofit. I tried to describe to her what I am interested in, and it just felt so insignificant. It brought back that same old question: What the heck am I doing just doodling away in my journal? Am I spending my time, my short time, on this earth well? How is this useful to me or anyone?

The author Oliver Burkeman once again provided insight, in a way that is a little surprising, by suggesting that what I do actually matters very little. In his book *Four Thousand Weeks*, he gently introduced the idea of cosmic insignificance therapy by suggesting that "what you do with your life doesn't matter all that much—and when it comes to how you're using your finite time, the universe absolutely could not care less." This is pretty contrary to any message I have ever received, but once I considered it, I realized it was also undeniably true. Burkeman explains: "You almost certainly won't put a dent in the universe. Indeed, depending on the stringency of the criteria, even Steve Jobs, who coined that phrase, failed to leave such a dent." Some people may find this realization disturbing, but for me, it brings certain relief.

Of course, I know what I do matters: I try to make the world better and believe that even small kindnesses alter the universe, but there is a realistic humility here that allows me to just be me and not measure my worth or how I spend my time against some sort of unrealistic or exaggerated metric of usefulness.

There is such freedom here. If I lose the notion that what I do must be significant, it frees me up to pursue what interests me. And who knows, could it be that what feels like play has its own kind of significance?

Another gift of cosmic insignificance theory is that it brings me back to earth, to the here and now. As Burkeman explains: "Truly doing justice to the astonishing gift of a few thousand weeks isn't a matter of resolving to 'do something remarkable' with them. In fact, it entails precisely the opposite; refusing to hold them to an abstract and overdemanding standard of remarkableness, against which they can only ever be found wanting, and taking them instead on their own terms, dropping back down from the godlike fantasies of cosmic significance into the experience of life as it concretely, finitely—and often enough, marvelously—really is."

Making a simple sketch helps me see what is here now. Playing with stamps or colors helps me enjoy the tactile nature of the moment. Asking what I make to be important layers on a stifling heaviness. It is hard to play when I am trying to be important.

Requiring what I do to always be useful or remarkable leaves something essential out; there is a richness to life that exists entirely outside these ideas. Letting go of an imagined and illusory notion of importance helps me see what is actually here.

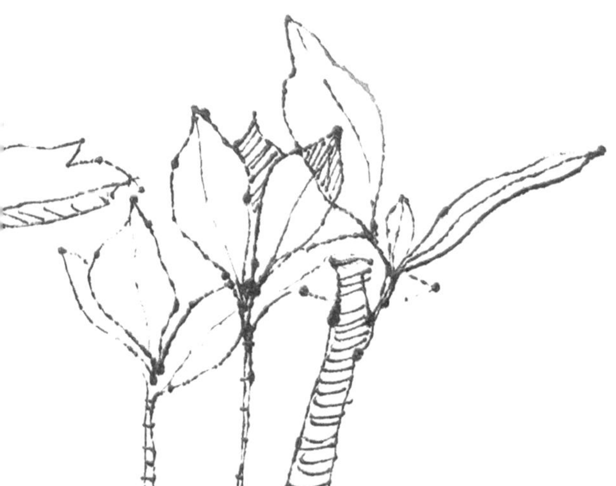

Play matters

Seeing art-making as play changes the game. Suddenly the considerations (Is it good? Is it useful?) fall away and we are left with just the movement of the making itself. Whimsy can find us, curiosity can find us, and possibilities open up.

And while play has value in and of itself, the benefits from play are wide-reaching: you play soccer and you get exercise, you play a board game and you build community, you do a crossword and you both relax and strengthen your brain. Play or humor can change a situation immediately; a lighter spirit often invites a more generous perspective.

Play is often the doorway to a more generative state. Lynda Barry spoke in the *New York Times* about the fruitful qualities of kids' play: "Adults think that kids playing is some nothing thing," she says. "But play is a different state of mind, and it can help us do so many things if we just allow ourselves to get back to it."

In another *New York Times article*, children's book author and illustrator Rowboat Watkins shares the advice he gives himself: "Whenever I feel hopelessly lost or stuck, sometimes the only thing to do is start playing with trash. Figuratively. And literally. Until I begin to see a way outside my own head. Sounds nuts, but it works. The only hard part is remembering to play in the first place. And being open to going somewhere different than where you thought you were headed. It's easier said than done, but always worth saying 'yes' to."

Sometimes it's hard to take this advice to just sit down and tinker with the materials at hand, but it is often the doorway to something new, to a place I wouldn't have found if I hadn't just messed around.

Play is lightness, whimsy, and fun, but there is another aspect of play that is deeper and more personal. In her book *Enchantment*, author Katherine May points out that playing means claiming time for ourselves. She defines deep play as a "flow toward the acts we love." She continues, "The skills of deep play took far longer to learn than anything I'd studied before. They meant asserting the awkward right to time, space, and solitude; making a shameful claim on my own creativity. They meant learning to trust my long-forgotten gut instinct and feel a yearning for my own work. They meant putting aside time to do things that seemed pointless to the outside world."

May sees play as doing what you are called to do without judging it or subjecting it to an outside view. It's allowing yourself to do what calls to you—this is what kids do so easily! Whether this results in something silly or serious is beside the point. It is about following your interests without worrying about any specific destination.

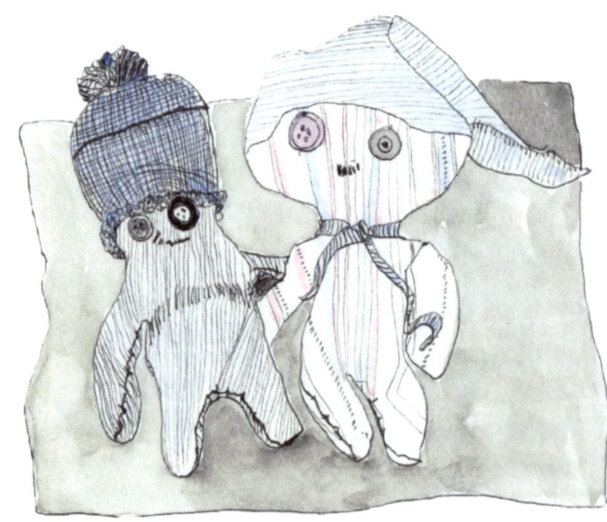

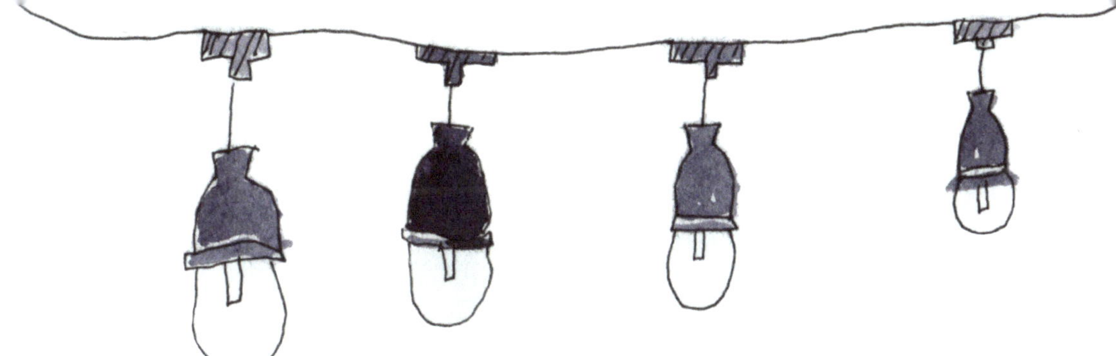

a hobby?

Before I started drawing and painting regularly, the idea of art-making seemed like a serious endeavor. Then, at some point, I remember explaining to my friend Kathy that drawing and painting were new hobbies, and suddenly—it all felt a whole lot lighter.

Is a hobby where adults get to play? I am not sure, but I know that, for me, approaching art-making in the spirit of fun rather than trying to make serious or important work is not only more enjoyable but also brings the focus back to process. It becomes less of a "telic" activity and more of an "atelic" activity—it turns what could be work into play.

Saying "I have a hobby" certainly sounds different than saying "I am an artist." I think that is interesting if nothing else.

In *Four Thousand Weeks*, Oliver Burkeman notes that hobbies are perceived as a little silly, if not downright worthless: "Yet it's surely no coincidence that hobbies have acquired this embarrassing reputation in an era so committed to utilizing time instrumentally. In an age of instrumentalization, the hobbyist is a subversive: he insists that some things are worth doing for themselves alone, despite offering no payoff in terms of productivity or profit."

I love this. I am being subversive when I scribble away! I am subversive when I call it a hobby! Heck yeah—let's have a revolution of fun.

What happens when you describe something you like to do as a hobby? Does it bring a lightness?

Take Rowboat Watkin's advice and just sit down and allow yourself to play with whatever you have at hand. What happens?

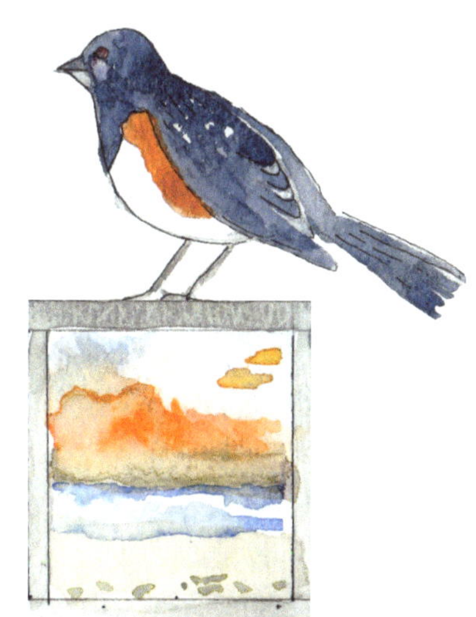

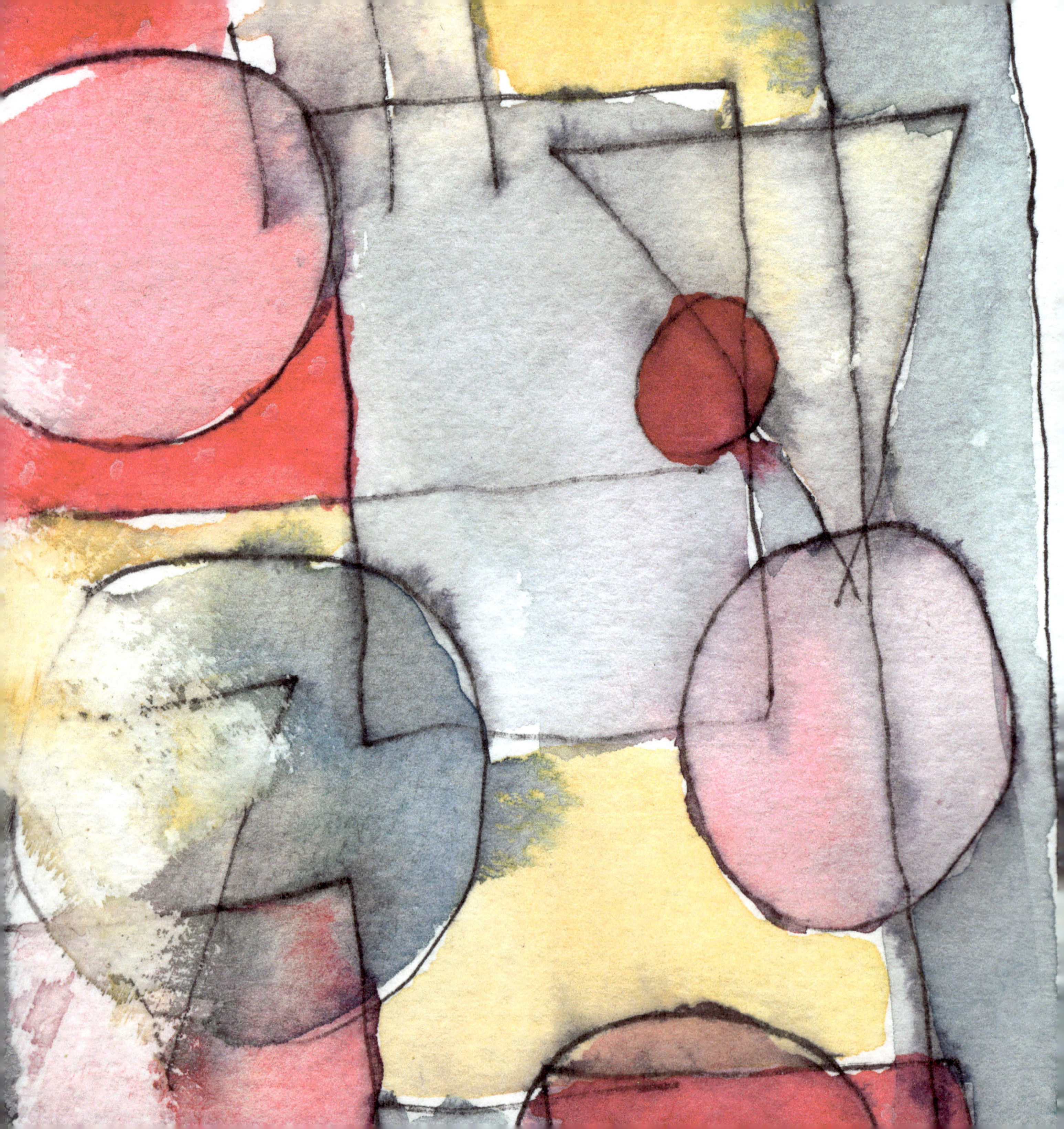

Possibilities

Try a series

Keep a journal or a sketchbook

Try gel prints

Experiment with collage

Enjoy stamps + stencils

Illustrate words

Write comics + stories

Ways to learn more

Try a series

There are so many ways to have fun with art! By poking around a little, I found some things that are easy to try. From journals to gel prints to collages and beyond, the possibilities are endless.

I took one design course in my twenties at a community college. The only thing I remember is that the professor suggested that repeating something can make it more interesting. I am not sure that always works, but sometimes, doing more than one of something is gratifying in a way that a single image isn't. Plus, you can evolve as you go, which is always satisfying.

Drawing boxes to do little drawings in can provide structure. You can build complexity and tell a story in a simple way.

I did this series of pears early in Jude Siegel's class, and it felt like a real breakthrough. It inspired me to keep going. Pears are great shapes to work with because they are both lovely and simple.

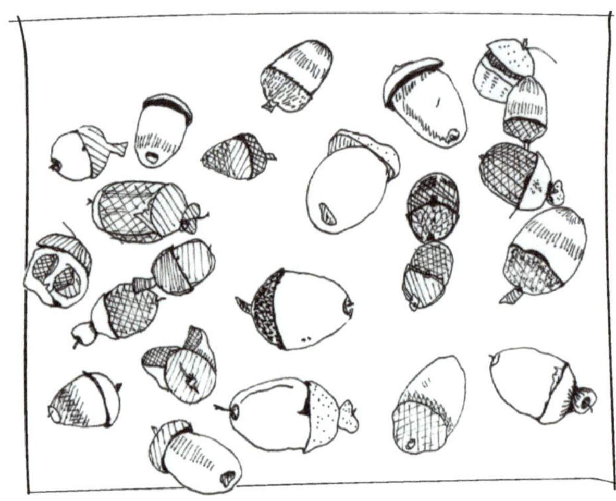

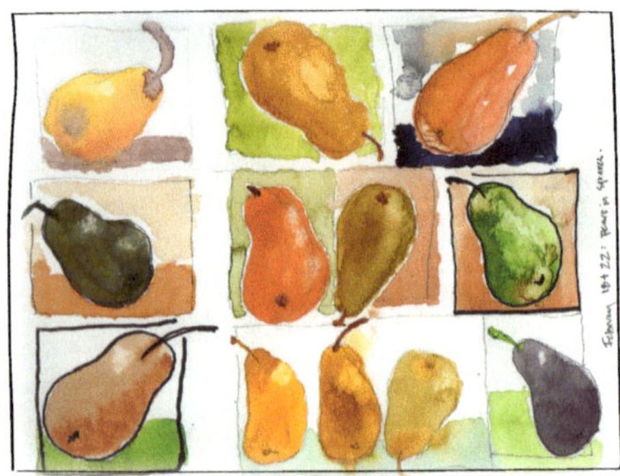

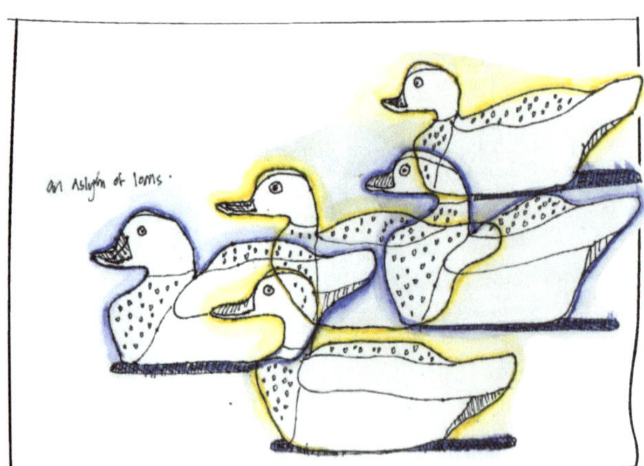

try this

Draw some simple pear shapes and try shading them. Add colors to the pears and the background.

try this

Find a group of something: acorns, buttons, seeds, anything, and draw them.

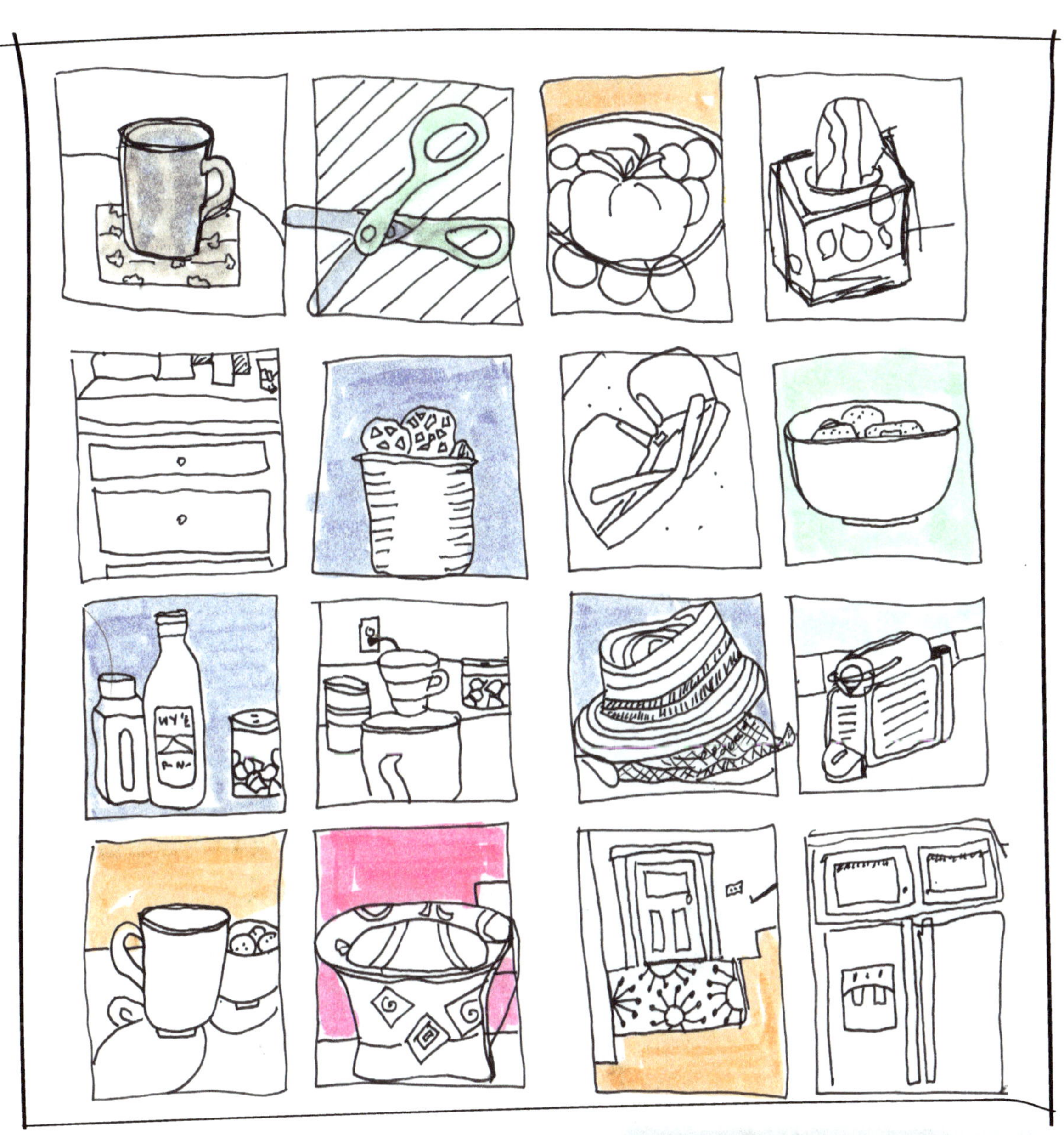

try this
Divide your page into boxes and draw a little
something in each one.

keep a journal or sketchbook

A journal or sketchbook is in itself a series. A drawing or a note gains complexity and richness when placed in the context of days. There is something satisfying about surrounding your drawings and musing with more of the same; they inform each other, and no one thing has to stand naked on its own.

I consider my journal less of a thing and more of a place for an ongoing conversation. Lynda Barry suggests "thinking of one's compbook as ... a <u>place</u> not a <u>thing</u>." What does it mean to think of my journal, not as a thing? For me, it means there is a sort of continual back and forth rather than a static state of completion. In my journals, I ask questions, paste things in, use stamps and gel prints, sketch images, paint paint blobs, copy text from books I am reading or lectures I am listening to, and note things I have noticed. Anything goes. I like to think there is a conversation in the pages between me, ideas, images, and other mysterious things. It is a process.

What ends up on the pages is what I have noticed and recorded at a single moment. It is simply impossible for me to work in my journal in the past or in the future. Adding to a journal page requires being present to the moment at hand.

A journal or sketchbook is also a playground. My sketchbook invites me to try stuff out, make mistakes, and go a little wild. And then to move on. What I learned from Jude Siegel initially (that my journal is only for me) is essential. As Cat Bennett explains in *The Confident Creative*, "Our sketchbooks can be messy and really ought to be. If we take too much care it's not a sketchbook but a scrapbook, something precious, something else. If we take too much care, something's getting in our way—perhaps a sense that it needs to be this way or that, or that someone's looking over our shoulders."

When I complete a journal, I get a palatable sense of satisfaction. After writing the dates on the spine, I place it next to my other journals on a shelf. I am never in a hurry to complete one, but when they are done, they have a completeness about them that is just satisfying, wacky pages and all. And yet, should I pick one up and thumb through the pages, there I am again, listening to that ongoing conversation. I don't know what it says about me, but I seem to be a much wiser person in my journal than I feel I am in real life.

Often, people use their journals as a place to collect words, images, ideas, lists, everything, and anything else. In *Learning by Heart*, Jan Steward suggests keeping "a sense diary": "A sense diary is a tool that enables us to become aware of and retain details often lost or imperfectly remembered ... The sense diary is your expandable vault in which to store words, ideas, and images." In this way, your journal can be a source of inspiration and a source for further work. What makes it fun is the freedom to do whatever you want.

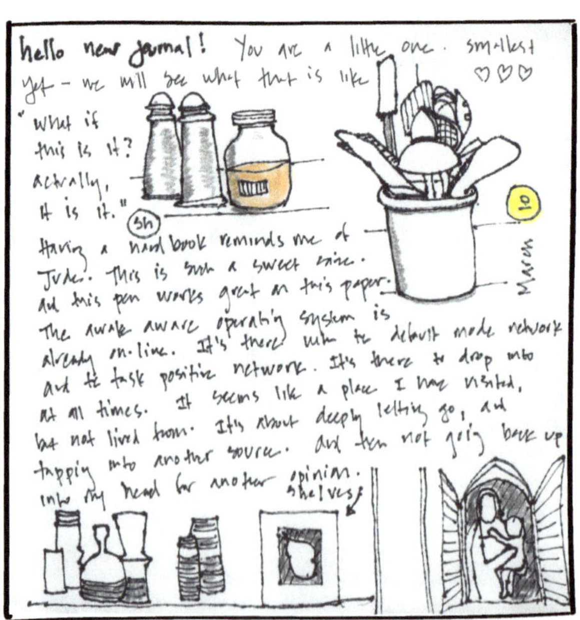

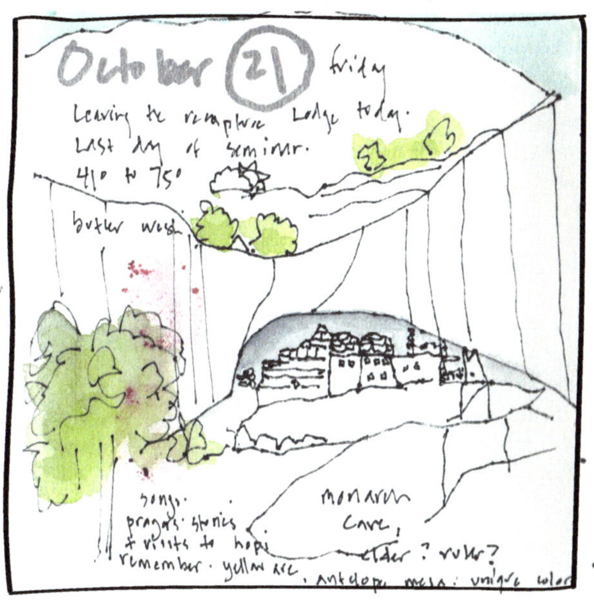

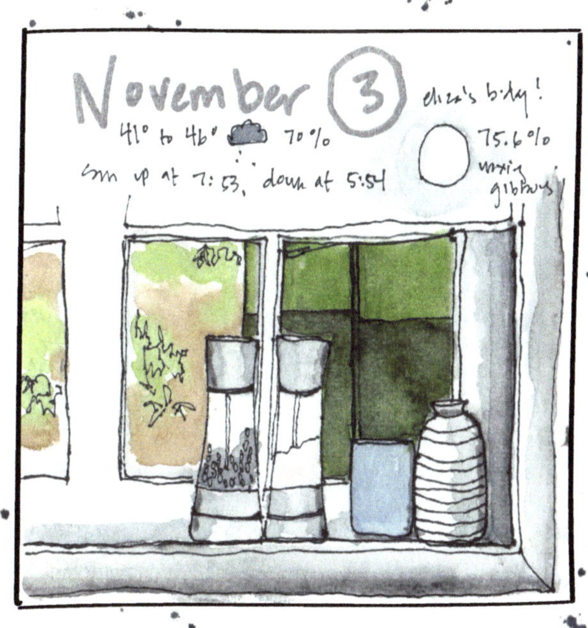

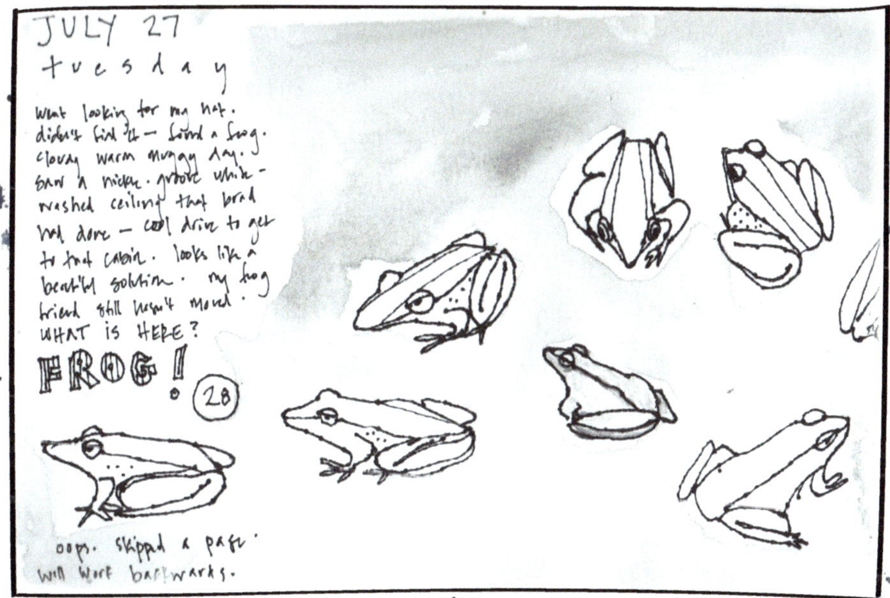

try this

If starting a journal seems intimidating, try saving and collecting anything you like: doodles, drawings, grocery lists. Put them in a folder to view at the end of the week. Then, take a look: What do you have there? Can you staple them together? Paste them on a page? This can be a way to sneak up on keeping a journal.

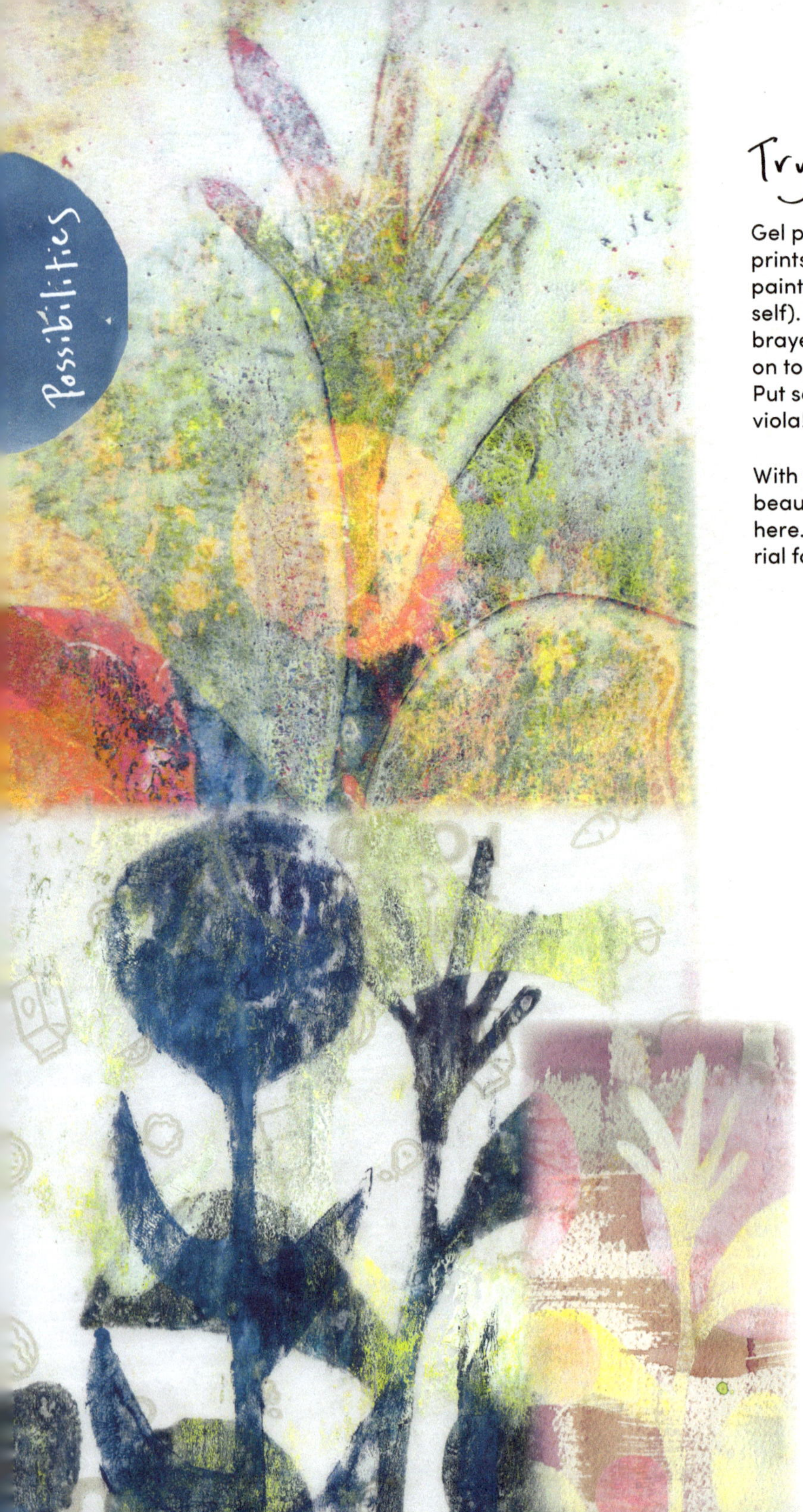

Try gel prints

Gel prints are downright addictive. To create gel prints, you need a gelatin block, a brayer, acrylic paints, and some stencils (which you can make yourself). Basically, you put the paint on the block, use the brayer to spread the paint, put your stencils down on top of the paint, and then put your paper on top. Put some pressure on the paper, then pull it off—and viola! You have made a print.

With this simple technique, you can make absolutely beautiful monoprints. There are so many things to try here. You will surely end up with lots of collage material for future projects. Really, this is pure fun.

try this

Get a small gelatin block, a small brayer, some paper, and just a couple of acrylic paints you can mix.

Cut some small, simple shapes out of some sturdy paper.

Place a dab of paint on the gelatin block. Spread the paint into a thin layer with the brayer. Put down the shapes you made on top of the now-painted gelatin block. Press the paper on top, then peel off. What happened?

Move the shapes and repeat? Try a different color? Experiment! If you start simply and small, you can always rev it up later.

Experiment with collage

There are two ways I end up collaging. The first is when I use collage to cover up a mistake. This is actually super fun and gets me to see my mistakes as invitations. The second is when I want to add complexity and richness to my page with different materials. If you get in the habit of randomly pasting in images and textures in pages you plan to work on later, when you get there, you will have something unexpected to work with. It is inspiring to encounter an already started page. You can also go back later to work on pages, adding layers and textures.

Collage brings richness and complexity to a page. It also can also reflect a truth about our lives. Jason Farago wrote an article on collage art for the *New York Times* entitled "An Art Revolution Made with Scissors and Glue": "Cut out your place in a world of fragments ... Too much media, too many images, too fast, too fragmentary. As regards to the creation of art, the circumstances can feel hopeless sometimes. But you can still find your way forward in a world broken to pieces. Glue them together in a new way and let the seams show."

Carrying a glue stick and little-kid scissors has become part of my kit. I never know when I am going to find something I want to glue into my journal. Life is filled with bits and pieces; it's gratifying to collect and combine them in new ways.

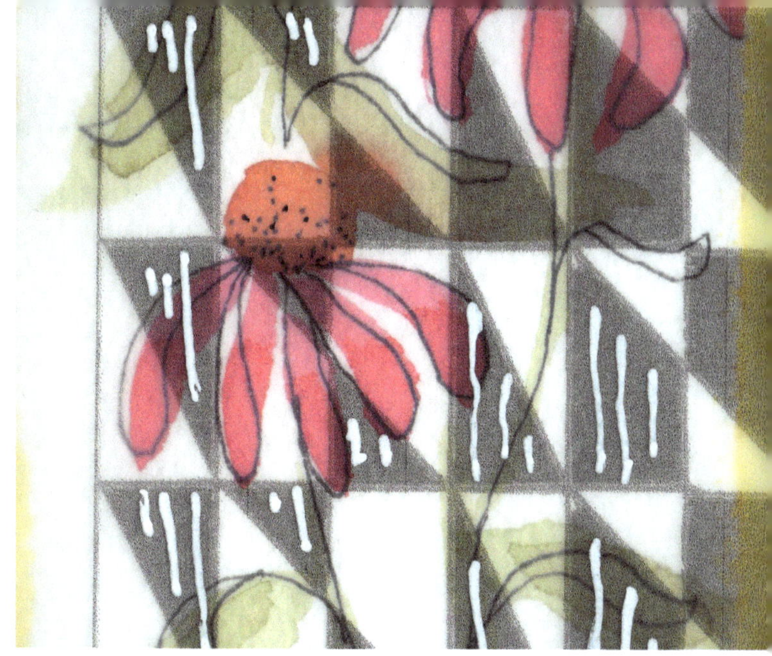

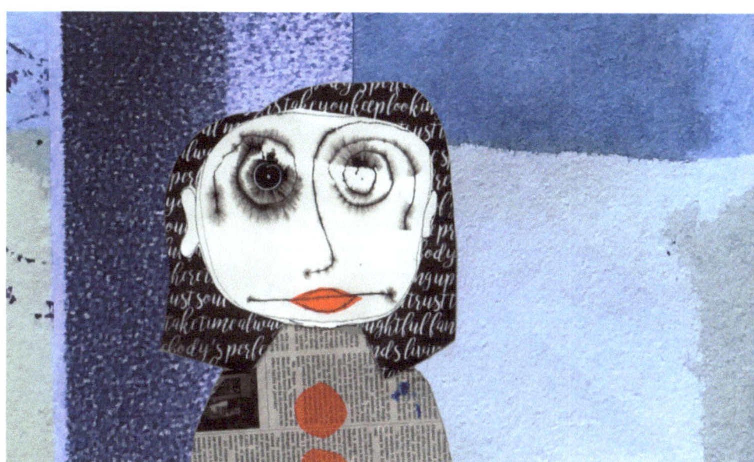

If you can access a copier, you can endlessly resize images, creating rich textures and interesting patterns.

You can turn colored images into black and white. It is a little amazing how helpful a copier can be.

Collect images you like. Newspapers and magazines are good sources. You don't need to use them right away. You can save them for a later moment or paste them onto a blank page to work on later.

Enjoy stamps + stencils

I admit it—I started out by turning my nose up at stamps. They seemed, well, too crafty. My husband teases me when he sees me using sparkly watercolors: "What, are you a teenager?" he laughs. He jokes, but there is a long tradition of art with a capital A turning its back on different forms of making. There is a whole crafty world of possibility out there, and there is no need to limit ourselves.

There are more stencils and stamps than I could ever imagine. Online, you can find numerous mixed media workshops and videos. This is a big universe; it is fun to poke around a little and explore.

joy is found in little things

may
1

Go ahead and get a full-page stamp—
one with an interesting texture. Then,
get a waterproof ink pad and stamp
some pages before you intend to work
on them (either loose sheets or in your
journal). This brings richness and texture
to a page and gives you a head start
when you get to that page.

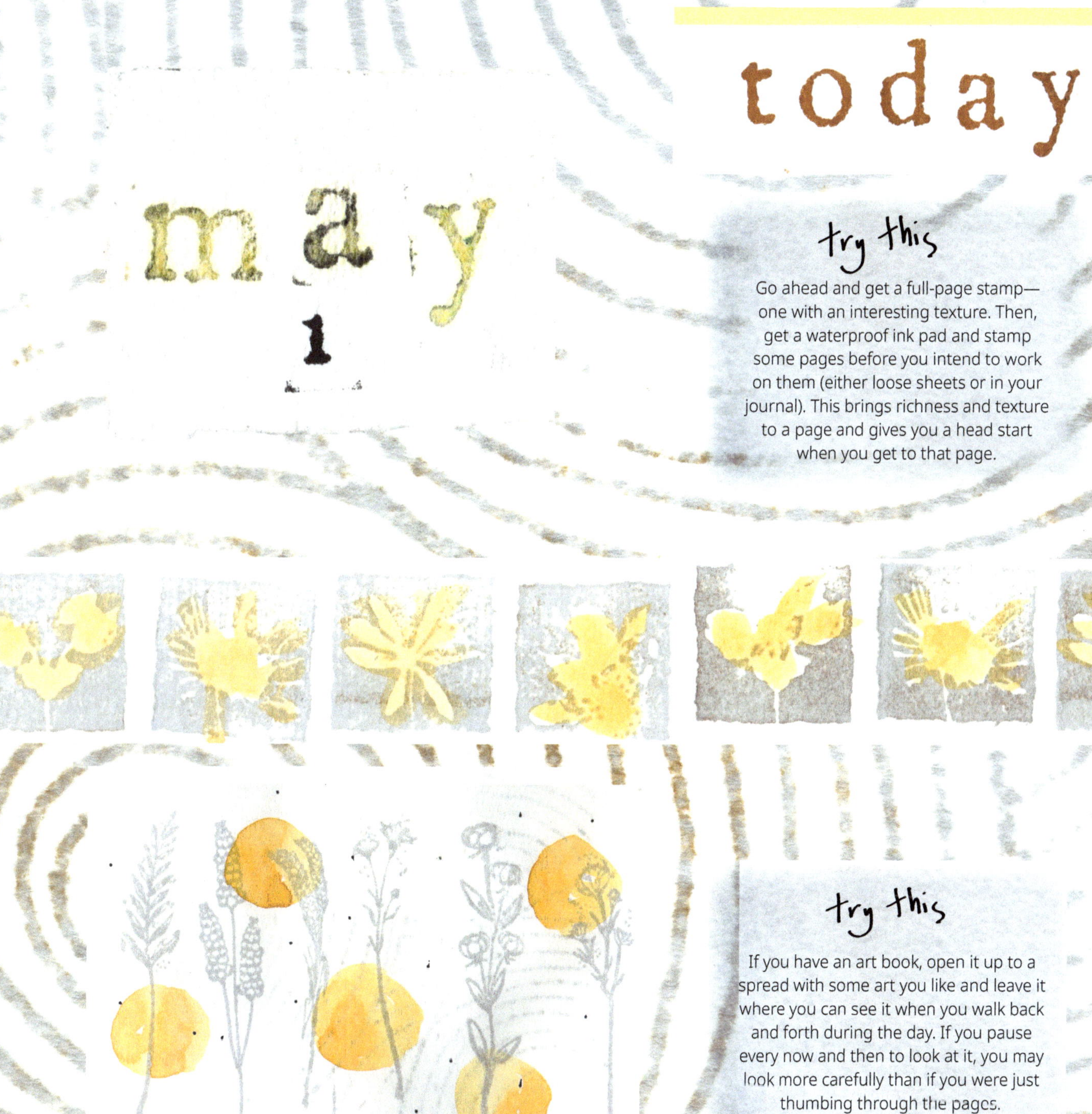

If you have an art book, open it up to a
spread with some art you like and leave it
where you can see it when you walk back
and forth during the day. If you pause
every now and then to look at it, you may
look more carefully than if you were just
thumbing through the pages.

Illustrate words

I often print out quotes and poems. Words can be
such a beautiful counterpart to images.

This I that is mine is tired
Worn out at the knees
From too much
Pulling weeds
Angling light
Fertilizing
Hard business
That of curating
A private paradise
Magnolias to plant
Vines to trellis
Tulips to tame.
Roses to put in glass
As in a fairytale
Orchids' heavy heads
Following your pacing.
What work indeed
To order
This symbolic network
Of petals, sepals, carpels, stamens, pistils
Frenetically self-reproducing
Honey, nectar, seeds, honey, nectar, seeds
In pursuit of that thing
Called harmony with oneself

by Haley Stewart

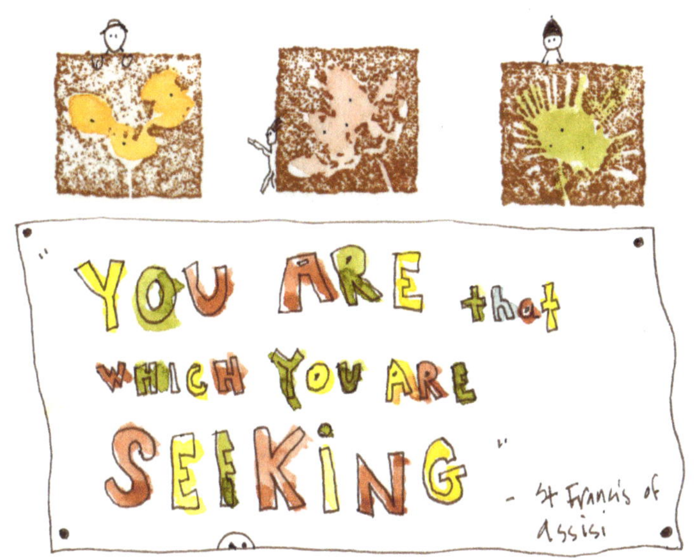

"YOU ARE that WHICH YOU ARE SEEKING"
- St Francis of Assisi

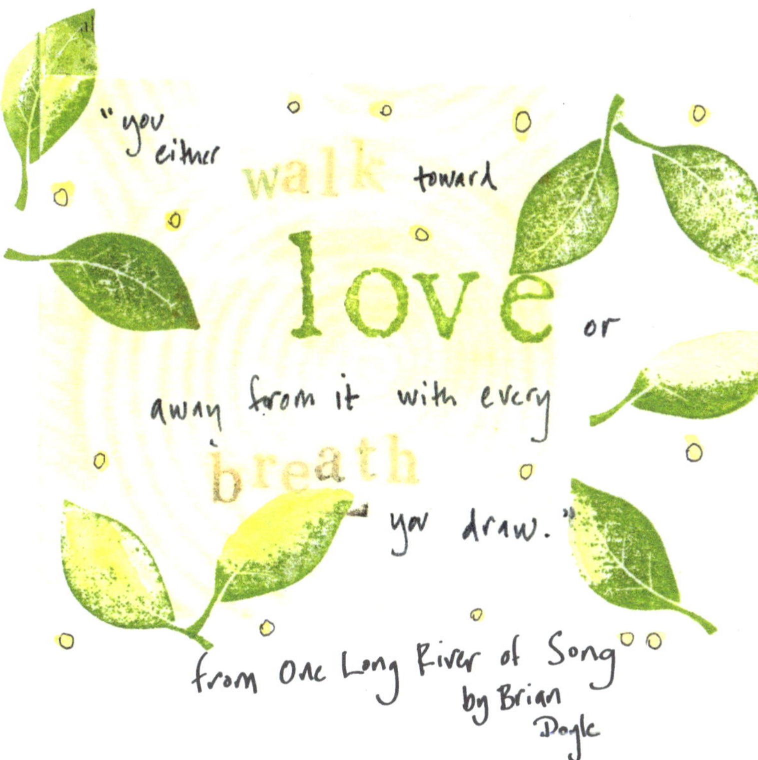

"you either walk toward love or away from it with every breath you draw."

from One Long River of Song by Brian Doyle

try this

If you find a quote, word, or poem you like, you don't have to use it immediately. I have an envelope labeled "words" on my table that has just that—words. When the time comes, I look through it to see what fits the page, project, or moment.

Write comics + stories

I would like to do more storytelling. I have to remind myself that my stories are just for me; otherwise, it becomes too hard. If I can just let myself go, it feels good for my brain and is freeing.

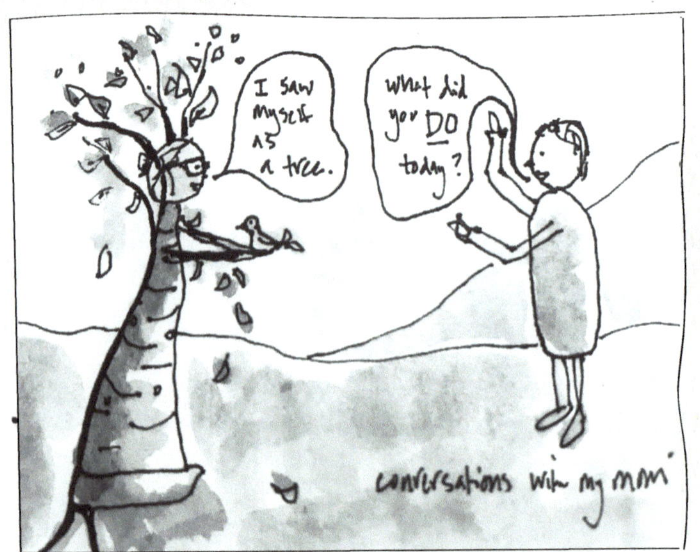

conversations with my mom

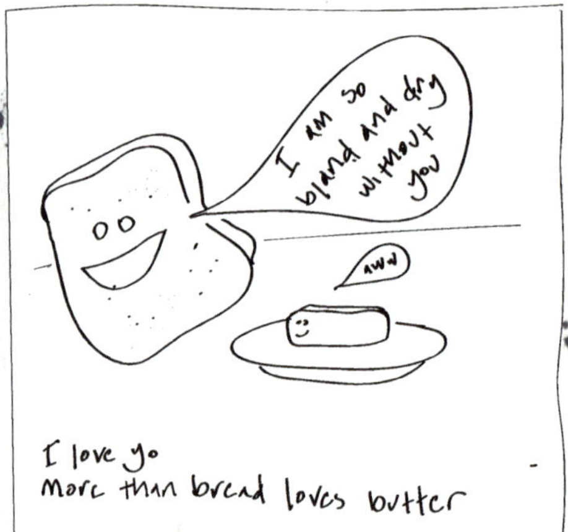

I love yo more than bread loves butter

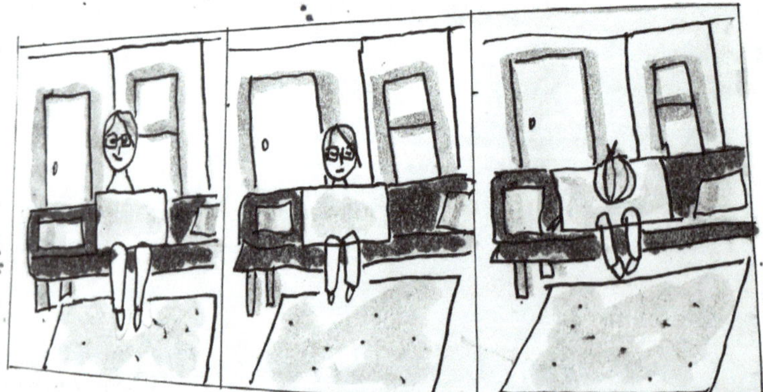

Too much computer time

resource

Lynda Barry's book *Making Comics* and *Cartooning: Philosophy and Practice* by Ivan Brunetti are both helpful and inspiring books for exploring making comics.

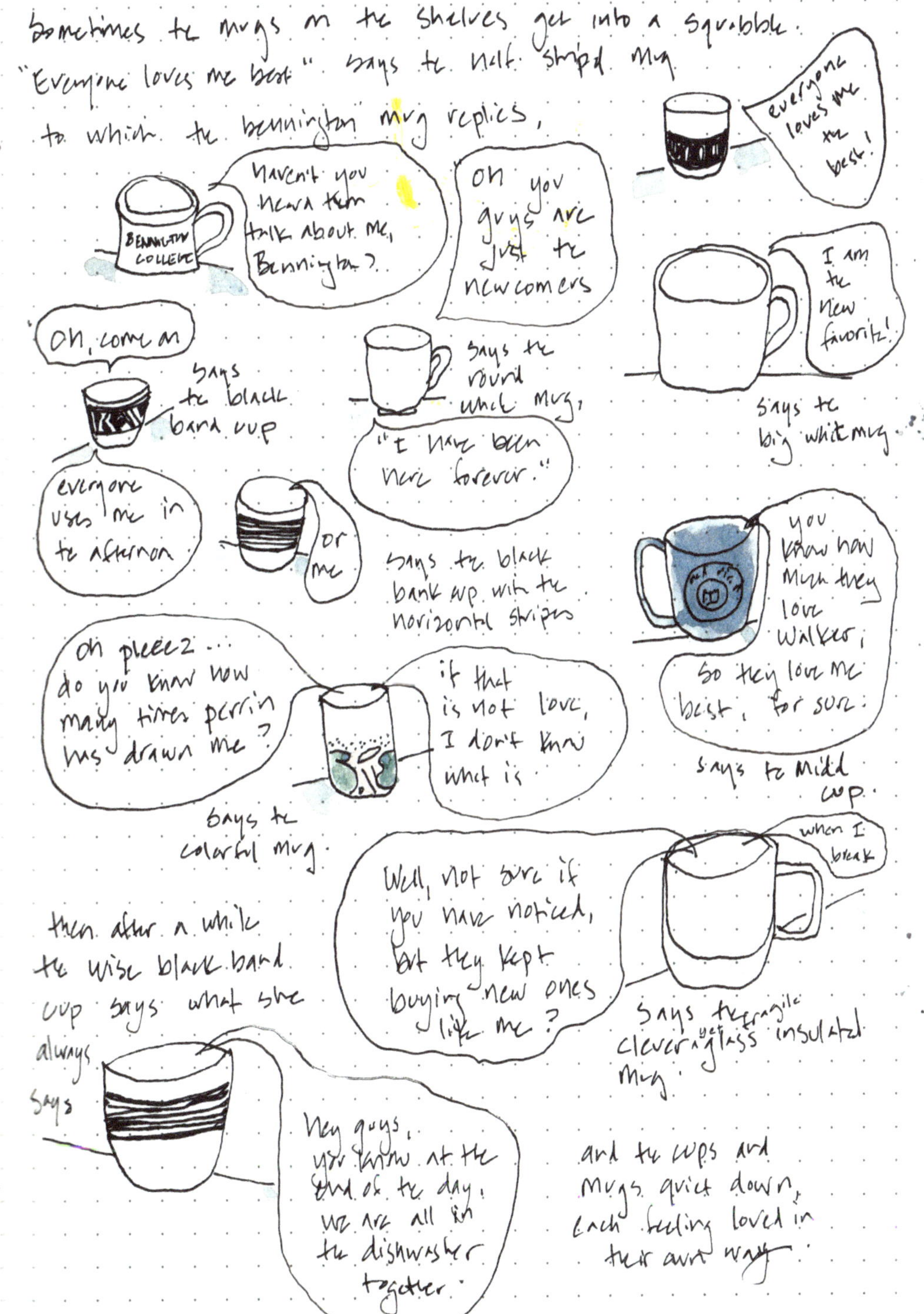

Sometimes the mugs on the shelves get into a squabble.
"Everyone loves me best" says the half-striped mug
to which the bennington mug replies,
haven't you heard them talk about me, Bennington?
oh you guys are just the newcomers
everyone loves me best!
I am the new favorite!
Oh, come on
says the black band cup
says the round white mug, "I have been here forever."
everyone uses me in the afternoon
or me
says the black band cup with the horizontal stripes
says the big white mug
you know how much they love Walker, so they love me best, for sure.
says the Midd cup
Oh pleeez... do you know how many times perrin has drawn me?
if that is not love, I don't know what is
says the colorful mug
when I break
Well, not sure if you have noticed, but they kept buying new ones like me?
says the fragile yet clever glass insulated mug.
then after a while the wise black band cup says what she always says
Hey guys, you know at the end of the day, we are all in the dishwasher together.
and the cups and mugs quiet down, each feeling loved in their own way.

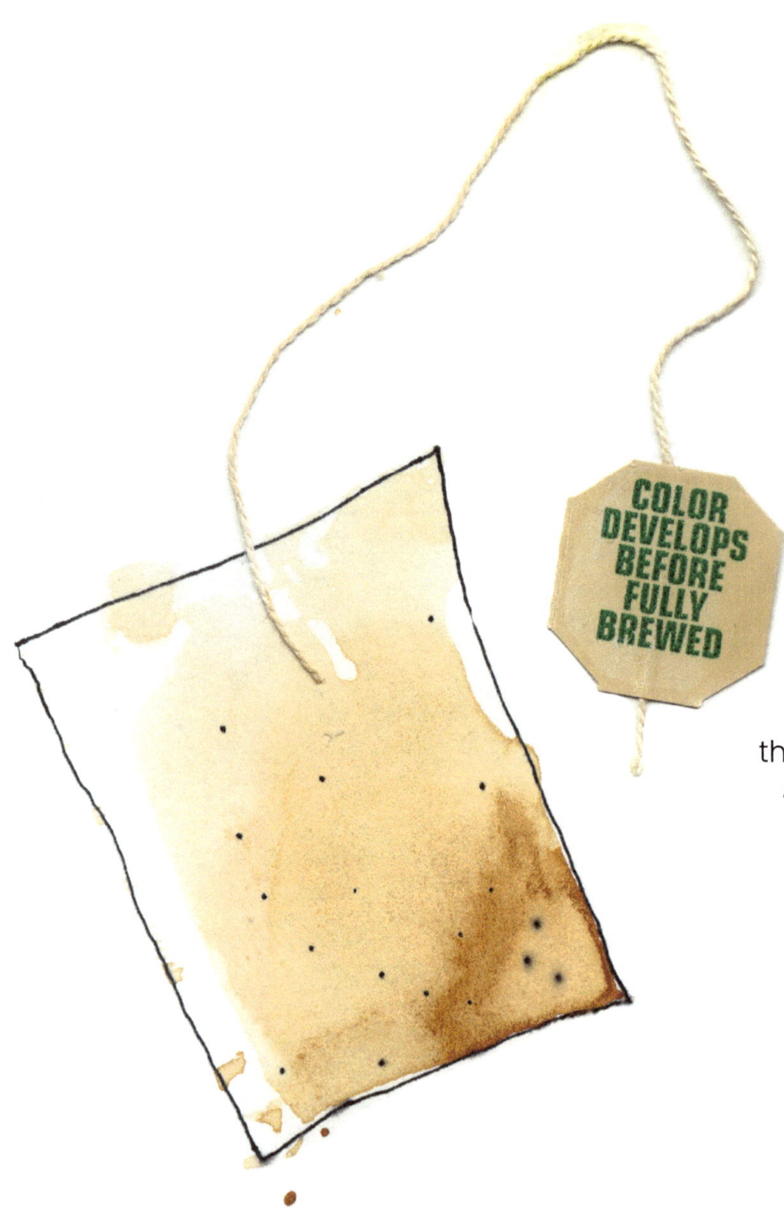

In his preface to his father's book of collected poems, *Ask Me*, Kim Stafford writes about his father's response to a listener's comment:

"At a reading, following one of his deft, quiet offerings, a listener helplessly spoke aloud, 'I could have written that.' And William Stafford, looking kindly at the speaker, replied, 'But you didn't.' A beat of silence. 'But you could write your own.'"

- Kim Stafford

Ways to learn More

Take a class

When I take a class, I always learn something. And it makes me practice! I often learn as much from other students as from the teacher. I have taken classes at a local art center, a community college, and online.

Explore online

Not surprisingly, there are many resources online. If you Google any material, technique, or color, you will find free videos on YouTube and websites with great information.

Visit a museum

I find museums incredibly inspirational in small chunks. However, it is easy to get overwhelmed and stop seeing things. Therefore, I like to look at fewer art pieces, spending a longer time on each one. This can be hard to do because you just know there are so many good things to look at.

Find a book

Hooray, just hooray, for libraries! Get a library card if you don't have one. There is nothing like a library card to make me feel rich. You can check out books on drawing, creativity, colors, mindfulness ... the list goes on! Sometimes, I can even find an art book about a specific artist. Because I am just borrowing them, I look at many books. Often, I am not looking for anything in particular—I never know what will spark my interest. You can find inspiring illustrations in children's books.

Look at social media

I am not a social media user because I find it too distracting, but I know others use Instagram and other social media platforms to find artists, view art, and learn more.

Check out art events

There is always something cool to see.

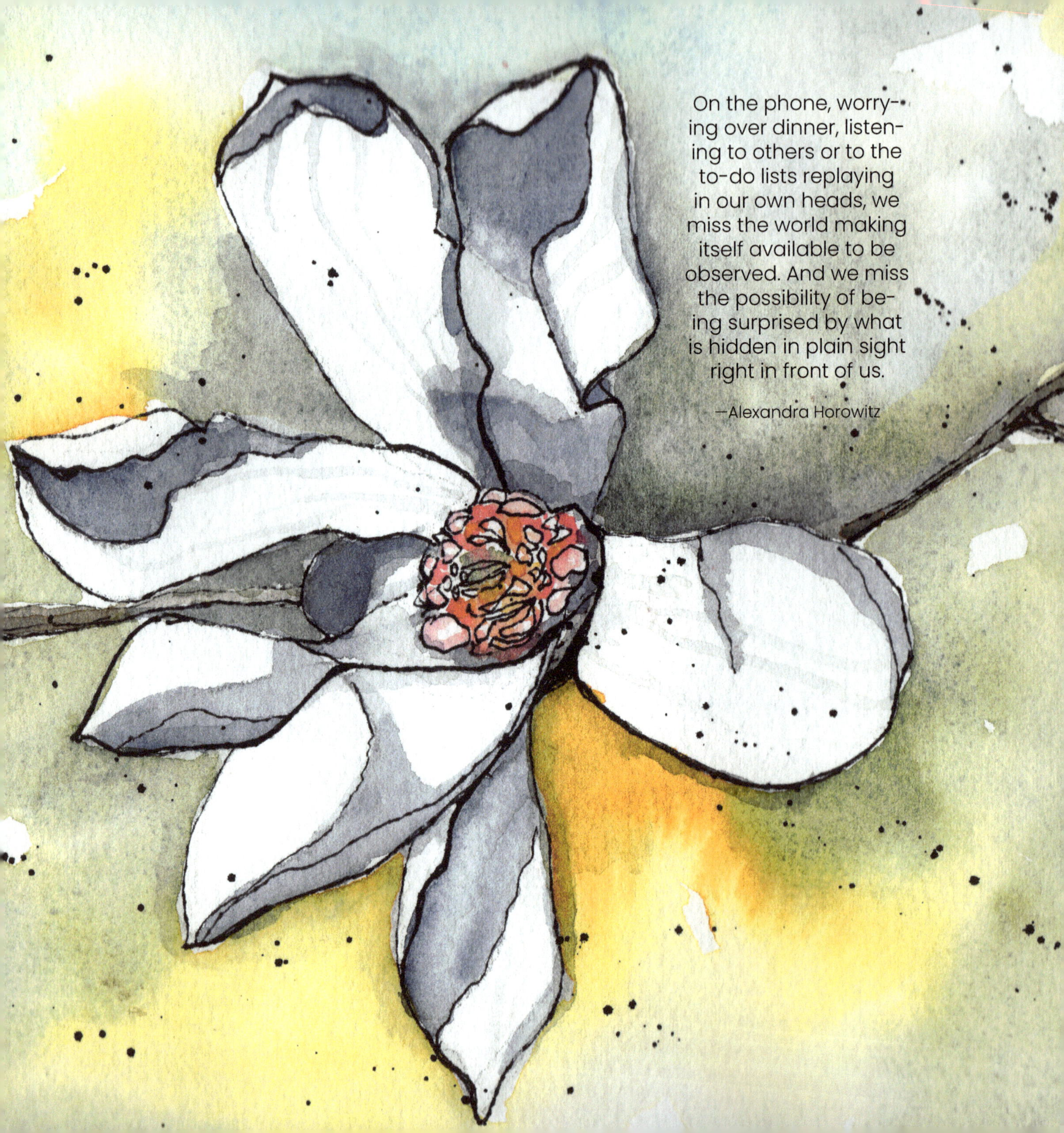
On the phone, worry-
ing over dinner, listen-
ing to others or to the
to-do lists replaying
in our own heads, we
miss the world making
itself available to be
observed. And we miss
the possibility of be-
ing surprised by what
is hidden in plain sight
right in front of us.

—Alexandra Horowitz

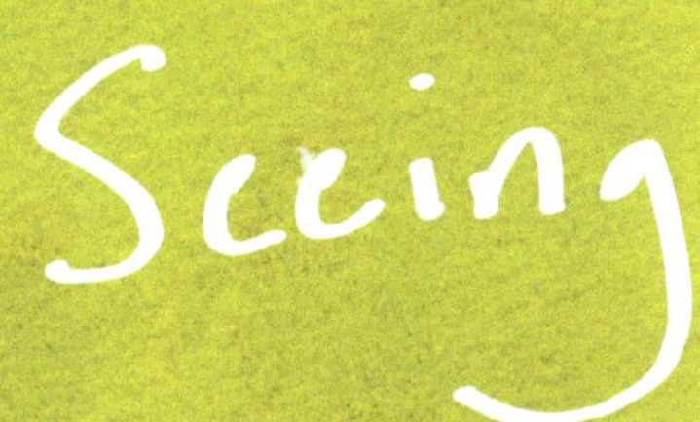

Seeing

Looking vs. seeing

Looking strategies

Tips for seeing

Looking vs. Seeing

Whenever my eyes are open, I am looking, and yet, I often don't see what is right in front of me. How can this be? We know we do this because we have all had the experience of driving to a destination without remembering seeing anything on the way or newly seeing something that has always been there.

This ability to look without seeing has everything to do with how our brains work. Human brains evolved to be efficient, and because of that, we use shorthand to look at pretty much everything. Instead of getting distracted by the branches of the tree or the color of its bark, our brain labels a tree as a tree and allows us to keep going. This is great for activities like driving and walking, but it makes it more challenging if you are interested in knowing what a tree looks like.

When you carefully look at something, say a glass of water, it is incredibly complicated. No wonder our minds have to simplify visual information—there is a lot going on! Without this ability to filter and generalize visual information, it would be very difficult to move through the world. My brain is continually predicting and constructing what I see; when my brain thinks it knows what something is, it stops looking.

Our brains' ability to predict and construct the world is truly amazing—and it can also make seeing harder. If my brain tells me an object is just an object, it can be hard for me to see it accurately. I have to remind myself to continually look.

Our tendency to be consumed by thoughts also makes it harder to see. Our thoughts construct their own version of the world. When we are caught up in our thoughts, we see only them—not the world.

In both cases, the tendency of our brains to interpret the world can keep us from seeing. We can get around just fine, but we overlook much of what is around us. As artist Jan Steward says in *Learning by Heart*, "Looking is not the same as seeing ... But seeing begins with looking."

Artists are people who have developed their seeing muscles in much the same way as weight-lifters develop their muscles—by constant, disciplined use.

—Corita Kent + Jan Steward

Practice looking

So, how do we move from looking to seeing? Well, I have to practice looking.

Because I habitually overlook the every day, I have to be intentional about my looking. Left to its own devices, my attention will wander here and there, lost in thought, predicting what will happen next, not really seeing what's around me. I have to actively practice looking to focus my attention and start to see.

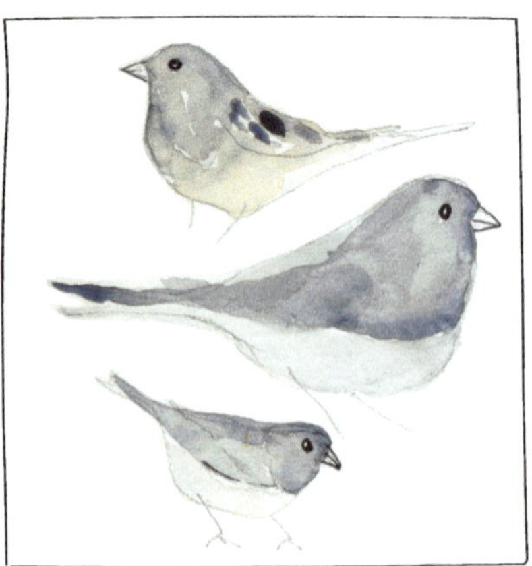

Looking Strategies

There are many different ways to practice looking. Here are seven that I find helpful.

1. Look carefully + draw

Put aside any idea of what the object is and any expectation of what your drawing should look like. Bringing careful attention to something can help you see it.

2. Look for something specific

You can pick anything to look for. Our world is filled with content, but looking for something specific will help you see more.

3. Collect what you see

Having a place to record or collect what you see, sense, smell, or hear will prompt you to look more.

4. Look for source

Being open to everything as a source opens your senses.

5. Put on a pair of goggles

Filtering what you are seeing can help you see more of it.

6. Look wide

Opening up your focus can help you see more.

7. Just look

Reminding yourself to look can be a quick way to restore awareness.

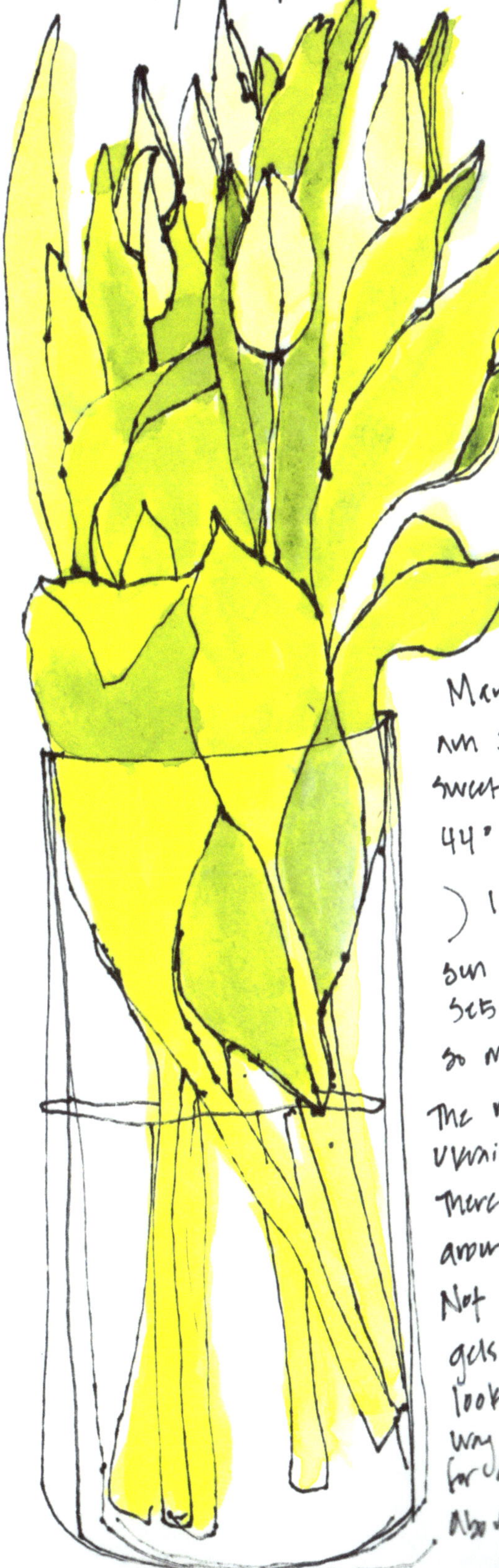

try this

Just look at something, anything, and draw what you see. Take your time and really look. Don't concern yourself with what your drawing looks like because that is not what you aim for; you aim to practice seeing what is actually there, not what you think is there.

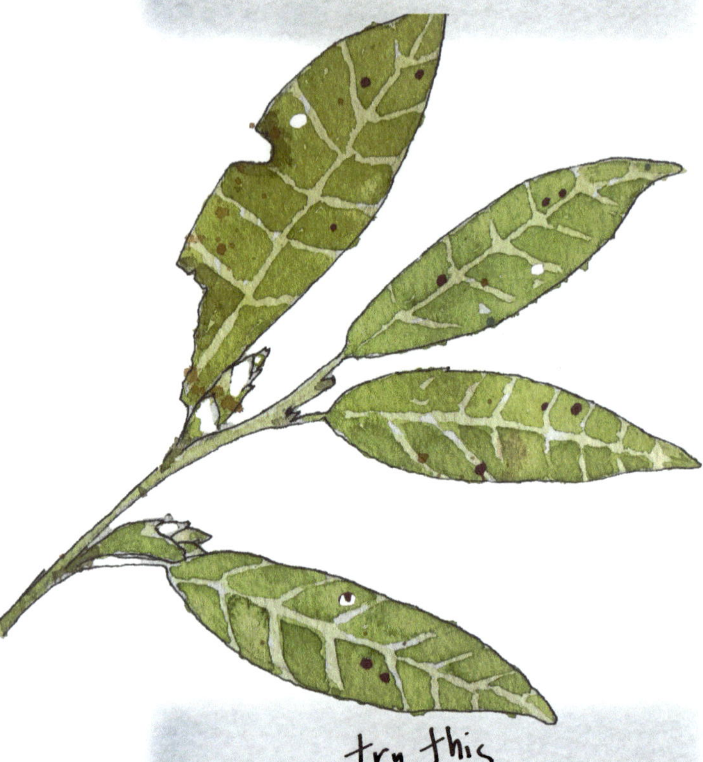

try this

The shapes of leaves and their growth habits are endlessly fascinating and easily observed. You can wander around outside just noticing all the different shapes. You could take a moment to sketch them. Or you could clip off a branch to bring inside to sketch later.

Look carefully + draw

One favorite way I practice looking is to place my attention on some everyday object and draw it. I start by reminding myself to be patient and really look. I look for contours, shapes, and values. I remind myself to look more at the object than at my paper.

Sometimes, the shapes, values, and contours I see are unrecognizable as the object, but if I just draw what I see, it magically becomes recognizable. Somehow, the act of paying attention and attempting to faithfully record what I see goes beyond my concept of the object and helps me see it.

Something about the simple act of looking and drawing helps me connect to an object, calms me down, slows time, and helps me be in the world rather than in my head. It can feel like a meditation.

Sometimes, the object and process of drawing completely capture me, but at other times, my mind natters on about something completely different or begins evaluating what I am doing. When this happens, I invite myself to return my attention to the object anew. Doing this kindly is important; after all, it is not like I have done something wrong—this is just how it goes.

Interestingly, the same is true when I meditate; sometimes, my mind bounces around, while other times, it lets go and opens up. I try to simply notice what is going on and not get involved in any thoughts. The aim is to be aware rather than to get things right or achieve a certain state of mind. Beginning over and over again when I get lost in thought, both in drawing and in meditation, is the practice.

Look for something specific

When I am out and about in the world, looking for something specific helps me develop my "seeing muscles," which in turn helps me notice more.

In her book *On Looking*, author Alexandra Horowitz examines how knowing something exists and looking for it allows us to see more. Horowitz takes mostly the same city walk with a child, her dog, and nine different experts. Each companion experiences and sees different things on their walk. As the experts share with Horowitz what they see, she learns what they know and is newly able to see what they see. For example, her walk with a geologist suddenly opens her eyes to the fossils in the limestone in the city all around her. Horowitz suggests that only when we have some knowledge of a thing can we look for it; we have to know about the fossils to see them.

Horowitz's walks primed her to see things she might have otherwise overlooked. She notes that part of this is due to a sort of seek-and-find aspect to looking—that we can set ourselves up to find things when we decide to look for them, "Your own internal monologue about what you are doing in any given moment actually affects what you will see in the moment. If you know you are looking for the knife, it will be easier to find."

You make the world more colorful by looking for colors. What you look for, you will find. Or maybe, more accurately, what you don't look for, you won't find. Looking for something specific sharpens my attention.

There is an overwhelming amount of stimuli on a city street. Looking for something specific allows me to see something I might otherwise overlook. It gets me out of my conditioned way of looking at the world. I often challenge myself to look for specific things when traveling a familiar route—anything from chimneys to electrical wires to combinations of colors.

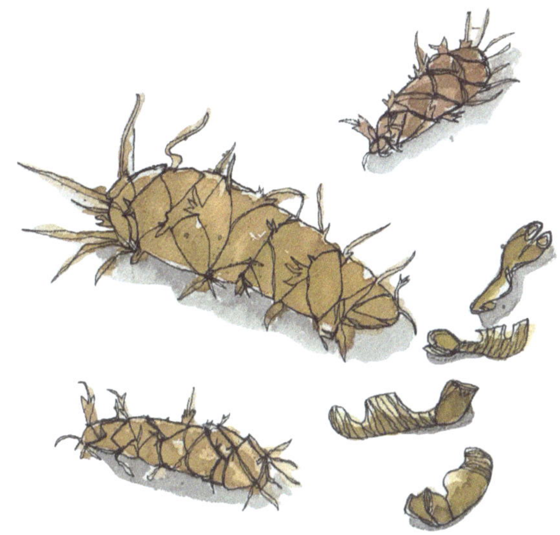

In his engaging book *The Art of Noticing*, Rob Walker has collected numerous prompts for looking for specific things, from looking up to looking for something new to creating your own looking scavenger hunt. Walker's book is filled with ideas for pushing yourself to notice things that are easily overlooked.

resource

In *The Art of Noticing: 131 Ways to Spark Creativity, Find Inspiration, and Discover Joy in the Everyday*, Rob Walker has collected generative and varied looking prompts from many different sources.

resource

On Looking: Eleven Walks with Expert Eyes by Alexandra Horowitz is an astute and delightfully written book about looking, attention, and observation. In it, she examines the point of view of nine experts, her toddler son, and her dog.

try this

Sometimes, finding regular time to work in a journal is just too hard. That happens, but you don't want to keep yourself from journaling because you don't have regular time for it.

It could be a once-a-week, once-a-month, or once-in-a-blue-moon journal.

try this

One of the prompts in Barry's book *Syllabus* suggests taking thirty seconds and writing down something you overheard during the day. This exceptionally generative prompt can transform an errand from a task to a treasure hunt. In the grocery store, I find I am not just filling my cart but also keeping my ears and eyes open, wondering what I can report in my journal later in the day.

try this

When you are out and about, look for things you might want to draw. Most of the time, we can't stop and draw on the spot, so take a picture of anything that catches your interest. Later, you can come back to that photo and draw it.

Even if you never end up drawing it, looking for something to take a photo of prompts you to notice more.

Collect what you see,
sense, hear, or smell

Keeping a journal, notebook, or sketchbook is, in part, an extended-looking strategy. The open page is an ongoing prompt, an empty space asking to be filled. Since most of my days are spent in familiar places doing familiar things, the prompt of the page prods me to look.

Keeping a sense diary, as Corita Kent and Jan Steward suggest in *Learning by Heart*, is another way to prompt yourself to look. To find things to put in your sense diary, you have to look around.

In her book *Making Comics*, Lynda Barry explains why keeping a daily diary is important: "The diary isn't about what you see, it's about being in a state of seeing ... The daily diary exercise is meant to be a form of physical practice for both your real eyes and your mind's eye. It's about increasing your capacity to gaze and to listen and most importantly, to notice what you notice."

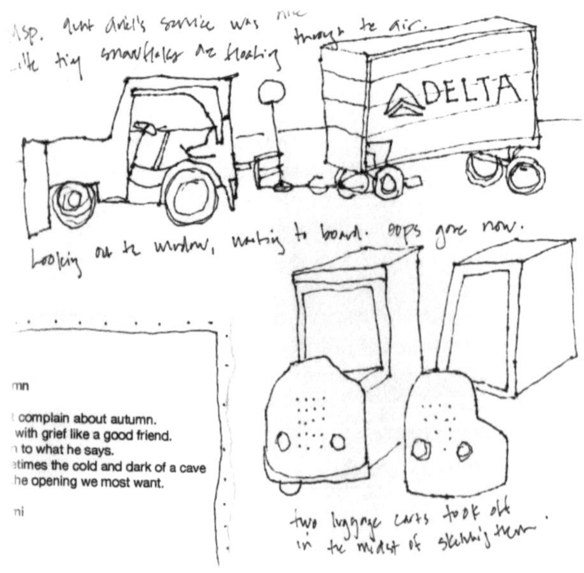

art, a souvenir, or something else?

After lunch, I sketched a tall tumble mustard plant. I did it quickly, in fifteen minutes, and the wind pushed the stems around, making it hard to keep my eye on the same part of the plant. It was a beautiful afternoon. A turkey vulture swept through the meadow and silenced the ground squirrels, who must have been hunkered down in their tunnels.

The tall tumble mustard was highlighted against a bank of white oak trees with yarrow plants scattered around their trunks.

My sketch looks rough, crude, and jerky. But it asked me to pay attention. I had to sit quietly and look. Would I have seen the yarrow mingled with the grasses around the base of the mustard if I hadn't taken this time?

What do I see when I look at this sketch? If I choose to see only the lines, I could get disappointed. If I choose to see that moment instead, then it becomes alive and sings of the beauty of the day and the blessing of being there to record it. I could wish my sketch were different, or I could simply accept it and be grateful for being able to record that moment.

You know, I think I will go with that.

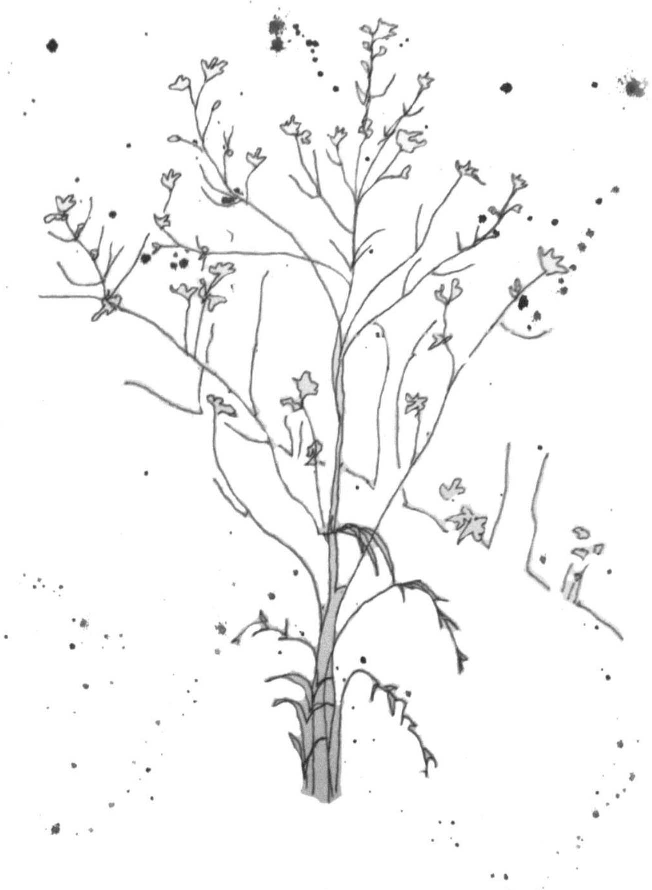

Look for source

The "state of seeing" that Lynda Barry refers to in *Making Comics* reminds me of another looking strategy I use: prompting myself to look for source. What is source? Source is anything I notice that can serve as inspiration. Birdsong can be source, a smell can be source, a pattern or color can be source. I don't think of it as an inspiration I immediately put to use; it is a more open-ended gathering. When I am looking for source, I am asking *What is here?* This feels both arty and Zen to me at the same time.

Shards of Light

We're only here for a minute …
We're here for a little window.
And to use that time to catch
and share shards of light and
laughter and grace seems to me
the great story.

—Brian Doyle

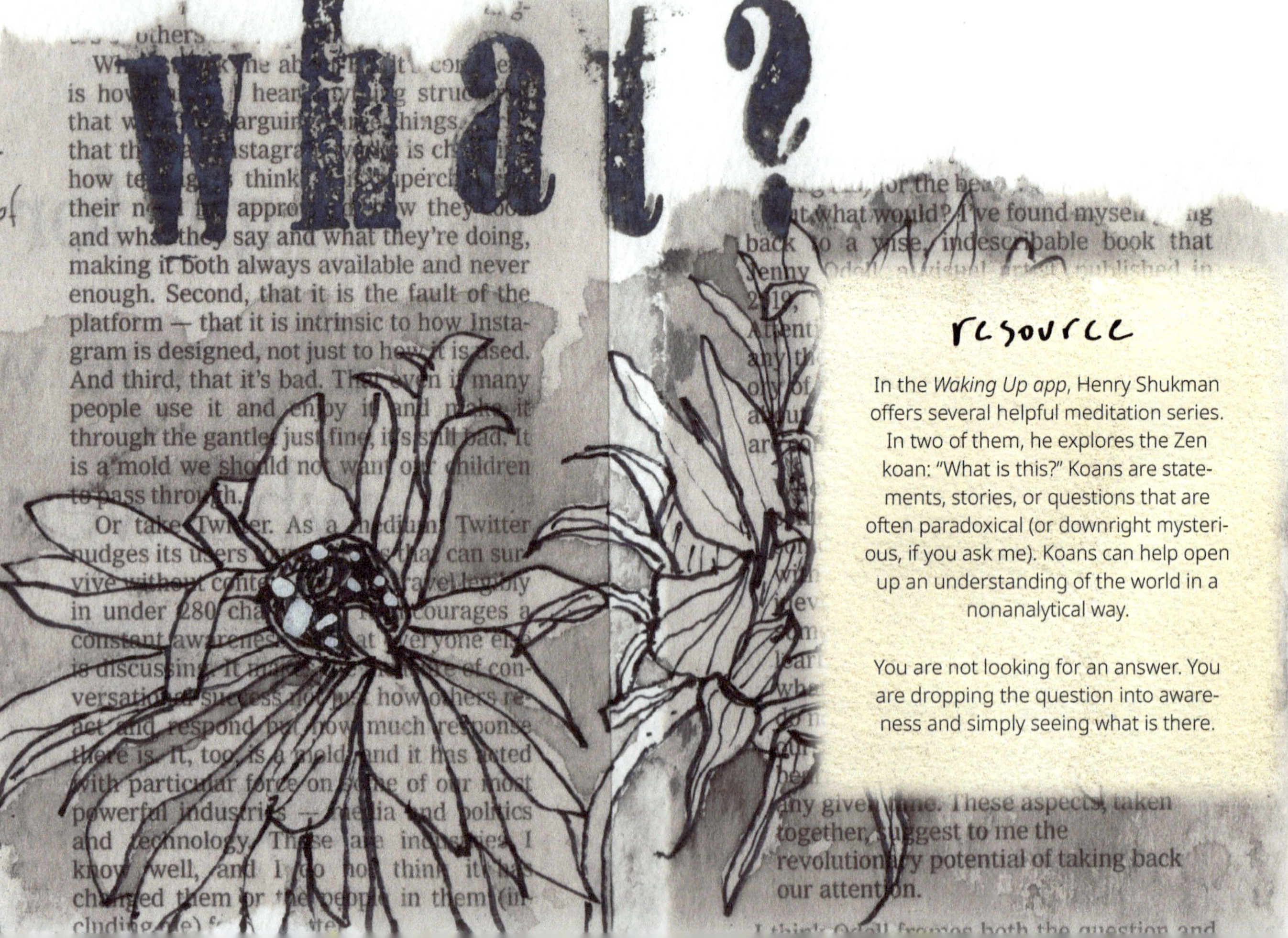

resource

In the *Waking Up app*, Henry Shukman offers several helpful meditation series. In two of them, he explores the Zen koan: "What is this?" Koans are statements, stories, or questions that are often paradoxical (or downright mysterious, if you ask me). Koans can help open up an understanding of the world in a nonanalytical way.

You are not looking for an answer. You are dropping the question into awareness and simply seeing what is there.

Put on a pair of goggles

For a while, a prompt in my journal was to put on "wonder goggles" and look for wonder. This is great because it pushes me to look for things to wonder at, naturally ushering in awareness and joy. In *On Looking*, Alexandra Horowitz explains why it's an effective strategy: "Blinders and googles are ways of physically restricting what you can, and expect, to see in the world; the brain has its own internal mechanism. By thinking about what you are looking for, or anticipating what you might be looking at, your brain grows biased to see it; biologically, the neuronal processes are primed to spot objects that fit your expectation."

In her book *Enchantment*, Katherine May says we find wonder by looking for it: "I think I'm beginning to understand that the quest is the point. Our sense of enchantment is not triggered only by grand things; the sublime is not hiding in distant landscapes. The awe-inspiring, the numinous, is all around us, all the time. It is transformed by our deliberate attention. It becomes valuable when we value it. It becomes meaningful when we invest it with meaning. The magic is of our own conjuring. Hierophany—that revelation of the sacred—is something that we bring to everyday things, rather than something given to us."

When May says that it is our looking, our quest, that imbues everyday objects with wonder, it helps me answer a question I have about my wonder goggles: Am I looking for something special here? Something extraordinary? One of the themes that runs through this book involves non-seeking. Relinquishing seeking can be a wise and fruitful practice. When I look for wonder, am I seeking? Or am I simply trying to rub my eyes to see more clearly what is already there?

May suggests that attention itself is transformative; it is our attention that matters, not necessarily what we turn that attention to. Is attention the magic that transforms looking into seeing?

The trick of wonder goggles is that they help me find wonder in the everyday; they help highlight the extraordinary that lives in the ordinary. Putting on a pair of goggles is another great way to help me see.

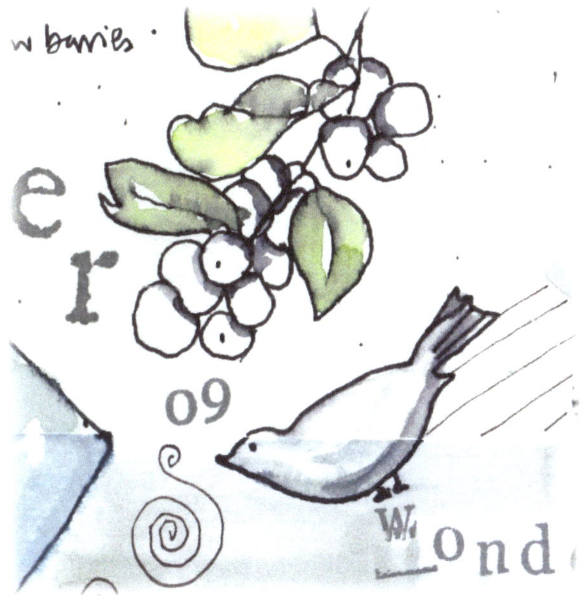

Go ahead and put on some wonder goggles. What do you see? Can you draw it? Or write about it? Or just mentally note it?

Look wide

There is another sort of looking I use, one that is less directed and more intuitive. In this sort of looking, things come to me rather than my trying to look for something specific. I set aside any expectations and try to open my mind up. Everything and anything can be absorbed. It is a sort of panoramic looking. This doesn't happen in a heady way; instead, I like to imagine that I am absorbing the world around me. When I see something, I just take it in. I don't have to do anything with it. I can just marinate in the experience of seeing it.

Corita Kent describes an exercise that promotes a similar sort of looking: "There is an exercise I've learned lately, and that is to be quiet and look at an object or space directly ahead of you. Keep a soft focus and also allow your attention to reach past your peripheral vision, left and right. In addition, place your attention on top of or above your head. All of these directions—front, right, left, above—being looked at with a kind of diffuseness. You try to have a clear moment when you are empty and open to things around you. You see them new—your vision is cleansed and you can make contact with what is really there, uncluttered by old thoughts and prejudices. Always be ready to see what you haven't seen before. It's a kind of looking where you don't know what you're looking for."

You could call what Corita terms "old thoughts and prejudices" concepts. The rawness of sensation or data we collect about anything is often papered over by concepts we place upon them. We often need to unpeel the concept from the thing itself to actually see the thing. Corita says this separation from concepts is essential in creating: "When you get past making labels for things, it is possible to combine and transform elements into new things. Look at things until their import, identity, name, use, and description have dissolved."

The practice of separating the concept of a thing from the thing itself can invite a mystery that moves us from looking to seeing. Sam Harris speaks to this experience: "No such litany of concepts or connections can account for the mystery that looms whenever you just look at something closely, anything, however commonplace, and realize that while you might have volumes of information about it, you don't have the slightest understanding of what it is in itself … We confront the mystery of being in every moment, but we don't notice it because this mystery is tiled over with concepts."

The wide-reaching implications of this experience are explored by Jenny Odell in her book *How to Do Nothing: Resisting the Attention Economy* when she notes, "Practices of attention and curiosity are inherently open-ended, oriented toward something outside of ourselves. Through attention and curiosity, we can transcend our tendency toward instrumental understanding—seeing things or people one-dimensionally as the products of their functions—and instead sit with the unfathomable fact of their existence, which opens up to us but can never be fully grasped or known."

What this shows us, as Odell neatly puts it, is "how endlessly strange reality is when we look *at it* rather than through it." There is a wonderful transcendent nature to this sort of looking—that can take us right out of our conditioned ways of looking and thinking and allow us to see the world anew.

try this

Sometimes, I try to notice what is *not* calling for my attention. This can be particularly interesting when you are a passenger in a car.

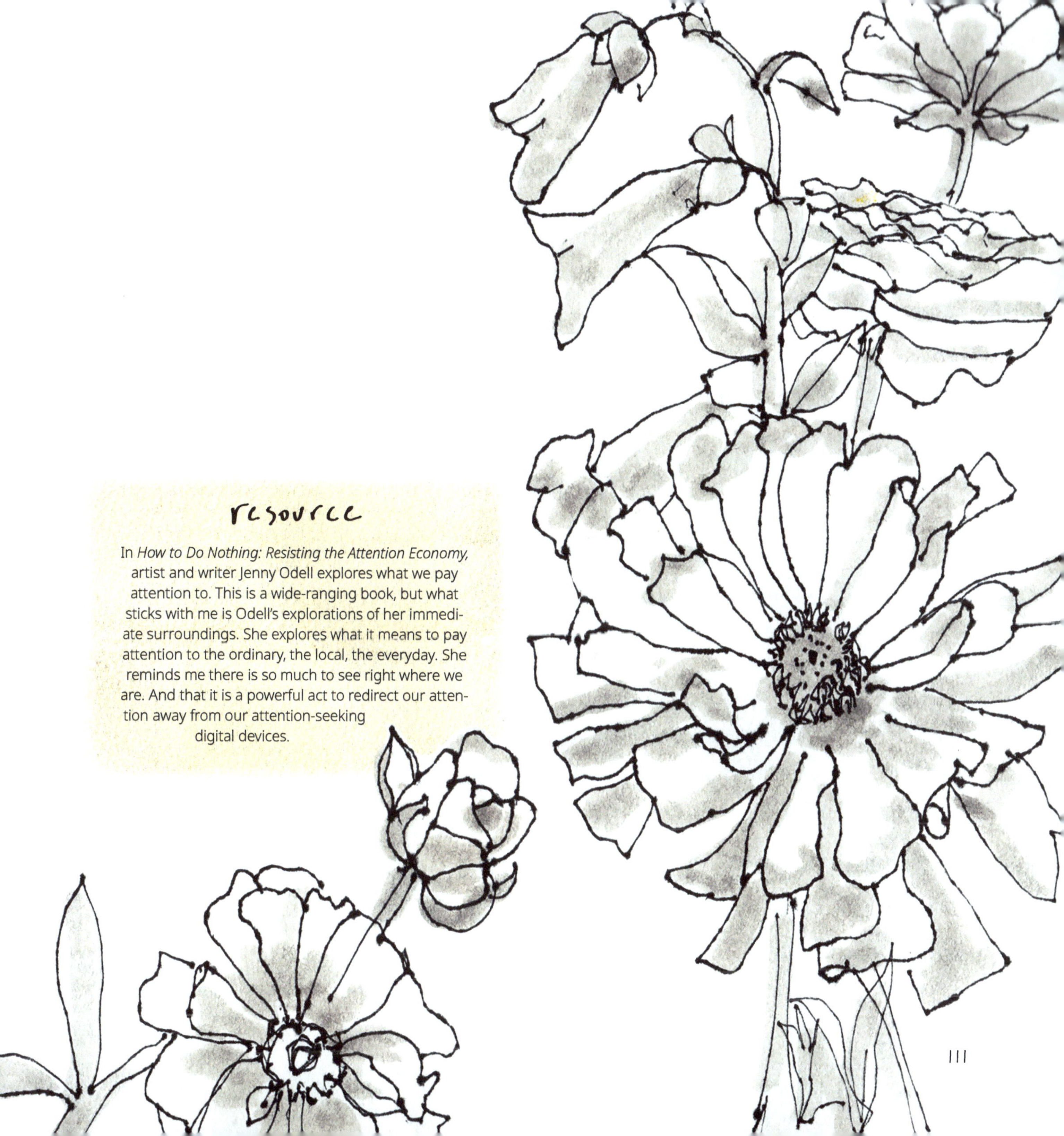

resource

In *How to Do Nothing: Resisting the Attention Economy,* artist and writer Jenny Odell explores what we pay attention to. This is a wide-ranging book, but what sticks with me is Odell's explorations of her immediate surroundings. She explores what it means to pay attention to the ordinary, the local, the everyday. She reminds me there is so much to see right where we are. And that it is a powerful act to redirect our attention away from our attention-seeking digital devices.

Just look

Whether I am looking wide or looking closely, just remembering to look is surprisingly helpful. Remembering to look when I am caught up in something restores some awareness. It reminds me of how mindfulness teachers suggest placing attention on the breath when we get lost in our thoughts. Reminding myself to *just look* is a quick, powerful way to get me out of my head and back into the world.

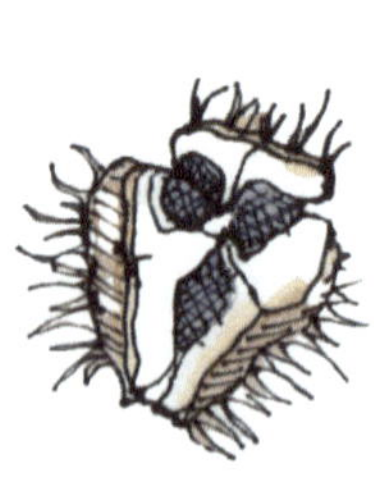

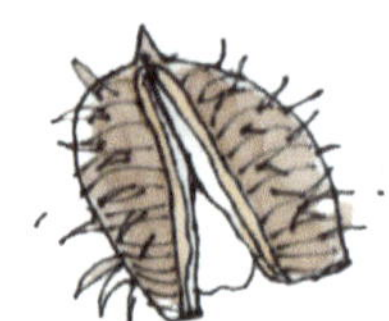

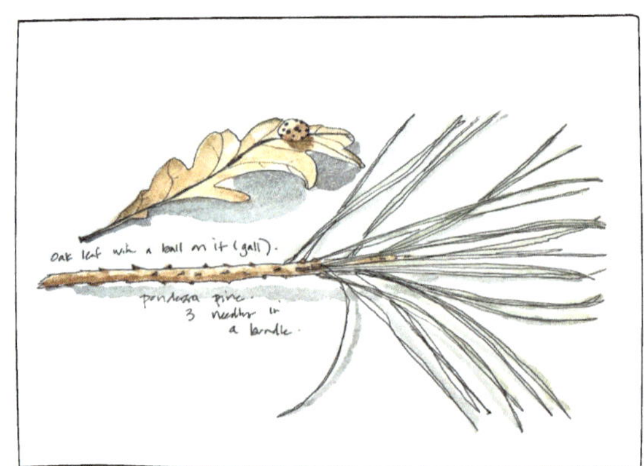

try this

If you notice your thoughts are rattling around, try just looking.

You can look outside or look at stuff in your house.

Look with a wide perspective and an open mind. It is a quick way to shift what you are paying attention to.

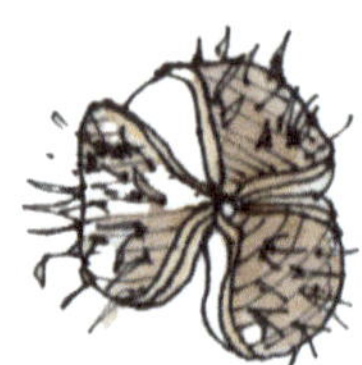

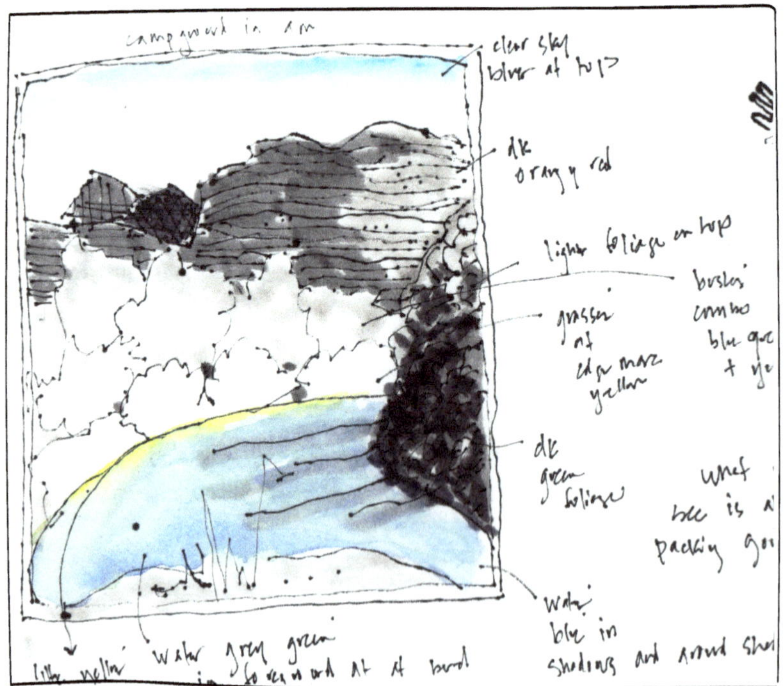

Tips for Seeing

These are all ways of coaxing your brain to step outside of its conditioned way of looking since our conditioned way of looking can blind us to what is actually there. These are especially helpful when it comes to drawing.

1. Look for shapes

Try to see big shapes first, then look for little shapes. Simplify what you see. Doing this helps you start to edit right away. As one of my art teachers liked to say, "We are not copiers; we are artists."

2. Look through a viewfinder

You can make or buy a viewfinder. This helps your brain focus on a part of the picture, discarding information that might otherwise get in the way. You can also use a viewfinder to focus on just a small part of something and, in doing so, see worlds you might have otherwise overlooked.

3. Look for value

Look for the light and dark areas. Sometimes, identifying three values—light, medium, and dark—can help simplify what you are looking at. Squinting your eyes can help.

4. Look for color

Making a small circle with your finger and looking at a color can help you see the color more clearly.

5. Look for negative space

Negative space is the space that surrounds a shape rather than the shape itself. By looking at the negative space rather than the object's shape, you can see what is actually there instead of getting lured into seeing what you expect to see.

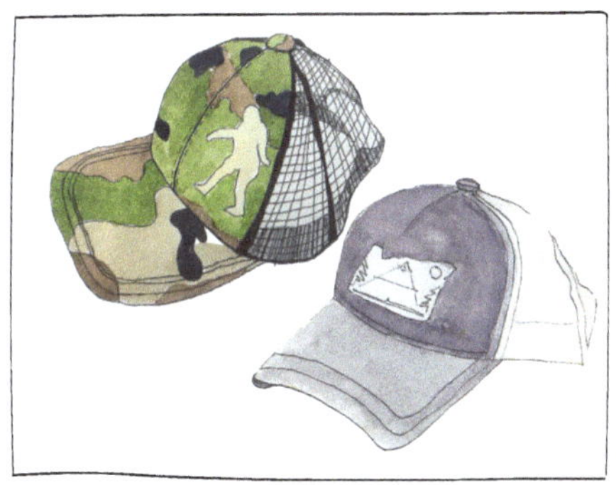

6. Look upside down

Turn a drawing upside down and then copy it. This is a great way to take your brain by surprise.

7. Flick your eyes back and forth

To see if a shape is drawn correctly, you can quickly flick your eyes back and forth from the shape you are drawing to the shape on your page. Somehow, it overrides my brain and allows me to see more clearly.

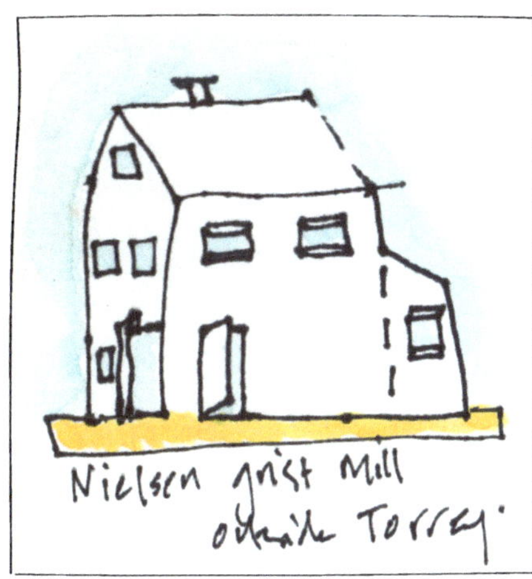

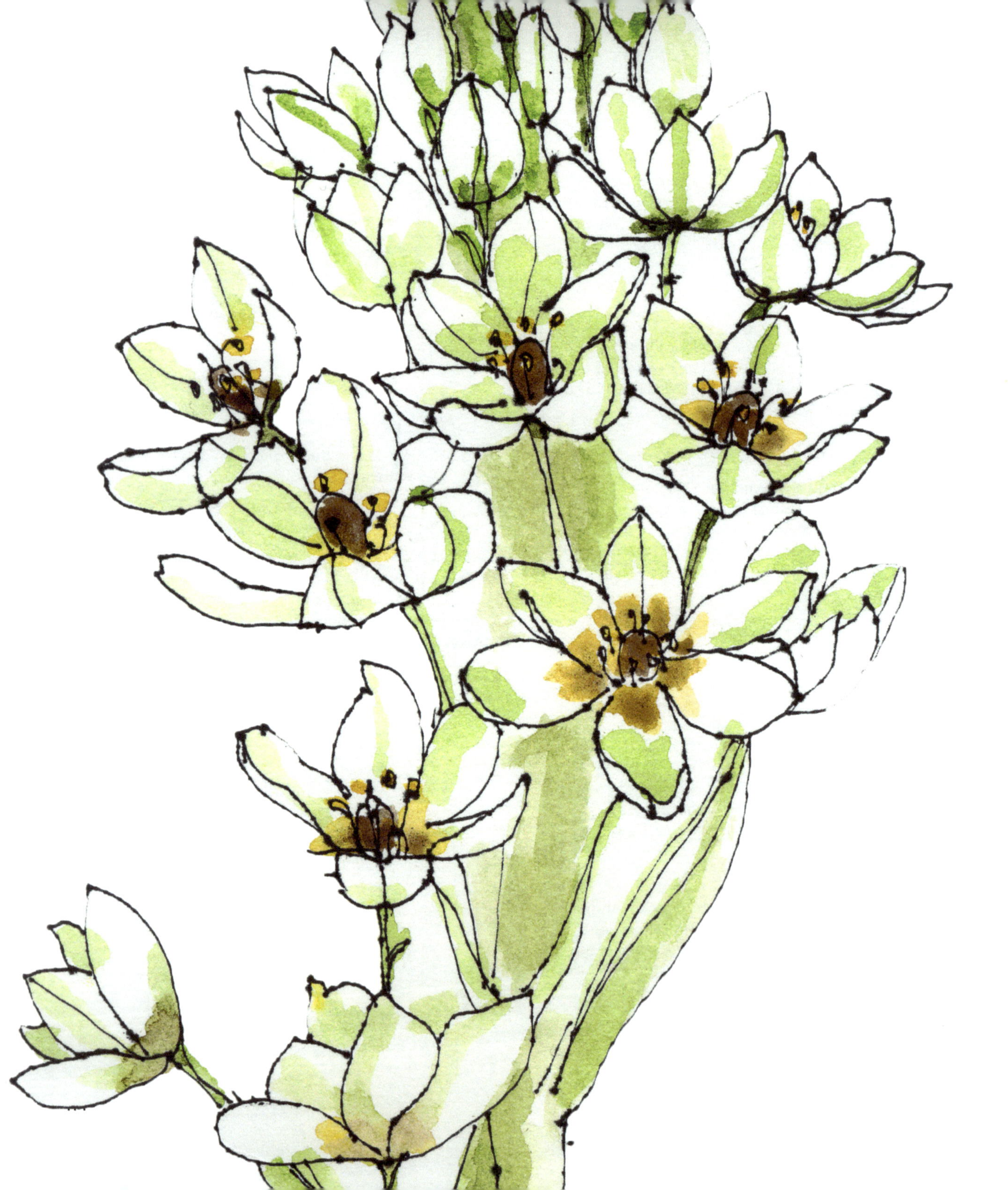

Mystery + paradox

Dropping the search

Taking the path as the goal

Effort + effortlessness

Am I an artist?

Love

Combining opposing ideas—straddling—is a vital part of design and far more common to both art and life than is generally realized. Too often we approach drawing as a discipline in which there is a right way and a wrong way of doing things. The idea that opposites can exist side by side can be perplexing to those of us brought up to see things as either/or, true or not true, correct or incorrect.

— Bert Dodson, *Keys to Drawing*

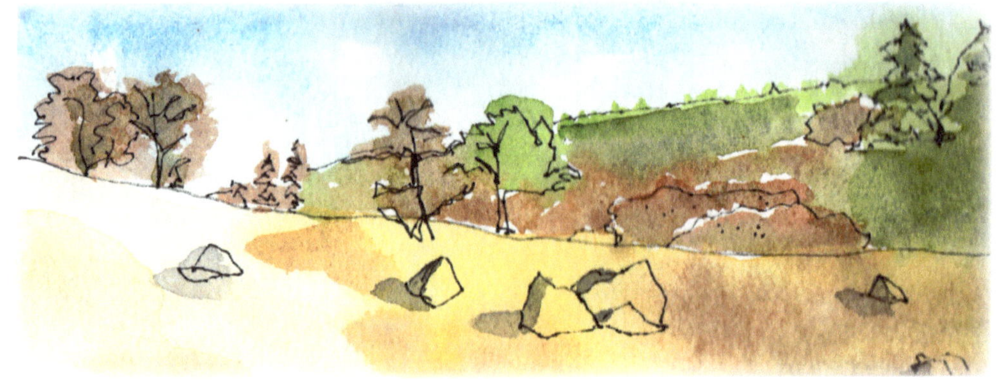

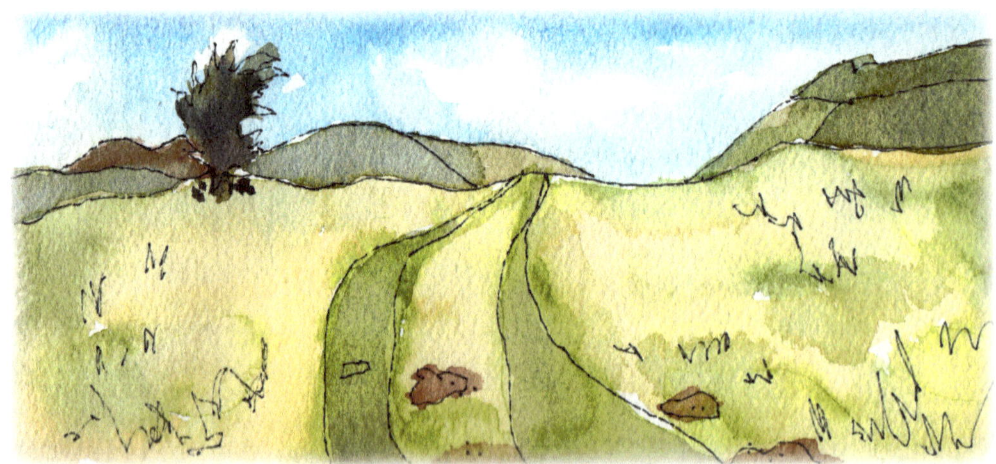

Dropping the Search

The power of mysteries and paradoxes is that they invite exploration. When you can't settle something definitively, you keep looking. We yearn for certainty, but when you think you know a thing, you stop wondering. Here are some mysteries and paradoxes in art and awareness that intrigue me.

I first discovered the paradoxical joy of dropping the search in the hills of Mosier, Oregon. I was riding my bike, and it was very easy and enjoyable. I saw many things: birds, colors, shapes, and clouds. It was easy because I was riding very slowly. My reason for riding so slowly was to keep my heart rate low. I was following an exercise training plan that specified my effort should be in a low heart rate zone 80 percent of the time.

I discovered that I like moving slowly, even if it doesn't make me healthier. I see more things and am more relaxed; it is more fun. I realized I could abandon the whole idea of training and simply enjoy the ride.

I made a similar discovery in meditation. When I first began meditating, I pushed myself, looking for change, hoping to become a calmer, more gracious person. But I started to see that my desire for change seemed to make things harder.

I began to see that I was on a never-ending search for improvement. Whether it was health, enlightenment, or art, I was never okay with being; instead, I was always intent on improving and changing. I was focused on the goal, never just okay being where I was. This stance is what meditation teacher Joseph Goldstein calls living with a "forward lean"—always searching to become rather than to be. He advises: "There is nothing to become ... Stop that forward lean ... The essence of the practice is not becoming anything ... but dropping back into not wanting."

So I started to wonder: Could I drop the search for competence in art and enlightenment in life? Just thinking about it, I felt an instant source of relief. What is that all about? I thought because, on the face of it, it seemed absurd. How can dropping the search for competence in art and enlightenment in life be a good thing? I wanted to be enlightened, an artist, and skilled! How could I possibly drop those desires?

But my bike riding had taught me something. In meditation, I was learning that dropping back and letting go was the key to finding my way. And as I created more, I found the quiet joy of making things just for myself.

Now, my goal is to be okay with where I am. What I started in search of—changing myself—is no longer my goal. I am beginning to understand that what I have been looking for has been here all along.

So is dropping the search how I find my way? I have heard it said that the person who begins the search for enlightenment is not the same person who finds it. Maybe the same thing is true of art.

Taking the path as the goal

The mindfulness concept of taking the path as the goal is about perceiving the journey as the destination. In other words, rather than practicing to become something or change anything, the practice is the thing itself, not just the means of getting somewhere else. The oft-given advice to engage in the process and let go of the outcome is relevant to this concept (although implied in this advice is that there is a destination, and engaging in the process is the best way of getting there.) However, if you truly understand your path—your practice—to be the goal, there is no gap between where you are now and where you want to be. You just are where you are. The abundance in this thinking is frankly exhilarating.

Sam Harris describes how this unfolds in meditation: "The ultimate practice of mindfulness is to notice the inherent freedom of awareness again in this moment, and if you can recognize it, you will be unable to seek it by any other means. There is no time to seek it or to hope for it because there is no distance between the moment you notice that you've forgotten and the moment of remembering. The openness of consciousness is available at any time we recognize it. How can you hope for what is fully available now? You can't. You can only remember to enjoy it, and that is how actual freedom, the ultimate goal of meditation, becomes the path."

So, how does taking the path as the goal relate to making art? Thinking this way, I feel every bit of practice is complete and not just a stepping stone to something else. Instead, a moment of practice can stand happily on its own—and not wait for some future achievement to validate it.

It means I can fully inhabit and be satisfied with what is happening now instead of holding my breath and wishing I was somewhere in the future with more time, competence, or experience. It makes me more attentive to and content with the present moment. It is also just more fun.

Sell your
cleverness and
buy bewilderment.
Cleverness
is mere opinion,
bewilderment is
intuition.

—Rumi

When I take the path as the goal, I disentangle myself from ideas of utility, competence, and recognition. This can be hard to do. Thinking of myself as a beginner helps. If I am always a beginner, there is no better, more accomplished self for me to chase after. I can stop viewing myself as always seeking and consider that I have already arrived. And yet, I can't stop doing because doing is the goal. It is not just practice—it is the destination itself.

You know, maybe I need a better name for practice.

try this

Can you take five minutes and sit quietly and just rest without seeking anything?

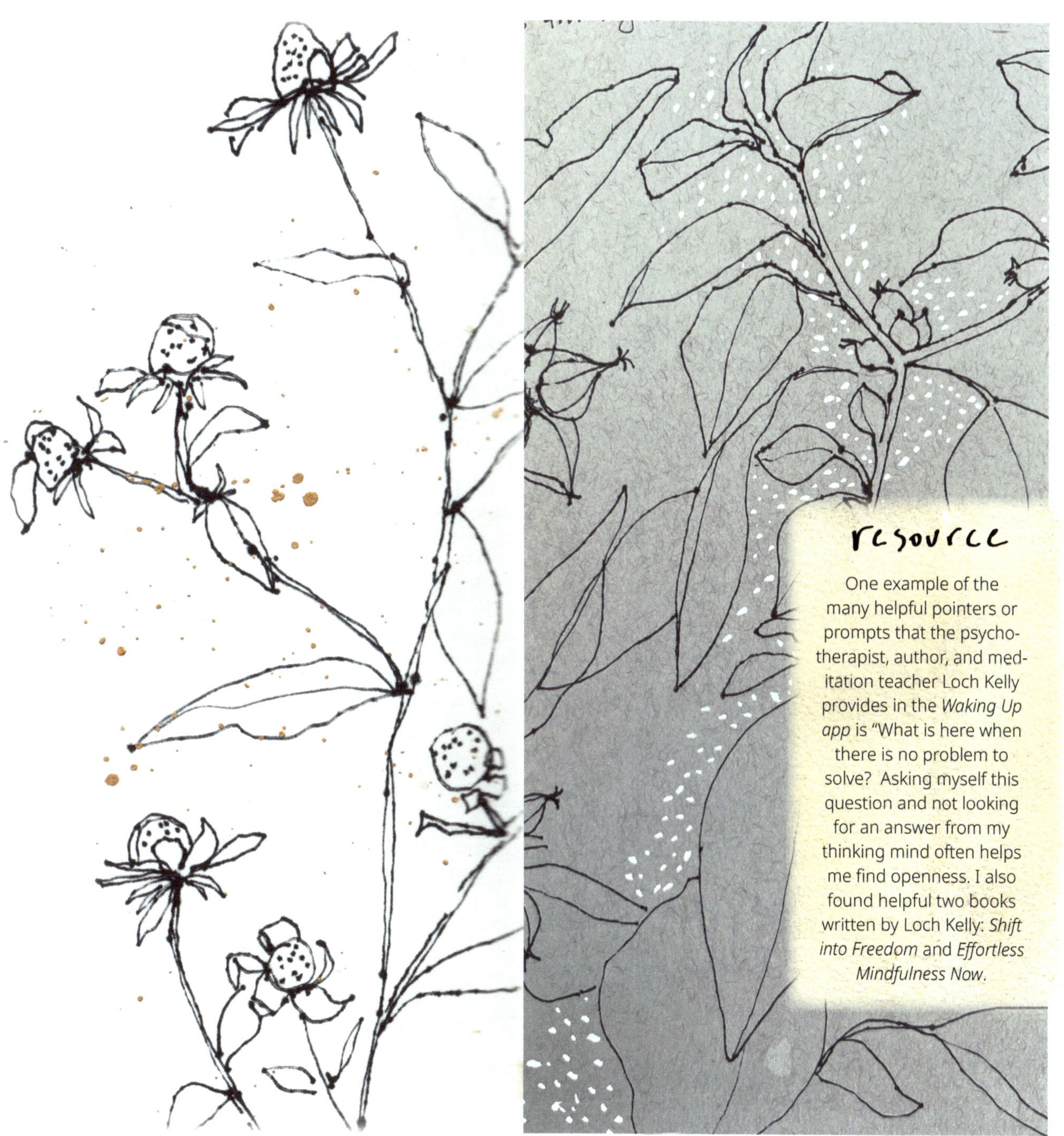

RESOURCE

One example of the
many helpful pointers or
prompts that the psycho-
therapist, author, and meditation teacher Loch Kelly
provides in the *Waking Up
app* is "What is here when
there is no problem to
solve? Asking myself this
question and not looking
for an answer from my
thinking mind often helps
me find openness. I also
found helpful two books
written by Loch Kelly: *Shift
into Freedom* and *Effortless
Mindfulness Now*.

Effort + effortlessness

When I rest and relax my always-doing self, I become aware of how much is going on all the time, outside of my control. While it can feel as if I am in the center of all experience, a doer and a striver making things happen, if I pay attention, I can see that it is not quite that simple. Sensations, thoughts, feelings, and even movements come and go. If I look to see where it all comes from, it is a bit of a mystery.

But it is not as if everything will work out if I do nothing. There is a tipping point to explore, a shifting balance between effort and effortlessness, thinking and intuition.

In his book *The Path of Aliveness*, Christian Dillo speaks to this balance of effort and effortlessness in the image of a bird laying an egg. A bird needs to lay an egg and sit on the nest for the egg to hatch. But turning the egg into a bird is beyond the reach of the mother bird. Likewise, in writing this book or making a drawing, what I can do is sit on my nest; whether the egg hatches or not is really beyond my ken.

There are any number of places where you can see this. You start something and put something into motion, but much of what happens is beyond your control. Making art can be a place where you actively explore this paradox. This relationship between effort and effortlessness can be conceived of as (effortful) thinking and (effortless) intuition.

I usually start by thinking: What are the big shapes? How are they related? Where will the drawing go on the page? What is happening with the perspective? With the values? And then, at some point, I have to let something go; if I don't, I end up feeling tense, having less fun, and my drawing looks stilted.

Letting go allows intuition to come into play. You may not know why you chose that exact color, drew that line, or wrote that word. If you investigate where that choice originated, you will find it is a bit of a mystery.

However, thought continues to be helpful; it may help me correct a proportion or understand why something is not working and how to improve it. The illustrator Cat Bennett speaks to this balance in *Making Art a Practice* by saying, "There's no need to think too much, to question or get caught in endless debate of this or that. Just trust, go for it and see what happens." But she also says, "In drawing, 'Let me put a line here' may be a very useful thought. 'I think I'll abandon this drawing; it's going nowhere' may also be a helpful thought, or not."

While I may not have a choice of what thoughts can come into my mind, I do have a choice as to which thoughts I listen to and converse with. Helpful thoughts differ greatly from unhelpful worries about talent, competence, or results. In mindfulness, thoughts are often described as clouds that obscure the bright clarity of an open mind. Unhelpful thoughts cloud the process of art-making and block creativity.

Art can be an opportunity to explore both the effort of helpful thinking and the effortlessness of letting that thinking go, allowing your intuition to surface. Our society is invested in analytical thinking—we are comforted by giving and receiving logical explanations. We like to make sense! But there is quite a bit of experience that we can't know in any rational way, experience that we can only sense or feel. Feeling your way into things is a different approach than thinking your way through things.

It is easy to overestimate the importance of thought and underplay intuition, so I often feel the need to give a little shout of encouragement to my intuition. Intuition involves trusting myself—or, maybe more accurately, trusting in something mysterious that I can't define but I can feel is there.

It can feel like magic because it is outside of our thinking mind's control. There is some sort of dance we do with the world, and the more I pay attention, the more I realize there is something deep and mysterious that is both part of and bigger than me. Small wonder Elizabeth Gilbert titled the book she wrote on creativity *Big Magic*.

The making of connections defines and makes possible creativity. These processes tap into what we know and feel, but have not yet (or cannot be) articulated. They elude the rational, conscious mind—which tends to constrict, label, categorize, and demand logical explanation.

—Jan Steward

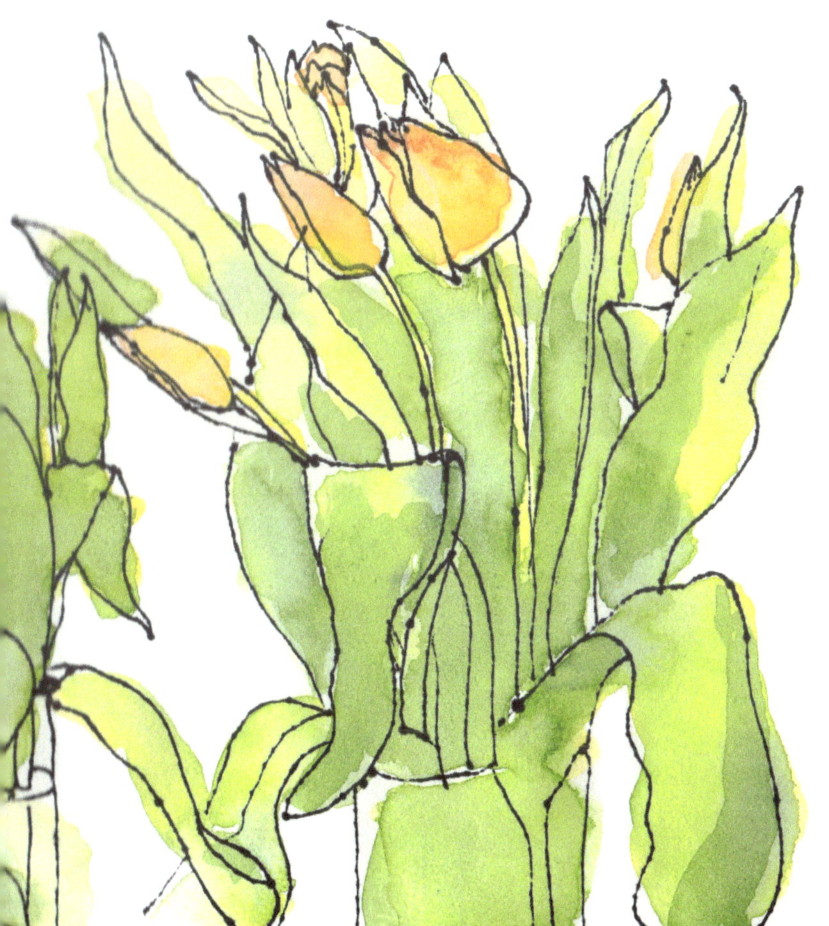

try this

Draw something. Anything. When you are done, take a look at it. Can you explain why you drew something a certain way?

Can you even explain how you got your hand to move?

Am I an artist?

There is a paradox at the center of identity: Thinking of myself as an artist can be helpful, but how can that be if I have come to understand that the entire notion of self is an illusion?

When people ask me if I am an artist, I hesitate, unsure what to say. "Well," I usually mumble, "I like to do art." I struggle with an answer. To be an artist, do you have to make money with your art? Do you have to make art every day? Is it a mindset? Do you have to have studied it? I imagine there are many ways to define an artist, but I am not sure a definition would help me.

Because I get tripped up by the idea that we have a fixed sense of self that can be neatly categorized. If I identify as an artist, I am giving myself a label that places me in a sort of conceptual box. Even though that label could be defined in many ways, it still puts me either in or out of the box.

I think our desire to label ourselves and others comes from a desire to simplify complexity. The world is ever-changing, and people are complicated! Maybe it is just a way to simplify things so we can stop thinking so much.

Identifying as anything becomes puzzling if you come to understand that who we are changes minute by minute; we do not have fixed identities. What we can think of as our self is actually a conceptual idea of who we are that masks our continually changing natures. I may consider myself to be an outgoing person, but I then find myself in a social situation and feel shy. So then, what am I? Am I a shy person or an outgoing person? Well, it depends. Our selves are more fluid than we often envision them to be.

When I spend time inquiring into the nature of my self, it simply disappears. It is not something I believe or a concept I understand; it is something I experience. What I have found through looking and meditation is that I am more of a process than a thing. And that I don't have an experience, I am identical to it. These two realizations (which come and go) radically change my perception of self. It is the kind of thing that sounds obscure and weird until you experience it. There is a mystery here I will never understand.

And, of course, I have a self. I have habits, inclinations, memories, and ways of being that are unlike anyone else's—and art can make me more aware of those inclinations. I have gotten to know myself better by working in my journals. (What is this odd attraction to dots and circles?) And there is no doubt that we are all different selves. If you give the direction to draw a car to any group of people, no two cars will be the same. Isn't that just fantastic?

So why does any of this matter? There is an inherent freedom that comes from recognizing that the boundaries of self are not fixed. At any moment, we are free to respond to the world without narrowing and reducing the experience through the lens of self. I can let go of any egocentric thinking about myself and just do stuff. I can step out of my own way.

resource

In the *Waking Up app*, author, retired psychotherapist, and teacher James Low elucidates teachings from both Buddhist and Dzogchen traditions with humor and clarity. He is a wonderful teacher if you are interested in learning more about how a fixed sense of self is an illusion.

But then again, when I woke up the other morning and was thinking about my day, I asked, *What would Perrin, the artist, do?*

I realize how incredibly goofy that is, and it runs right up against the recognition that I am not a fixed self, but there is something there.

I wasn't looking for an egocentric answer. I realized I could also ask what other Perrins would do: What would Perrin, the mom or friend, do? Or what would Perrin, the activist or helper, do? But for whatever reason, *What would Perrin, the artist, do?* strikes closest to home. The first thing I notice when I ask it is that I relax.

I relax and allow myself to pay attention, to slow down, and to look more closely at what is here. This relaxation, attention, and looking usher in gratitude; I feel grateful for being alive and able to see what is here in this beautiful, fractured, and imperfect world.

Surprisingly, I realized the answer at first has absolutely nothing to do with making art. What does that mean? How could Perrin, the artist, not make art?

Does the relaxing come from letting go of the idea that I am the doer and driver? Does it somehow mean that I am relaxing into the day as it arrives? And that making things, for me, involves a non-negligible amount of letting go? Does it mean that the real art is in slowing down, paying attention, and seeing?

I want to keep asking these questions. I want to remember that each moment brings me the opportunity to keep looking, be a beginner, and see the world anew. And I guess it doesn't matter to me whether that is being an "artist" or not.

It's not about being anything, really. It is about seeing that the door is always wide open.

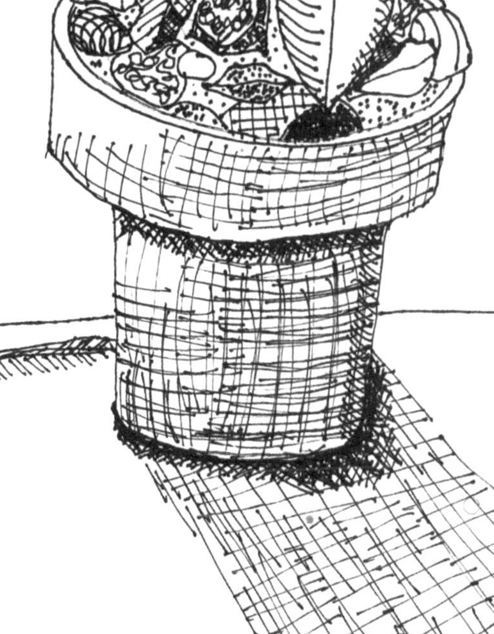

Try sending wonderfully imperfect homemade cards. Making and sending a homemade card is an act of love, but it is easy to get hung up because you think it needs to be really good. It can be hard to let that go—here are some things you can try.

Use stamps for the lettering. My handwriting can wobble all over the place, so I often use stamps for the main words.

Paste a drawing, painting, or bit of color or pattern on the front of the card. Because I never know when I will make a big splotch, if I start out planning to paste something on, it takes the pressure off.

Quick, silly little sketches can be a delightful addition to a card.

Collect bits and pieces of your work to paste on the front of a card. You will be amazed at what can work.

love

Making something can be incredibly frustrating while at other times it is magical fun. You start with nothing and then there is something. And it is not exactly clear how it all happens. Did I mean to do that? You see something you have drawn or written and you wonder: What the heck? Where did that come from?

It didn't exactly come out of nothing. You have to have had at least a little time and a little place to make something. Without some sort of creative structure, it is hard to make anything. You also have to have something in you that wants to be known. What emerges is some sort of mingling of what your hand does, what you have seen, and what wants to be expressed. There is some sort of co-emergence with the world. There is a lot of mystery here.

But once made, there it is. This thing you have made can make you happy, it can make you sad; it becomes subject to all sorts of scrutiny. Much of this is simply beside the point, but it is alarmingly easy to get hung up at this stage. We can saddle our creation with so much baggage, it just sort of sinks.

But you don't need to do this. You can use awareness and love to view what you have made.

Yes, love. Let's talk about love. For me, love is at the center of it all, as sappy as that sounds. I keep drawing when I am compassionate to myself. Sometimes I think making things is an act of love, but we overcomplicate it with thinking and a false sense of self. Are all acts of creation little acts of love? No matter what they look like? Is sitting down to draw an act of love, no matter the results? Is making something a love letter to the world? I like to think it is.

I am struck by how both making things and looking are ways of exploring the world. When we look more and make more, we expand our awareness and become more alive to the world. We can say, Yes, this is what I want, this is how I want to live; we can choose looking— or making—or both as ongoing practices in our lives.

In *Enchantment,* Katherine May suggests this is a lifetime endeavor that we will never complete: "Seeking is a kind of work. I don't mean heading off on wild road trips just to see the stars that are shining above your own roof. I mean committing to a lifetime of engagement; to noticing the world around you, to actively looking for small distillations of beauty, to making time to contemplate and reflect."

Actively looking is a commitment we can choose to take on. When you are puzzling over the colors in a leaf and then look up, your ability to see color everywhere is heightened. When you look closely at the values and shapes of an object, you find your attention sharper when you turn your eyes to the rest of the world. When you are alert to the world around you, it becomes more vividly alive. Both looking and making art cultivate an awareness that helps me see.

This seeing doesn't mean becoming blind to the difficulty of our lives. The news is always going to be bad, and our lives are brief and marked by loss. But actively practicing looking is a way of opening up the lens, gaining a wider perspective, adjusting for our human proclivity to drift toward fear and negativity. As the Buddhist teacher James Low says, even in times of difficulty the blackbird sings. I simply have to listen.

And of course, it is okay just to have fun. It is also okay if I don't practice every day. And it is even okay if I stumble around blindly for days at a time. After all, this is what it means to be human. But then suddenly I will remember: All I have to do is look.

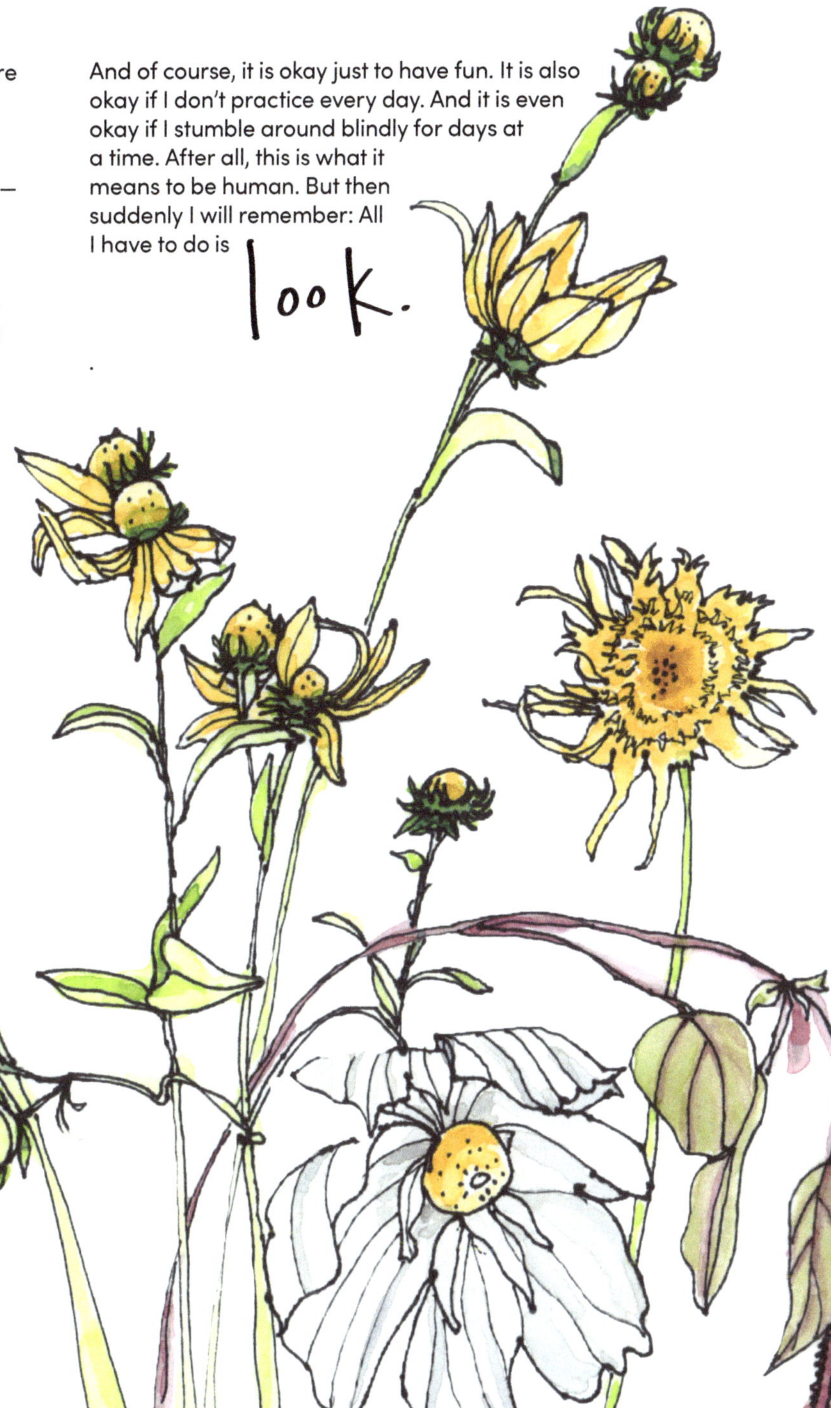

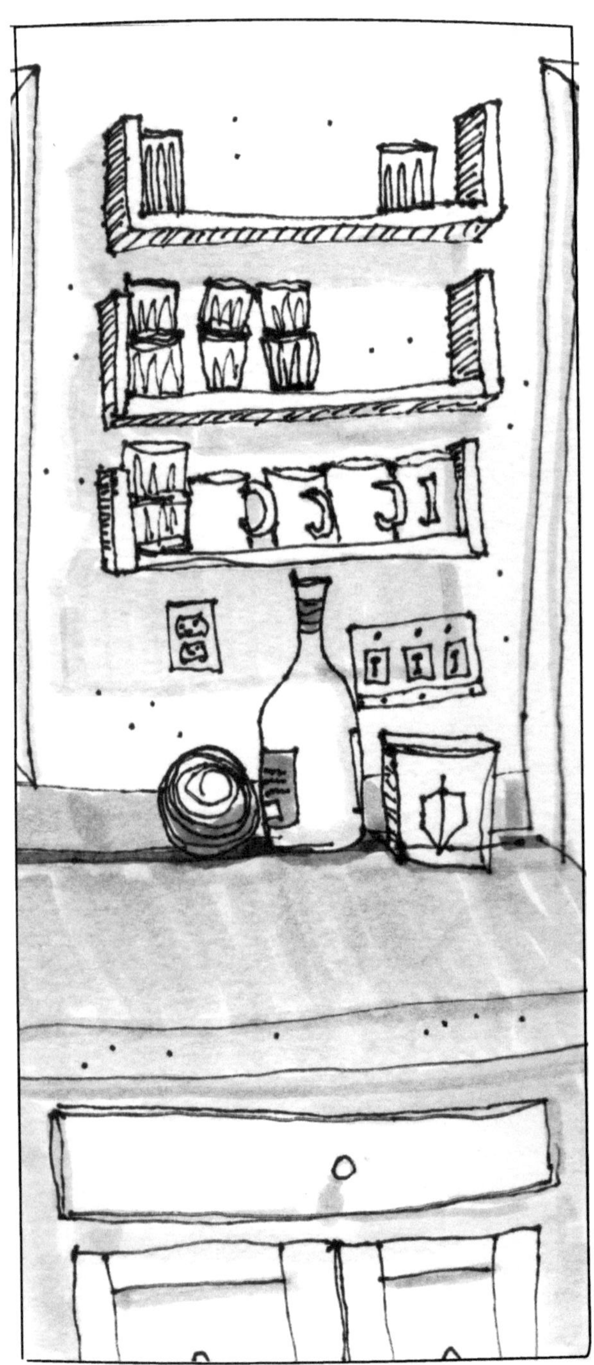

Resources + references

"17 things i made" (YouTube video)
by Amy Krouse Rosenthal

"A Genius Cartoonist Believes Child's Play Is Anything but Frivolous"
by David Marchese

"An Art Revolution Made with Scissors and Glue"
by Jason Farago

A Pacific Northwest Nature Sketchbook
by Jude Siegel

Atomic Habits: An Easy and Proven Way to Build Good Habits and Break Bad Ones
by James Clear

Big Magic: Creative Living Beyond Fear
by Elizabeth Gilbert

Cartooning: Philosophy and Practice
by Ivan Brunetti

Drawing from Life: The Journal as Art
by Jennifer New

Effortless Mindfulness Now: Awakening our Natural Capacity for Focus, Freedom, and Joy
by Loch Kelly

Enchantment: Awakening Wonder in an Anxious Age
by Katherine May

Everyday Matters: A Memoir
by Danny Gregory

Four Thousand Weeks: Time Management for Mortals
by Oliver Burkeman

Frederick
by Leo Lionni

How to Do Nothing: Resisting the Attention Economy
by Jenny ODell

Keys to Drawing
by Bert Dodson

Learning by Heart: Teachings to Free the Creative Spirit
by Jan Steward and Corita Kent

Making Art a Practice: How to Be the Artist You Are
by Cat Bennett

Making Comics
by Lynda Barry

Midlife: A Philosophical Guide
by Kieran Setiya

On Looking: Eleven Walks with Expert Eyes
by Alexandra Horowitz

One Long River of Song: Notes on Wonder
by Brian Doyle

Passing for Human
by Liana Finck

"Praise for intelligence can undermine children's motivation and performance"
by Claudia M. Mueller and Carol S. Dweck

Shift into Freedom: The Science and Practice of Open-Hearted Awareness
by Loch Kelly

Stop Look Breathe Create: Four Easy Steps to Mindfulness Through Creativity
by Wendy Ann Greenhalgh

Syllabus: Notes from an Accidental Professor
by Lynda Barry

The Art of Noticing: 131 Ways to Spark Creativity, Find Inspiration, and Discover Joy in the Everyday
by Rob Walker

"The Art of Procrastination"
by Rowboat Watkins

The Creative License: Giving Yourself Permission to Be the Artist You Truly Are
by Danny Gregory

The Confident Creative: Drawing to Free the Hand and Mind
by Cat Bennett

The Essential Leunig: Cartoons from a Winding Path
by Michael Leunig

The Little Book of Being: Practices and Guidance for Uncovering Your Natural Awareness
by Diana Winston

The Path of Aliveness
by Christian Dillo

The Zen of Seeing: Seeing and Drawing as Meditation
by Frederick Franck

Urban Watercolor Sketching A Guide to Drawing, Painting and Storytelling in Color
by Felix Scheinberger

Waking Up app
(meditations by Sam Harris, Henry Shukman, James Low, and Loch Kelly)

What It Is
by Lynda Barry

"Why You Should Marry My Husband"
by Amy Krouse Rosenthal

permissions

"The Summer Day" by Mary Oliver
Reprinted by the permission of The Charlotte Sheedy
Literary Agency as agent for the author.
Copyright © 1990, 2006, 2008, 2017 by Mary Oliver
with permission of Bill Reichblum

Excerpt From "Of Power and Time" from Blue Pastures by Mary Oliver. Copyright 1995, 1992, 1991. Used by permission of HarperCollins Publishers.

"Untitled" Used by permission of Haley Stewart. Copyright 2019 by Haley Stewart.

Excerpts from *Learning from Heart: Teachings to Free the Creative Spirit,* by Corita Kent & Jan Steward, Copyright 2008. Used by permission of Skyhorse Publishing.

The Confident Creative by Cat Bennett published by Inner Traditions International and Findhorn Press, ©2010. All rights reserved.
http://www.Innertraditions.com
Reprinted with permission of publisher.

Making Art a Practice by Cat Bennett published by Inner Traditions International and Findhorn Press, ©2013. All rights reserved.
http://www.Innertraditions.com
Reprinted with permission of publisher.

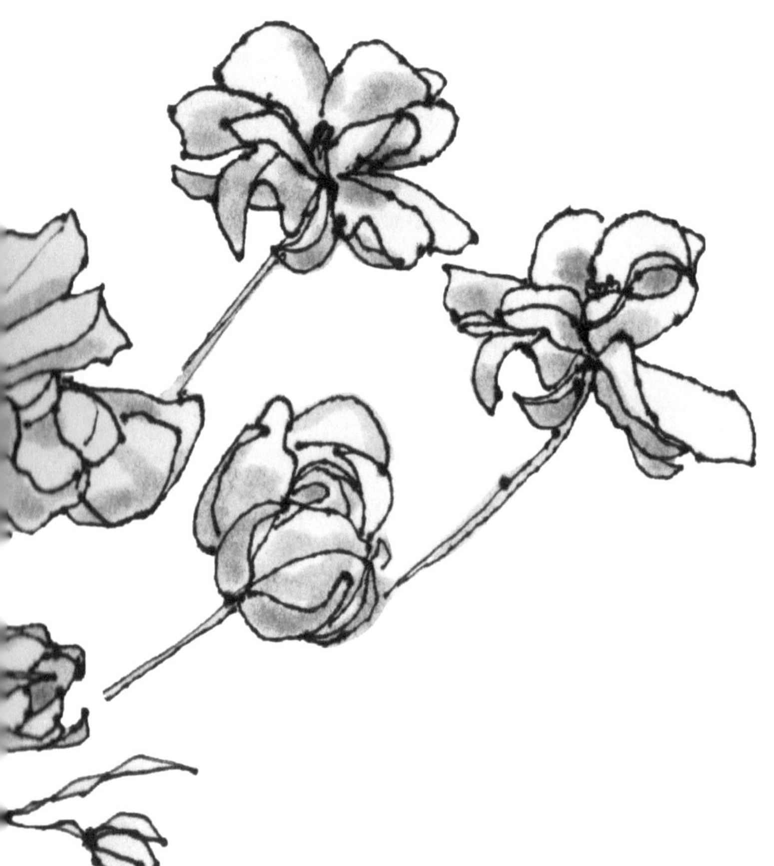

thank you

I wonder a lot about co-creation and co-emergence and where things come from. What a pleasure it is to wonder at all the people who have had a hand in creating this book! There are the many meditation and Buddhist teachers I have read and listened to, the artists who have shared what they know, and the many good people I have been lucky enough to spend time with.

My fellow art students taught and inspired me. My early teachers, Jude Siegel and Leslie Barnum, taught with such wisdom and warmth that they provided an ideal launching pad.

My high school friend Mary gave excellent advice and helped me steer this project. My friends Dani, Carmen, and Kathy all read the early parts of this book. They gave me warm encouragement, as did my friends Alison and Lisa, who, on numerous walks, listened to what must have seemed like an endless project. And I am indebted to Grace, who, on one walk when I was wondering what the heck I was doing, helped me see this book simply as an invitation. It was my dear friend Mary who suggested that I write this book; our walks and discussions of life struggles, creative and otherwise, make me both happier and wiser.

This is largely a DIY book. I am blessed with a wonderfully supportive family. My parents, Dave and Sally, and my three sisters, Betsy, Kate, and Emily, provide a foundation of love and strength; they let me know I am never alone.

Whenever I tentatively shared something I had drawn with my children, Haley, Walker, and Ella, they wholeheartedly urged me on. Their loving encouragement meant so much to me. Without it, I am not sure I would have continued.

Haley also waded through this book several times, helping me find my way. Ella and my husband, Brian, assisted in thinking about the layout and feel of the book. Seeing my silly little drawings displayed on Walker's fridge made me feel, well, like my drawings really were okay. All the drawings and paintings in this book are from my journals.

Two wonderful editors also helped. Thank you to Nina for encouraging me to rewrite this book and to Ashley for giving me the confidence to take the final step of publishing.

My husband, Brian, provided me with time and space and was unwavering in supporting this book. I am forever grateful for his grace in letting me find my own way in art while also happily answering all sorts of art questions. He has surrounded me and this project with love—and for that, I am truly thankful.

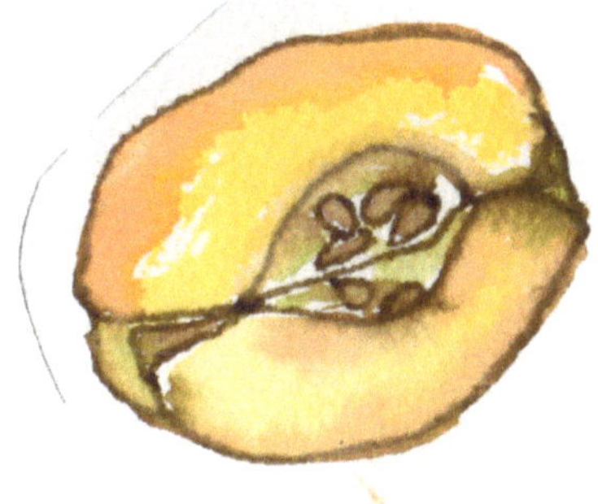

Who am I?

Well, now, that's a loaded question, isn't it? Probably not something to attempt to answer in a book concerning awareness, but still ...

I started my career at the dawn of desktop publishing, creating newsletters and catalogs. For a while, I was the creative services manager at The North Face. For years, I was a stay-at-home mom raising three remarkable people: Haley, Walker, and Ella. During that time I focused on marketing, communications, and fundraising efforts for non-profit organizations.

Along the way, I helped my sister Emily launch a brand consulting business, and my husband, Brian, start Electrify Now, a volunteer organization promoting electrification as part of the solution to the climate crisis. I have always liked making things.

I live in Oregon with my husband, Brian.

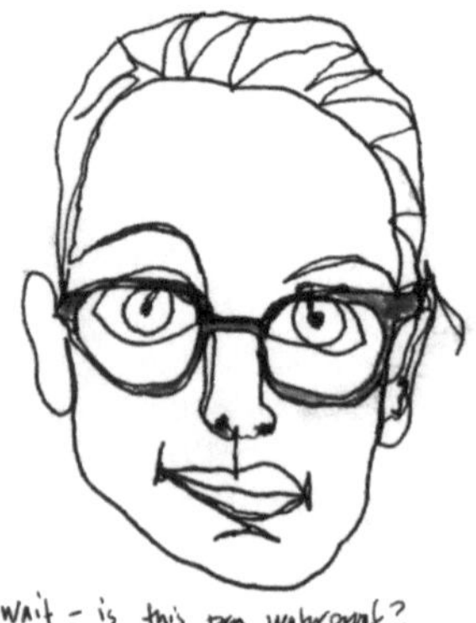